CHOOSING THE FUTURE FOR AMERICAN JUVENILE JUSTICE

YOUTH, CRIME, AND JUSTICE SERIES
General Editors: Franklin E. Zimring and David S. Tanenhaus

Homeroom Security: School Discipline in an Age of Fear
Aaron Kupchik

Kids, Cops, and Confessions: Inside the Interrogation Room
Barry C. Feld

Choosing the Future for American Juvenile Justice
Edited by Franklin E. Zimring and David S. Tanenhaus

Choosing the Future for American Juvenile Justice

Edited by Franklin E. Zimring and David S. Tanenhaus

NEW YORK UNIVERSITY PRESS
New York and London

NEW YORK UNIVERSITY PRESS
New York and London
www.nyupress.org

Library of Congress Cataloging-in-Publication Data

Choosing the future for American juvenile justice / edited by Franklin E. Zimring and David S. Tanenhaus
pages cm. -- (Youth, crime, and justice series)
Includes bibliographical references and index.
ISBN 978-1-4798-1687-3 (hardback) -- ISBN 978-1-4798-3444-0 (paper)
1. Juvenile justice, Administration of--United States. 2. Juvenile delinquency--United States. I. Zimring, Franklin E. II. Tanenhaus, David Spinoza.
HV9104.C46 2014
364.360973--dc23

2013045560

New York University Press books

Manufactured in the United States of America
10 9 8 7 6 5 4 3 2 1

Also available as an ebook

CONTENTS

ACKNOWLEDGMENTS

The idea for this volume was sparked by the anonymous reviewers who evaluated our proposal for the Youth, Crime, and Justice Series that this book now officially launches. Many people deserve our thanks for ensuring that a promising idea became a potentially useful book for those who care about children. These include our authors who presented drafts of their chapters in April 2013 at the Choosing the Future for Juvenile Justice Conference at the William S. Boyd School of Law at the University of Nevada, Las Vegas (UNLV); the session chairs and commentators (in order of appearance, Mary Berkheiser; James Forman Jr.; Ramona Denby Brinson; Anne Traum; Máximo Langer; Steve Wolfson, Clark County District Attorney; William Voy, Clark County Family Court Judge; John Valery White; Fatma Marouf; Michael Kagan; Ann Cammett; Donella Rowe, Deputy District Attorney Clark County; Jean Sternlight; Stacey Tovino; Rebecca Nathanson; and Catherine Cortez Masto, Nevada Attorney General); and the audience members who included juvenile justice practitioners and administrators from across the nation.

The Boyd School of Law and Berkeley Law provided essential and exemplary support for both the conference and this volume. UNLV Executive Vice President and Provost John Valery White nurtured the initial spark and Elaina Bhattacharyya, the Director of Strategic Initiatives at the Boyd School of Law, tended the flame. Elaina even found the contrasting images that now appear on the cover. As usual, Toni Mendicino of the Institute for Legal Research at Berkeley Law provided expert assistance in preparing this volume for publication. The

Criminal Justice Research Program at Berkeley Law has supported the book series and its volumes since 2010.

Finally, we thank our dedicated editors at NYU Press, Ilene Kalish and Caelyn Cobb, for their stewardship of this project. This included securing timely and constructive evaluations of the entire manuscript by Barry Feld and other anonymous peer reviewers.

Introduction

FRANKLIN E. ZIMRING AND DAVID S. TANENHAUS

The juvenile court and the system of juvenile justice that it produced was invented in Illinois in 1899 and is now 115 years old. While it is the youngest of the major institutions of Anglo-American law, it has also become the most popular. There are juvenile courts in all 50 American states and in almost all the nations of the modern world.

But while the mission of the court is universally popular, the moving parts of juvenile justice in the United States have been changing almost from the beginning. The basic principles of the court in 2014 still reflect the intentions of its founders, but the priorities and power relations in juvenile justice have changed importantly in the past half-century.

Enduring Principles

The first enduring principle of the juvenile court was the radical idea that the law should treat children differently from adults. This radical idea is also an old one, predating the American Revolution. The political philosopher John Locke argued that children's lack of reasoning capacity, which disqualified them from participating in government, also made them less culpable for their criminal acts. By the turn of the twentieth century, child advocates embedded the principle that children are different from adults—and thus require individualized handling of their cases—into the foundation of the world's first juvenile courts. That bedrock assumption is still alive and well in 2014.

A second principle is closely and inextricably related to the first. Once juvenile courts were established, children's advocates argued that children's cases should be diverted from the destructive dynamics of the criminal justice system. This diversionary rationale made increasing sense in a society in which the modern ideal of a sheltered childhood became nearly universal by the middle decades of the twentieth century. For example, children's advocates in Florida led a successful campaign in 1950 to amend the state's constitution, so that the Florida could establish a separate justice system for juveniles based on the diversionary principle. Every American state has a commitment to juvenile courts, and this diversionary hegemony is secure for the foreseeable future.

Changing Procedures and Priorities

While the mission of the court for kids has remained popular, the informal structure and paternalist assumptions of the court were sharply curtailed by the US Supreme Court in *In re Gault* in 1967. Children at risk of secure confinement were provided by *Gault* with the right to counsel and to due process in the adjudication of delinquency charges. These procedural changes in the court made both defense attorneys and public prosecutors much more important parts of juvenile justice.

The Get-Tough Era

In the 1980s and 1990s, in response to mounting concerns about juvenile crime, many states changed their laws to give prosecutors, instead of juvenile court judges, the authority to determine which court system would handle a particular youth's case. As a result, prosecutors now make the vast majority of transfer decisions. This dramatic departure from past practices threatened to undermine the longstanding principle that children are different. By the late 1990s, some critics even called for the abolition of the juvenile court.

Yet this so-called get-tough era ended at about the same time that the twentieth century became history. The moral panic over youth crime and the subsequent wave of transfer laws that characterized the 1990s largely abated after 2000. Since 2005, when the US Supreme Court abolished the juvenile death penalty in *Roper v. Simmons*, children's advocates have been on a winning streak before the justices of the high court.

Thus, the time is ripe to rediscover the first principles of American juvenile justice and to do less harm to young people. Justice Elena Kagan's clear statement about children being different from adults in *Miller v. Alabama* (2012), for example, is an emphatic reminder of why we created the juvenile court in the first place, and why no state has abolished its juvenile justice system.

* * *

This book aims to provide resources for choosing the future of the policies and institutions of the juvenile court's delinquency jurisdiction. The volume is divided into three parts.

The first section sets the stage for current reform discussions by profiling the attitudes and legislative changes that were the legacies of the 1990s. Chapter 1 concerns the youth homicide trends after 1985 in the United States and the fears they generated. Chapter 2 shows how public concerns and prosecutorial ambition produced legislation that reduced judicial and probation authority and increased prosecutorial power.

The second section of this volume identifies six important priorities for law reform in the immediate future. Michael Caldwell profiles the changes in law that were imposed on juvenile sex offenders and demonstrates the lack of fit between current policies and scientific evidence. Aaron Kupchik shows how the increasing presence and power of police in schools has become a disturbing part of the "school-to-prison pipeline." James Forman discusses a pioneering and successful effort to educate kids even while they are subject to secure confinement. David Thronson explores the consequences of policy choices that juvenile justice systems must make in cases involving immigrant youth. James Jacobs analyzes the conflict between the increasing availability of juvenile arrest and adjudication records and diverting young offenders from permanent legal and economic disabilities. Franklin Zimring provides a new approach to reducing the harms suffered by disadvantaged minority youth in juvenile courts.

The concluding section of the book searches for appropriate strategies and appeals to achieve progressive reforms in juvenile justice. Terry Maroney explores the promises and limits of appeals based on the evolving neuroscience of adolescent development. Zimring and David

Tanenhaus provide a consumer's guide to the rhetoric of law reform in juvenile justice.

The aim of this book is to close the gap between theory and practice in American juvenile justice, and to start a conversation about progressive reform that is both disciplined and practical.

PART I

The Legacy of the 1990s

The two chapters in this introductory section profile the changes in youth violence and in the legal framework of juvenile justice that happened during the 1990s in the United States. Chapter 1 tells the story of youth homicide trends from the mid-1980s to the early 1990s, when sharp increases in killings by youths and young adults generated fears of "juvenile superpredators" on the near horizon. But just when predictions of further increases in youth violence had reached a peak, the most substantial drop in youth violence of the twentieth century erased all the earlier increases. How could criminologists and policy analysts have been so wrong?

Chapter 2 shifts the focus from the ebb and flow of youth homicide to the legislation that public concern and prosecutorial ambition had provoked. The chapter shows that there were only minor changes in the jurisdiction of juvenile courts, but major shifts in the power of prosecutors to make transfer decisions without judicial oversight were both the primary objective and the most important result of the legislative bumper crop of the early 1990s.

The public alarm and legislative record of the 1990s are thus one very important dimension of a reform agenda for juvenile courts at the start of the twenty-first century. Prosecutorial power and the erosion of judicial and probation authority are both a feature of the current court and a problem that progressive reformers need to address.

1

American Youth Violence

A Cautionary Tale

FRANKLIN E. ZIMRING

A volume on reforms in juvenile justice presents its opening chapter on American youth violence for two reasons. First, concerns about youth violence had been driving the wave of state penal legislation in the 1990s. Second, youth violence because of its extremity is an obvious priority for citizen concern. Acts of life-threatening violence by young persons are important and troublesome events in developed nations for a variety of reasons—they are the most serious crimes young persons commit, and they test the degree to which legal principles can mitigate penal responses; they happen at the beginning of social and criminal careers, and may be signals of protracted dangerousness; they follow closely on periods of child development and dependence, so that the crimes of the young also clearly implicate failures of family, government and society.

But there were three special developments in the United States over the period since 1975 that compelled special scholarly concern with youth violence. The first special feature of the late twentieth century was a baby boom that propelled an expansion of children and adolescents all through the 1960s and early 1970s, just as crime rates in urban America were also expanding. Youth violence had become a much more important concern simply because there were so many more young people in the American mix.

The second special element of the period was an explosion of rates of youth homicide in urban areas during the eight years after 1984. The escalating rates of youth homicide started after the youth population peak (in 1975) during a period when the population of older juveniles was declining.

And this explosive increase in youth homicide touched off the third element of the story: predictions of continuing growth in American violence on the horizon, a moral panic in the media and government inspired by PhDs warning that "a bloodbath" was on the horizon that would be the result of an emerging generation of "juvenile superpredators." While the ink was still wet on these dire predictions, rates of youth homicide were already dropping—the beginning of an era of declining rates of lethal violence by youth unprecedented in magnitude in the modern era. The contrast between predicted and actual rates of homicide arrests for the middle term was five to one. James Alan Fox had projected a volume of juvenile homicide arrests of "almost 5,000 per year by 2005, as a result of demographic growth alone" (1996, 3), but then concluded that "we will likely have many more than 5,000 teen killers" (ibid). Yet the actual number of arrests in that age group in 2005 was 1,073.

This chapter will focus on trends over time in serious youth violence since 1975 and on what the catastrophic errors of the 1990s teach us about youth violence and the limits of criminological projection. The first section provides a profile of statistical sources on youth violence with emphasis on the distinctive features of violent crime during adolescence. The second section then profiles the age-specific trends in homicide after 1980 that provoked the moral panic in the 1990s, and provides details on the assumptions used to project future problems. A third section details the trends of homicide after 1994 for different age groups and suggests substantive reasons why the direction and magnitude of juvenile homicide was the reverse of that predicted. A brief concluding section applies the lessons learned since 1995 to a risk-averse discussion of future trends in youth homicide.

The jump in youth homicide in the mid-1980s was tied to a sharp increase in gun use by younger offenders. What happened after 1995 was a classic regression toward prior proportions of youth to total homicide that interacted with general declines to produce huge drops in youth violence. The regression scenario was not considered by the superpredator predictors of the mid-1990s. That error should not be repeated.

The prospects for future trends in youth violence are most likely to be in the same direction and magnitude as the rates for offenders over the age of twenty.

I. Youth Violence: A Profile

Two sources of information are available about the incidence and character of youth violence in the United States—official statistics from police and health departments, and survey research estimates that come from interviews with samples of the population about whether and in what respects they have been crime victims in the recent past.

Because the victims of an offense will frequently not know much about the offender, there are important limits to using such surveys to determine offender characteristics, even in violent episodes where the victim comes in contact with the offender. So most of the information available about the incidence and character of youth violence in the United States comes from police statistics.

But police statistics on the age of criminal offenders will not be available for the majority of all the offenses known to the police because an offender has not been identified. Detailed and accurate information on the age of criminal offenders can only be taken from cases where a particular suspect has been arrested or otherwise identified, and we will see later in this section that estimating the true prevalence of criminal offense responsibility from arrest or suspect counts is often problematic.

Official Statistics

There are five crime categories used in uniform crime reporting statistics that involve the immediate threat or imposition of personal injury—homicide, rape, robbery, aggravated assault, and assault. Homicide and rape are the most serious of the police classified offenses and also the lowest incidence crimes. The total number of intentional killings estimated by police statistics is around 13,000 per year, and health department death statistics stay quite close to this level. The number of rapes reported in the United States by the uniform crime reports is also small at just over 20,000, though this is regarded as a very substantial undercount. The two more frequent index crimes of violence, robbery and aggravated assault, are heterogeneous in severity. Robberies vary from unarmed extortions to dangerous encounters with loaded guns. While assaults must be aggravated by either an intent to injure or the threat to use a deadly weapon to be upgraded to the index categories, they vary

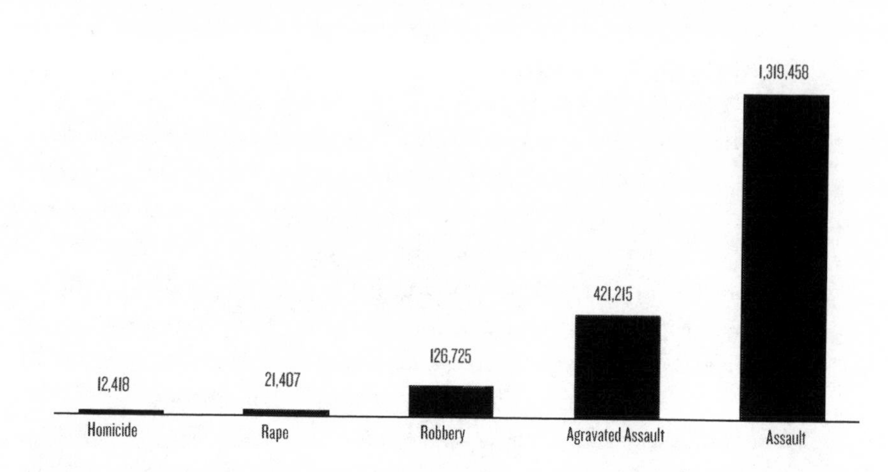

Figure 1.1. Police-Defined Crimes of Violence in the United States, 2009
Source: US Department of Justice, Federal Bureau of Investigation, *Uniform Crime Reports 2009*.

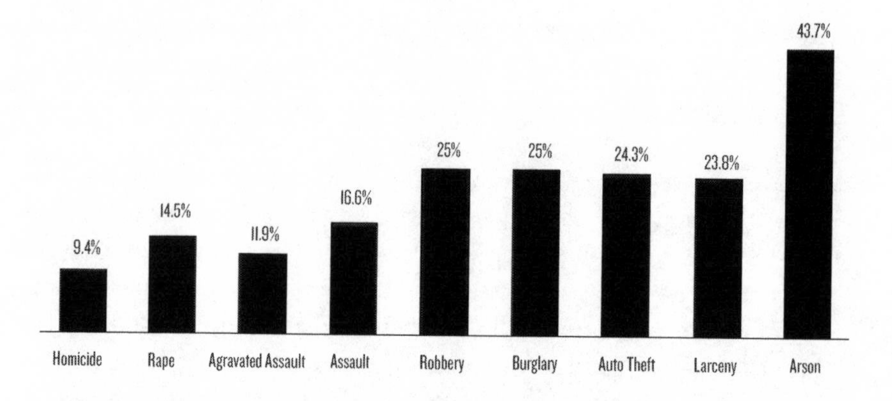

Figure 1.2. Under 18 Share of Arrests, Nine Offenses, United States, 2009
Source: US Department of Justice, Federal Bureau of Investigation, *Uniform Crime Reports 2009*.

in severity. Figure 1.1 shows the varying scale for police-defined crimes of violence in the United States in reports for 2009.

Using arrests as one measure of crime (because age specific detail can be added to it), homicides produce 2 percent of all index violent crime arrests in 2009. When arrests for the less serious assault category are added into the mix, homicide arrests are just over six-tenths of one percent of violence arrests.

Figure 1.2 provides some measure of the concentration of various violent crimes among younger adolescents by showing the percentage of all arrests for the eight index crimes and for nonindex assault in 2009.

The youth share of violent crimes is at the low end of index offenses for four of the five violent crimes. The fifth, robbery, at 25 percent, clusters with burglary and the other property crimes at almost twice the concentration of murder, aggravated assault, and rape.

But these police-based statistics both underestimate the amount and the concentration of violence among the young and overstate the youth share of violence. The first reason the under-18 share of arrests understates the relationship between youth and violence is that it cuts off the youth category pretty early in the developmental process. Adding in violent crimes up to age 21 or 23 would more than double the youth segment. The second reason that the under-18 share of arrests is an undercount is that official statistics do not fully reflect the assaults and fights among teens that are frequent during middle and late adolescence. Victim surveys identify the ages 15 to 19 as the highest assault age group, and the 12 to 15 group ties with young adulthood for second place (Zimring 1998, ch. 2). Teen males often don't report such conflict to the police and police will often take such events lightly if injuries are not severe. In one sense, however, arrest statistics exaggerate the amount of youth violence because younger offenders get arrested in groups, an issue I will return to later in this section (see Figure 1.4).

Is Youth Violence Different?

For the most part, patterns of youth violence resemble patterns of violence by older persons—concentrated in the same genders (males), the same kinds of conflicts, and the same disadvantaged minority segments of the community (Zimring 1998, 20–30).

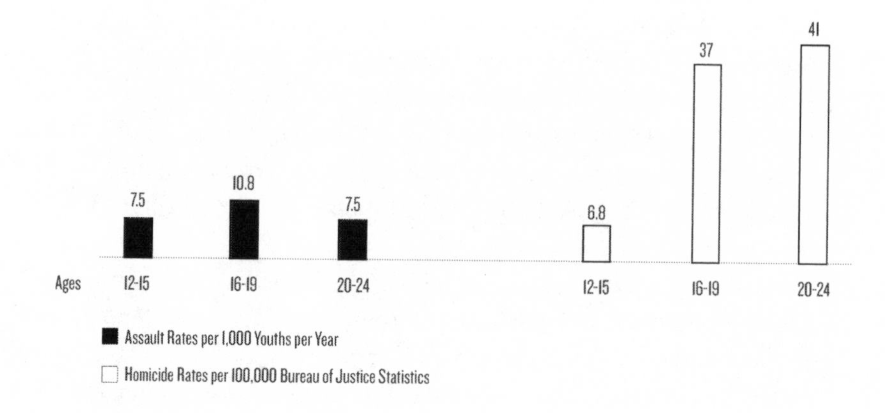

Figure 1.3. Male Homicide and Assault Victimization Rates by Age, 1991
Sources: National Center for Health Statistics (1991, 36); US Department of Justice, Bureau of Justice Statistics (1991, 24, Table 5).

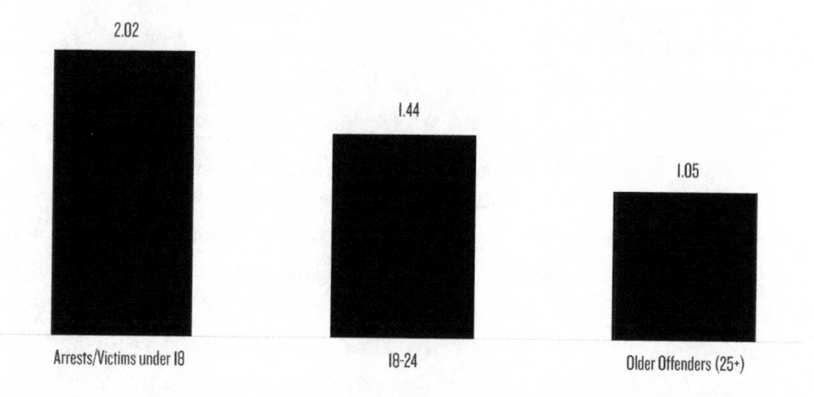

Figure 1.4. Ratio of Arrests for Homicide to Homicide Victims, United States, 2008–2009
Source: US Department of Justice, Federal Bureau of Investigation, *Uniform Crime Reports, Supplementary Homicide Reports.*

There are three important respects in which youth violence, particularly under the age of 18, differs from the behaviors found among older populations—high volume, low seriousness, and group involvement.

The high volume of violence during adolescence is not in serious dispute in the United States, but the extent to which it crosses gender and class boundaries and the degree to which very serious violence is broadly distributed among boys is not clear. The prevalence of assault among boys is substantial—but how serious are most of these male peer assaults? And while fighting is a relatively common rite of passage among boys in the teen years, we are less confident about the extent and severity of assaults initiated by adolescent girls. If arrest statistics are an accurate measure, assaultive behavior is even more concentrated in males during teen years than after (see Zimring 1998, ch. 3). But is the arrest rubric itself a product of police discounting of girl violence?

The high rates of youth assaults that are common are usually counterbalanced by the relatively low severity of most youth assaults. Figure 1.3 contrasts homicide and self-reported assault victimization rates for three age groups. I use 1991 data, which was close to the high point for youth homicide discussed in the next section.

The best evidence that youth assaults are less serious is that the youngest group in the figure has the same reported incidence of self-reported assault victimization (7.5%) as 20- to 24-year-olds, but a much lower homicide victimization rate (6.8 versus 41 per hundred thousand).

The third specific marker of youth violence is the very high prevalence of group involvement. The official statistics on almost all forms of adolescent criminality show high levels of group involvement. Figure 1.4 demonstrates this pattern for homicide by showing the ratio of homicide arrests to victims associated with the arrests for three different age groups in the United States from 2007 to 2009.

The group involvement and multiple arrests of juvenile offenders produce two arrests for every victim of this age group, while the oldest age group produces what is essentially a one-to-one ratio. The young adult rate is 1.44, between the juvenile and older adult ratios.

For most nonserious assaults, the net effect of undercounting offenses and multiple arrests is almost certainly to undercount total juvenile assaults and to underestimate the proportionate share of assaults committed by youth. For homicides, however, there is no undercount, and the much larger role of multiple arrests in the 1990s produces a significant overestimate of the proportionate share of homicide.

For homicides, a comparison of arrest rates for juveniles with arrest rates for persons over 25 is a very misleading indication of the risk to victims posed by the two age groups, because the number of victims generated by each 100 homicide arrests of juveniles is half that of the over-25 offender set. The impact of multiple arrests and the clearest way to correct the distortions produced by arrest patterns will be discussed later in this analysis.

II. The Late 1980s Homicide Epidemic and the Projections It Produced

The pattern of violent crime in the last four decades of the twentieth century breaks into three distinct suberas, as shown in Figure 1.5.

The first era of homicide experience was during the decade after 1964, when homicide rates doubled in the United States. The second era of fluctuation without a clear trend lasted from the mid-1970s to the early 1990s, when rates first dropped in the mid-1970s and then climbed back to the 1974 high in 1980, then dropped in the early 1980s only to go up again after 1985 to near the 1974 and 1980 high points in 1991. This second era was followed by nearly a decade of decline.

The trend line for homicide victimization between the ages of 15 to 19 provides reports every ten years from 1950 until 1980, and annual reports thereafter. The early 1980s level is approximately twice the 1950 rate but then spikes sharply after 1985 to peak at 20 per 100,000.

The last half of the 1980s was a particularly sharp disappointment in the United States, when homicide rates increased. Rates of imprisonment had expanded as never before and were expected to reduce crime through substantial incapacitation (Zimring and Hawkins 1995), and the aging of baby boomers also had reduced the proportion of the population in high-risk youth ages. Yet homicide and life-threatening violence increased almost as much as during the late 1970s, and the rebound of the late 1980s was concentrated among younger offenders. Some of the most dramatic contrasts over time were based on the increases in cases where municipal police identify the suspect as under

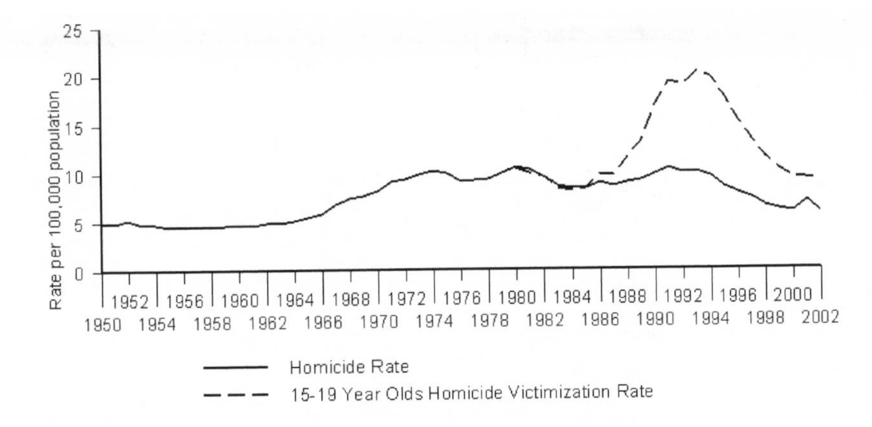

Figure 1.5. Homicide Rates by Year and 15–19-Year-Olds Homicide Victimization Rate in the United States, 1960–2002

Source: National Center for Health Statistics, 2005; Center for Disease Control and Prevention, *Health, United States 2004, with Chartbook on Trends in the Health of Americans*, National Center for Health Statistics (2004), Table 45 (Death Rates for Homicide, According to Sex, Race, Hispanic Origin, and Age: United States, Selected Years 1950–2002), 194, www.cdc.gov/nchs/data/hus/hus04trend.pdf.

18 when the crime was committed. The sharpest increases were noted in the monthly supplemental homicide reports that were the basis for James Alan Fox's 1996 analysis:

> Since 1985, the rate of homicide committed by adults, ages 25 and older, has declined 25%, from 6.3 to 4.7 per 100,000 as the baby boomers matured into their middle age years. At the same time, however, the homicide rate among 18- to 24-year-olds has increased 61% from 15.7 to 25.3 per 100,000. Even more alarming and tragic, homicide is now reaching down to a much younger age group—children as young as 14–17. Over the past decade, the rate of homicide committed by teenagers ages 14–17 has more than doubled, increasing 172%, from 7.0 per 100,000 in 1985 to 19.1 in 1994 (Fox 1996, 2).

Fox's 1996 report created a figure from the Supplemental Homicide Reports (SHR) of the FBI data adjusted to cover missing reporting sites, reproduced here as Figure 1.6.

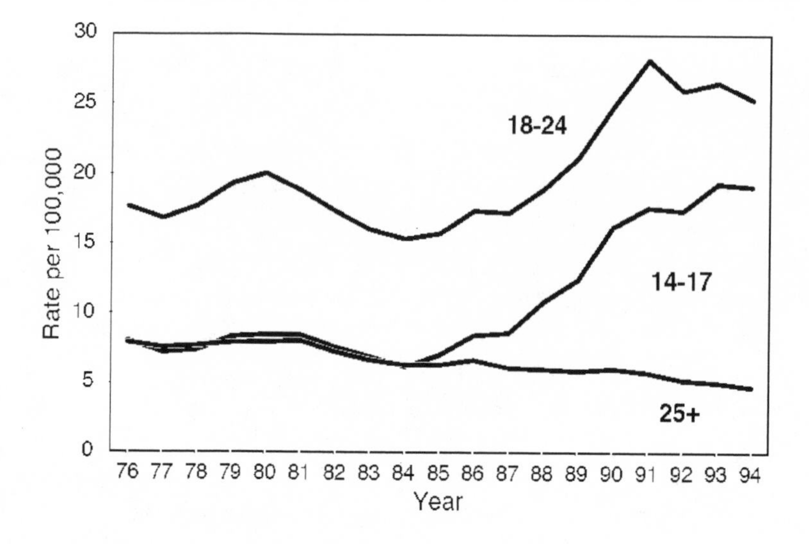

Figure 1.6. Homicide Offending Rate by Age
Source: Fox, 1996 (FBI, Supplementary Homicide Reports and Census Bureau, Current Population Survey).

The data in Fox's table was an estimated rate of offending and show a clear contrast after 1985 between sharp upward trends for juveniles and young adults and low rates for older groups, with some downward draft as well. In this analysis the rates of homicide offending were the highest for the young adult group, but the sharpest increase after 1985 was the 14- to 17-year-old group, with a peak rate 172 percent higher. Fox then constructed two projections, a high and a low projection for 2010, using the pre-1995 trends in his table. The low projection assumed that rates per 100,000 youth would stay at their peak 1994 rates for the next 15 years, and then adjusted the volume for each protected year by that year's population 14 to 17. Because the population in the age group expands, this method produces Fox's "almost 5,000 per year as a result of demographic growth alone" (Fox 1996). The second projection (Fox labels this one "high") assumes the offending rate will continue to expand as it had in recent years. This method produces a projected 8,000 "juvenile killers" by 2005. There is no express rationale for assuming the continued expansion of this peak rate for another decade.

Perhaps Fox was trying to imagine the worst outcome of any likelihood. There are a variety of indications that Fox was presenting these two versions of the future as exhausting the likely or possible trends. He labels one "low" even though it produces the highest volume of juvenile homicide offending ever by 2005, and calls the other (and even higher) projection "high," suggesting that he is exhausting the field of choice. But he never says why his low total assumes no decline from the peak rate in his historical series.

While James Fox spent most of his mid-1990s analysis on the arrest and suspect statistics of the prior decade, John DiIulio of Princeton emphasized the interaction of high mid-1990s crime rates with changes that were taking place in the age structure of the US population. Reviewing the SHR numbers in the Fox analysis, DiIulio concluded that "the youth crime wave has reached horrific proportions," but adds, "what is really frightening everyone from D.A.s to demographers . . . is not what's happening now but what's just around the corner—namely a sharp increase in the number of super crime-prone males . . . By 2005, the number of males in this age group [14 to 17] will have risen about 25% overall and 50% for blacks . . . Americans are sitting atop a demographic time bomb" (DiIulio 1995, 23–24).

DiIulio's demographic time bomb was based on two substantially inconsistent projection techniques. The first method was based on an assumption that fixed proportions of a youth population become serious offenders. The origination of this formula was DiIulio's teacher at Harvard, James Q. Wilson, who assumed that the 6 percent of Philadelphia boys born in 1945 who had five or more police contacts prior to age 18 were a fixed proportion of serious offenders. Wilson then argued that an expansion in the youth population of 1,000,000 produces 500,000 extra adolescent males. Extrapolating from the 6 percent chronic finding, Wilson tells us to expect "30,000 more muggers, killers and thieves than we have now" (Wilson 1995).

DiIulio used this logic, but with different time horizons and adjectives. He noted that the total population of boys under 18 was expected to grow from 32 million to 36.5, a total of 4.5 million, prior to 2010. Using the Philadelphia cohort 6 percent finding, he multiplied the 4.5 million additional male children under 18 in the United States by 2010 to project "approximately 270,000 more superpredators." The ninefold increase between the Wilson and DiIulio totals happens because the time period and number of extra youth are expanded, but also—and more importantly—because Wilson confines his analysis to adolescents while DiIulio assumes that 6 precent of *all* children alive in 2010 will be superpredators. The logic is still a fixed proportion of a variable population. As I pointed out, slightly more of these superpredators would be under age four in 2010 than over age 14 (Zimring 1997).

But DiIulio is not content to assume only a fixed proportion of criminal threats, noting that the offense severity profile increased between the two Philadelphia birth cohort juvenile eras: "Each generation of crime-prone boys has been about three times as dangerous as the one before it. For example, the crime-prone boys born in Philadelphia in 1958 went on to commit about three times as much serious crime per capita as their older cousins in the [first Philadelphia birth cohort]" (DiIulio 1995, 23–24). So DiIulio is ready to argue that the rate of serious youth crime is dynamic rather than constant, and that things have been getting worse. But if the rate and seriousness of youth crime varies over time, why should we assume that the 6 percent estimate of serious offenders is constant, or for that matter that the size of the youth population is a major variable in predicting the criminological future?

By the middle of 1996, complaints based on what Philip Cook and John Laub call "cohort effects" were taking center stage—allegations that the current youth generation were a breed apart (Cook and Laub 1998). In the coauthored volume *Body Count,* published in 1996, William Bennett, John DiIulio, and John Walters argue that the concentrated social disadvantages of fatherless families has created a high incidence of what they call "moral poverty" that all but guarantees violent criminal careers:

> Four of ten children go to sleep without fathers who live in their homes . . . We have come to the point in America where we are asking prisons to do what fathers used to do (196).

The impact of predictions based on projections of increasing youth violence on the political process was not small. In 1996, Rep. Bill McCollum of Florida, the chairman of the House Subcommittee on Crime, testified at a Senate hearing:

> Today's enormous cohort of five-year-olds will be tomorrow's teenagers. This is ominous news given that most violent crime is committed by older juveniles . . . Put these demographic facts together and brace yourself for the coming generation of "super-predators" (McCollum 1996, 2–3).

I do not mean to suggest that projections of increasing juvenile homicides—let alone nightmare predictions of coming generations of juvenile superpredators—met with universal academic acceptance. The Cook and Laub articles in *Crime and Justice* separated fact from science fiction with clarity and vigor (Cook and Laub 1998; Cook and Laub 2002; see also Zimring 1998). For the most part, however, the academic reaction to the demographic time bomb rhetoric was silence, whether respectful or not. The empirical criminologists whose cohort findings provided a framework for the Wilson and DiIulio predictions apparently did not participate in the public discourse about juvenile crime futures. And the prospect of impending juvenile risk seemed to offer rhetorical opportunities for the left (James Fox complaining about inadequate support for youth services), as well as Bennett and DiIulio's right-wing diagnosis of moral poverty and prescription of prison expansion. The demographic time bomb looked to be the next big thing in a period that had already endured the war on drugs and featured the "three strikes and you're out" phenomenon.

What Happened Next?

But what happened next was the most sustained and substantial decline in youth homicide in modern US history. Youth homicide arrests had actually begun to drop in 1994, so the low estimate in Fox's Figure 1.6 projection for 1996—the year his analysis was published—was already 33 percent higher than the actual FBI number. By 2005 the total volume of SHR homicide arrests and suspects under 18 had dropped by two-thirds instead of increasing by almost 40 percent, and this very large decline in homicide volume took place even as the youth population had expanded and the proportion of the youth population from traditional high-rate minority groups had also expanded. Every demographic determinant in the predictions made by Fox, Wilson, and DiIulio had come to pass, but the violent crime outcomes had been turned upside down. What turned Fox's 40 percent increase into a 67 percent

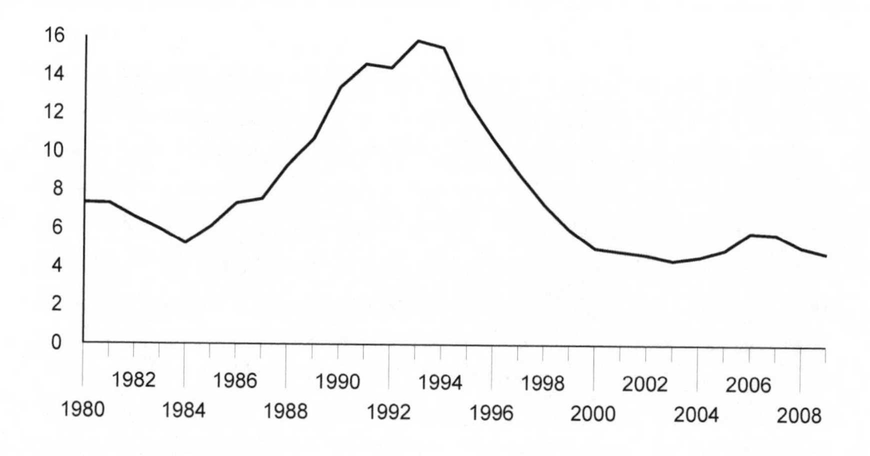

Figure 1.7. Juvenile Homicide Arrest Rates
Source: US Department of Justice, Federal Bureau of Investigation, *Uniform Crime Reports, Supplementary Homicide Reports.*

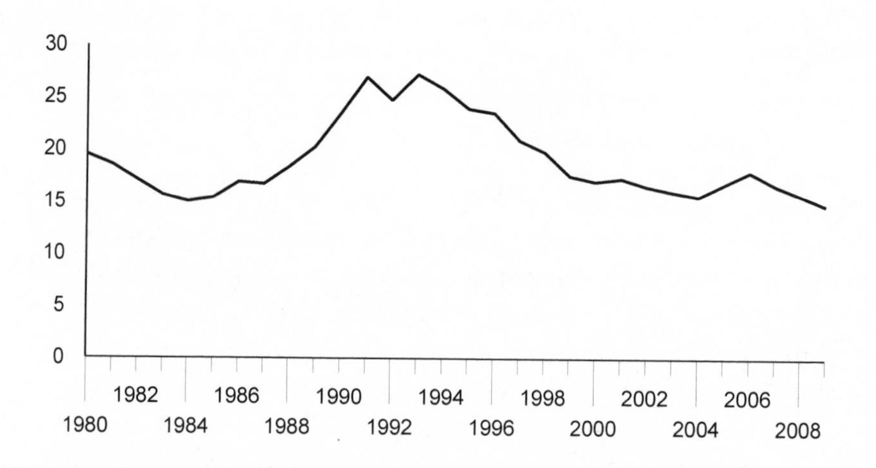

Figure 1.8. Young Adult Homicide Arrest Rates
Source: US Department of Justice, Federal Bureau of Investigation, *Uniform Crime Reports, Supplementary Homicide Reports.*

decrease was only one variable—the rate of juvenile homicide involvement. Figure 1.7 tells the tale by tracing the rate per 100,000 for ages 13 to 17 through more than a quarter-century.

After rising in the late 1970s, the youth homicide rate turned down sharply through the early 1980s before beginning the assent that was the centerpiece of the Fox and DiIulio concerns. Even as the alarms of the mid-1990s were being sounded, the rates of homicide attributable to juveniles began its steep and sustained drop.

In both the increase after the mid-1980s and its decline after 1993, the homicide patterns of ages 18 to 24 paralleled the rollercoaster ride of age-specific homicide rates, as shown in Figure 1.8.

The timing of the ups and downs for the two groups is very close, with a correlation over time of .95 (see Zimring and Rushin 2012, 13).

In retrospect, the predictions of a coming storm of juvenile violence were classic false predictions on a par with pushing Internet stocks in 2000 or recommending Greek government bonds in 2007. But was this simply bad timing, or was it also problematic criminology? The question is an important one, because discovering mistakes that should have been foreseen in 1995 can reduce the margin of error as we think about what should determine the character and rate of youth violence in the coming decades. Are there lessons to be learned, or is the recent history of forecasting on this topic an uncorrectable blind gamble?

III. An Anatomy of Catastrophic Error

The previous section of this chapter mentioned a few ways in which the methods and assumptions in the James Fox projections differed from those by James Q. Wilson and John DiIulio. There were, however, four problems manifest in all of the "coming storm" predictions that were errors in judgment even from the perspective of 1996:

1. The failure to recognize the plenary power of rate fluctuations in determining homicide trends;
2. The failure to account for regression to historically typical levels as a probable future outcome;
3. Assuming fluctuations in the number and demographic character of future population as a major influence on crime volume; and

4. Mistaking simultaneous movements in youth and young adult violence for juvenile-only cohort effects that signal long-term changes in rates of crime and violence as a group ages through the life cycle.

1. The Plenary Power of Rate Variations in Juvenile Homicide

What I am calling the plenary power of rates on the volume of juvenile violence was a central fact in the epidemic that led to coming storm predictions. The youth population actually decreased in the seven years after 1984, when killings committed by juveniles increased. All of the extra killings come from higher rates of killings attributed to juveniles. As a matter of strict arithmetic, *more* than 100 percent of the increase in youth homicide after 1984 came from rates going up, because the higher rates had to compensate for fewer kids. Since the period just prior to the mid-1990s had been dominated by variability in rates, the people making future projections should have been on notice that the dominant factor in future homicide rates would not be the number of juveniles at risk, but rather the trends in homicide rates per 100,000.

Sure enough, more than 100 percent of the *decline* in juvenile homicide that followed the dire predictions of the mid-1990s was also the result of rate changes because the youth population had expanded modestly. The extreme variability of homicide rates—almost tripling, then declining by two-thirds in just over 20 years—means that a 15 or 20 percent variation in total population will probably play a minor part in the total volume of serious youth violence. That which can be precisely estimated 10 and 15 years in the future—the population of youth and young adults—won't make much difference, and what will be the largest determinant of youth homicide—trends in rates—can't be predicted with any confidence.

The extreme variability in homicide rates that produced the Fox and DiIulio projections also should have worried Wilson and DiIulio away from expecting a fixed 6 percent of a youth population as violent. The variability of homicide rates from 1980 to 1994 undercut Fox's assumptions in a slightly different way. At no point in his analysis of the growth of youth homicide from 1984 onward does Fox suggest either an explanation for the upward slope or a behavioral model of what determines rate fluctuations. So Fox cannot explain the extreme fluctuations that he documents. But how can he predict future variations if he can't explain past variations? He never discloses this. Instead, he produces two straight-line models, each of which is based on a single assumption never justified. The "low" future merely assumes that the rate per 100,000 of juvenile homicide wills stay at its 1994 level (an all-time high) for the foreseeable future. The high projection model assumes that the upward growth in homicide rates will continue without interruption for the projectable future. A look back at Figure 1.7 will demonstrate that the actual variations in rate since 1980 conform to *neither* of these assumptions, with some downward variation after 1980 before an upward shift. So Fox had no behavioral or historical model to project future rates, despite the fact that rate fluctuations are the dominant feature in the magnitude of youth violence.

Both Fox and DiIulio believed that rates of youth violence would go up from 1994 levels. DiIulio mentions that the incidence of serious crime went up between the juvenile years of the 1945 cohort (1957–1963) and the juvenile years of the 1958 cohort (1970–1976), and suggests that this is likely to continue.

The behavioral emptiness of the Fox projections published in 1995 can best be illustrated by a parallel exercise of projecting juvenile

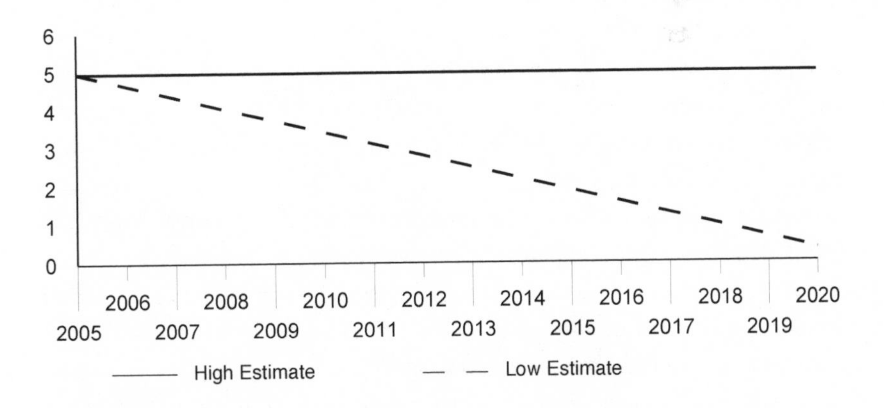

Figure 1.9. Straight-Line High and Low Volumes of Juvenile Homicide Projections, 2005–2020
Source: Author's projections.

homicide rates using 2005 as the base year. The high estimate, parallel to that of Fox in 1996, would take the 2006 rate of SHR juvenile homicides and assume it will continue with adjustments only for anticipated changes in the population ages 13 to 17. The low estimate would project continued downward rate levels.

Each of these projections assumes that juvenile homicide rate trends will do something they have never done before: either 12 years without significant change or more than 20 years of uninterrupted downward trend. Neither projection allows for an increase in juvenile homicide offending. Why? Have social or economic trends improved? No. But the crime trends preceding year one have changed.

For DiIulio, the 1995 assumption that crime trends would continue to get worse has been falsified. Will he still believe that a fixed percentage of the youth population will be juvenile superpredators?

One important vice of all the 1995 and 1996 predictions was that they didn't allow for the known variability of crime rates, despite the fact that rate changes had been the only significant moving part in the decade that produced their alarm.

2. Regression and the Lessons of History

When historical patterns have been cyclical, any straight-line projections that either forbid variation (the Fox low projection in Figure 1.6) or push it all in one direction (Fox's high projection) must assume that long-term historical trends have changed. And this ignores a very common pattern of statistical accounts of crime over time—regression toward long-term mean patterns. With respect to youth homicide, a very good illustration of this is a charting of the share of all homicide arrests attributable to persons under 18 in the United States. Figure 1.10 tells this story for the period 1980 to 2008.

What Figure 1.10 shows is that the percentage of total homicide arrests or attributions in the SHR increased over the period after 1984 to a rate double the level in the early years of the series, and then returned back to near the beginning proportion. The steep increase in the share of all arrests attributed to juveniles in the years after 1984 does not translate into any direct information on the future rate of juvenile offending, of course, because we would have to know future homicide

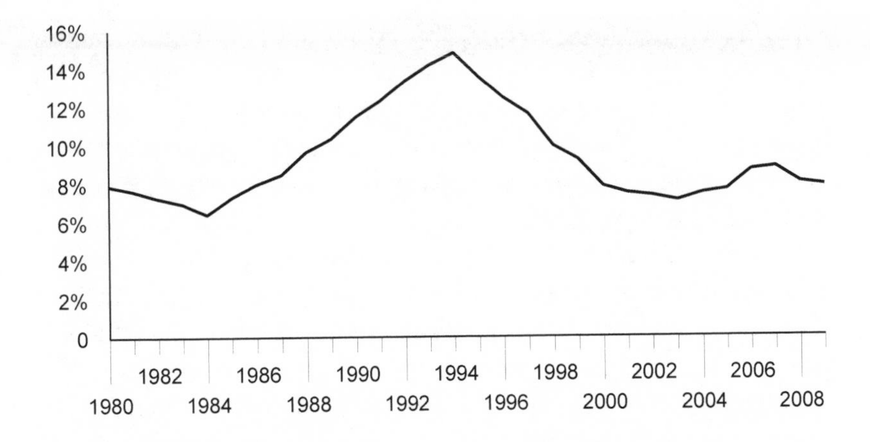

Figure 1.10. Juveniles as Percentage of Total Homicide Arrests
Source: US Department of Justice, Federal Bureau of Investigation, *Uniform Crime Reports, Supplementary Homicide Reports.*

offense rates for older offenders to translate any guesses we might have about the juvenile share of homicide arrests into estimates of juvenile rates. But the clear departure from historic patterns in 1984 onward puts forecasters on notice of important implications in assumptions they make about future trends. Take Fox's high projection for 2005 from the perspective of 1994. To maintain straight-line continuity from 1994, the historical pattern tells us that the proportion of total arrests attributable to juveniles would have to keep diverging from its historical levels. But we are also on notice that what had already diverged from an historic mean might also return to it. The perspective of a longer-term history should thus provide a caution against future assumptions radically different from historic relationships.

Paying close attention to historic relationships can also provide important information about the substantive implications of later changes. The pattern revealed in Figure 1.10 speaks directly to the substantive argument made by Donohue and Levitt in their now-famous argument that about half the 1990s crime decline in the United States should be attributable to the changes in the quality of the birthrate generated by the US Supreme Court abortion decision in 1973 (Donohue and Levitt 2001). I have an extensive analysis of this study in other writing (Zimring 2007, 88–103), and do not propose to revisit most of the wide range of issues that analysis discussed. But one argument made by Donohue and Levitt seems to me a textbook case in the substantive implications of regression. The clinching argument for these authors that crime declines in the 1990s were the result of 1973 changes in abortion rules was the fact that arrest data showing crime declines in the 1990s were concentrated in younger age groups: "Virtually all of the abortion-related crime decrease can be attributed to reductions in crime among the cohorts born after the abortion legalization. There is little change among older cohorts" (Donohue and Levitt 2001, 382).

But recall that Donohue and Levitt are examining the period after the early 1990s in Figure 1.10 when the proportion of arrests for homicide attributable to youth is dropping, and they are noticing the same pattern for young adults. What they argue is that this youth-only pattern of decline shows that the lower rate of unwanted births produced a lower rate of crime and violence among teens and young adults in the 1990s.

But Figure 1.10's data provides a new perspective for evaluating this claim: lower than what? If the arrest share of youth had declined to levels in the late 1990s that were much lower than in earlier eras, then that would be evidence that the crime tendencies of the young had shifted from normal expectations. But what Figure 1.9 actually shows for juveniles is a return to normal patterns of juvenile homicide market share 7.3 percent in 1983, versus 9.7 percent in 2009 after peaking in the intervening years. The problem is that there was no *Roe v. Wade* to hold the 1983 levels down, so why should we conclude that it was *Roe v. Wade*'s effect that pushed the youth share back to near its 1983 level in the late 1990s?

Figure 1.11 shows trends over time in the percentage of total arrests attributable to suspects under 18 for violent index offenses.

The first lesson from Figure 1.11 is that homicide and robbery have much larger increases and subsequent drops. The second pattern is that any increase in the juvenile share for violent crimes, much more modest than homicides, also falls back in the late 1990s, but the level of violence arrests for juveniles doesn't return to its 1983 level for violence—not good news for the Donohue and Levitt expectation of a uniquely large drop for the young. For property crime, by contrast, the concentration

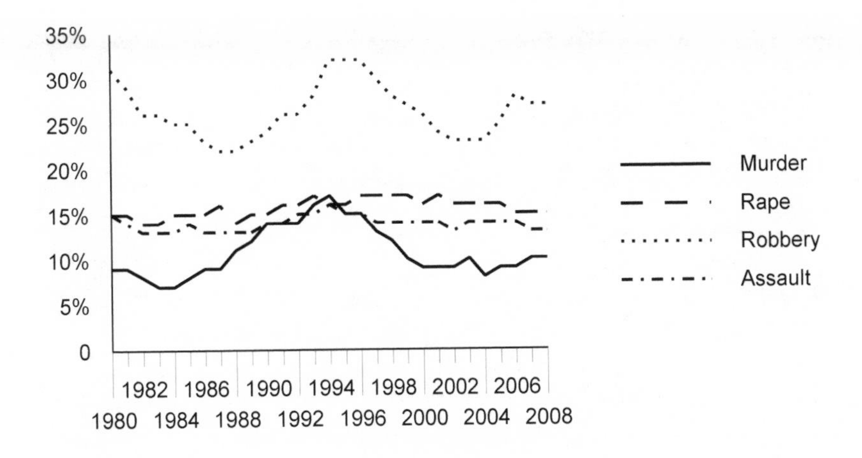

Figure 1.11. Juveniles as Percentage of Total Arrests for Violent Crimes
Source: US Department of Justice, Federal Bureau of Investigation, *Uniform Crime Reports, Supplementary Homicide Reports.*

of arrests under age 18 declines in the 1990s to levels below the 1983 starting rates—better news for an argument that expects lower-than-historical concentrations for the post-*Roe* cohorts.

GUN AND NONGUN JUVENILE TRENDS

One important disaggregation of trends in youth homicide provides important information on the source of the sharp increase in total youth homicide. Figure 1.12 separately shows trends over time in firearms and nonfirearms killings involving at least one offender under age 18.

All of the growth of homicide cases involving youth after 1980 was firearms homicide. The three decades of nongun killings show no pronounced increases ever, and a downward tendency throughout. Gun homicides first drop in the early 1980s and then triple during the decade after 1984, before dropping below the 1990 rate for every year after 1998. That the entirety of the increase is gun cases suggests that the increase after 1984 is not due to a change in the character of the youth population, but rather to the interaction of kids and guns. And the sharp and restricted nature of this increase is also a further suggestion

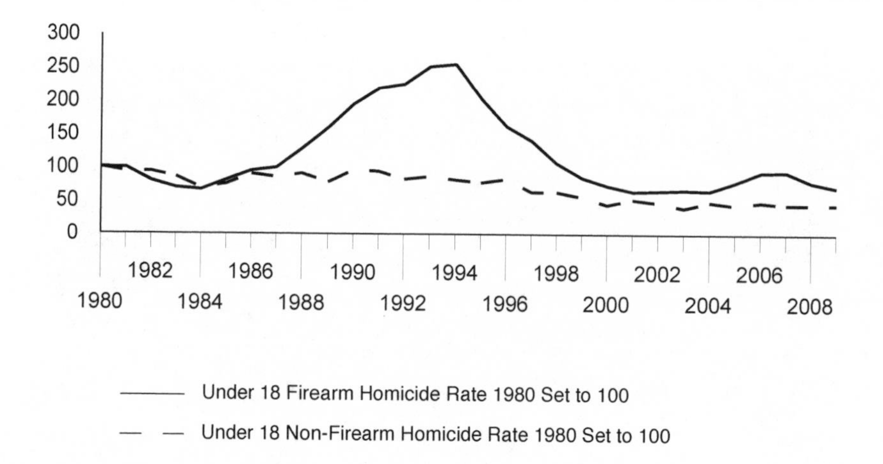

Figure 1.12. Trends in Juvenile Firearm and NonFirearm Homicide Rates, 1980. Set to 100
Source: US Department of Justice, Federal Bureau of Investigation, *Uniform Crime Reports, Supplementary Homicide Reports.*

that a regression, in this case a gun-specific regression, might be on the horizon. Figure 1.12 is pretty convincing evidence that the character of the juvenile population didn't change in the 1990s, only the character of instruments used in many violent assaults.

As a precautionary principle: for any projections based on historically atypical periods, regression toward more normal statistical values must be regarded as a plausible rival hypothesis to consider. The possibility of a return to historical normal patterns is so obvious that any set of projections that do not provide this alternative is presumptively deficient. Only convincing evidence of irreversible structural change should rebut the presumption that regression cannot be ignored. There were no such indications in the 1990s—only anecdotes and adjectives to the effect that this generation was very dangerous and the next one would be even worse.

3. *The Folly of Demographic Determinism*

This is not an appropriate venue for a comprehensive discussion of the relationship between population fluctuations and rates of youth crime in the United States. But one aspect of the moral panic of the 1990s makes a brief excursion into demography necessary. The academic and political vendors of the coming storm of juvenile violence all argued that a major expansion of adolescents was on the American horizon. James Q. Wilson opened the bidding with a million more teenagers in the short term; DiIulio upped the ante to 4.5 million extra young people to derive his 270,000 juvenile superpredators, and characterized the population developments on tap as "a demographic time bomb." Congressman McCollum prophesized that "today's enormous cohort of five-year-olds will be tomorrow's teenagers," and placed the major emphasis for his coming storm prediction on the expansion of the youth population.

Looking back at this particular American moral panic, there are two empirical puzzles that stand out. The first puzzle is that the population trends that were on the horizon for the 20 years after 1990 were really quite modest. Figure 1.13 reproduces a figure from an earlier analysis of the 1990s panic that shows the share of total population ages 13 to 17 at five-year intervals.

The proportion of the US population in the 13 to 17 age bracket varies over the 50 years after 1960, from a low of 6.7 percent of the population to

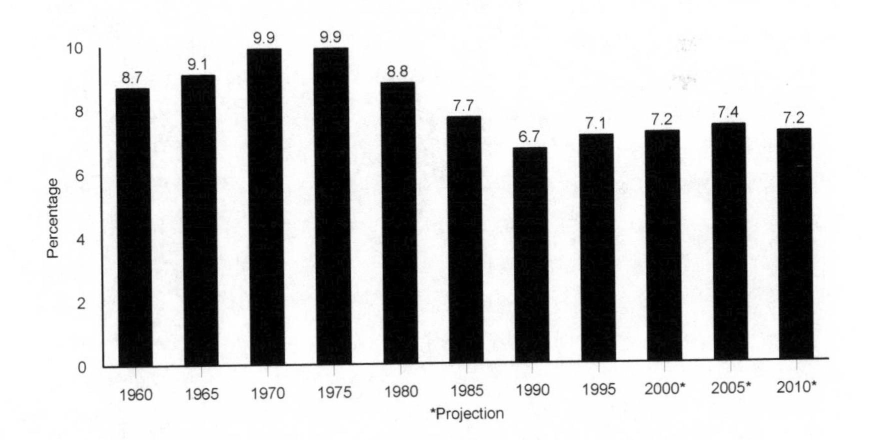

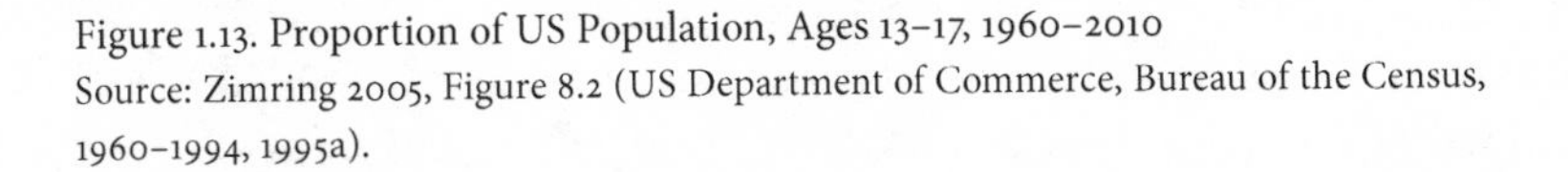
Figure 1.13. Proportion of US Population, Ages 13–17, 1960–2010
Source: Zimring 2005, Figure 8.2 (US Department of Commerce, Bureau of the Census, 1960–1994, 1995a).

a high of 9.9 percent. The demographic projections viewed with alarm in the 1990s were a very modest increase in the youth share—from the 6.7 percent low point in 1990 to 7.2 percent in 2010. The postdemographic time bomb youth cohort would be a *much* smaller share of the total population than 13- to 17-year-olds had been in the low-crime era of 1960 (7.2% versus 8.7%). There were only two reasons why the numerical count of teens would go up at all by 2010: the fact that total population was expanding, and the significant fact that 1990 was the very lowest youth share of the time series. The 7.2 percent concentration projected for 2010 would be the third lowest in the half-century after 1960. By post-WWII American standards, the concentration of youth expected for 2010 was *below average.* And that should have been easy to determine in 1995.

The second reason why worry about the size of a youth population was an odd concern for 1995 was the lack of any indication in the years after 1975 that the size of the youth cohort was a major determinant of the youth violence problem. Recall that 1990 was the post-1960 low point in the youth share of total population. It was also the middle of the youth violence epidemic that launched the moral panic. A corollary to the fact discussed earlier that more than 100 percent of the rise in youth homicide was caused by changes in rates per 100,000 kids is that the size of the youth population played no role in the process. It turns out that the post-1990 modest expansion that Bill McCollum worried about also played no role in the decline of youth violence, but the worry merchants of 1996 had no reason to know this. They *did* know, however, that that crime rates had been the only problematic moving part in producing the epidemic of the late 1980s. Why didn't the lack of any demographic impact on the upswing deter them from assuming the negative impact of any future population growth? Some speculation is required to answer this question, and that brings me to the final element of this methodological autopsy.

4. The Case of the Counterfeit Crime Cohort

The American birth cohort that was the subject of the projections by Fox, Wilson, DiIulio, and McCollum was too young to have any track record of criminal behavior in 1996. McCollum was predicting violence for five-year-olds. Fox was projecting the number of apprehended killers in a group of children between three and seven years old for the period a decade in the future, and he asserted that the lowest volume this new group would generate would be at the highest rate that age group had experienced in the 15 years in his chart. Why? He was projecting this 1994 rate (at minimum) on a 2005 set of 13- to 17-year-olds, because he must have been assuming that the forces that pushed up the rates of adolescents in the 1980s and 1990s were structural shifts in urban settings or populations that would not be reversed in the proximate future. But what were those these changes? The report complains about the lack of public support for child development in general terms, but presents no model. The only data to inform the future in Fox's calculations were previous years' rates. Why shouldn't the average rate from 1980 to 1994 be his middle range forward estimate? Because Fox assumed things had changed, but the evidence for this is missing from the analysis—and it was literally off his chart.

DiIulio and associates had a verbal description for what they thought had driven up the homicide rate—"moral poverty"—and they argued that these social and demographic features were the cause of the sharp increases in rate. But this is an assumption in DiIulio, and there is no discussion of one-off environmental and situation features of the 1980s that might not have similar impact in future years. Two examples of potentially nonpermanent impacts of the era mentioned by others were crack cocaine (see Blumstein and Wallman 2000), and sharp fluctuation in gun use (Cook and Laub 1998). For the cohort of kids born after 1985, the assumption in the coming storm warnings was that permanent social or demographic changes made a peak rate in an older generation the minimum legacy of the new generation.

Because the evidence for the permanent impact of the 1980s and 1990s changes was so weak, the out-of-hand rejection of regression or return to normal ratios is unjustified. But this must have been the reason why intelligent people made simple mistakes.

The supreme irony is that this same generation of kids, the "enormous cohort" of five-year-olds that scared Congressman McCollum and presidential nominee Robert Dole, became a blessed low-crime population group of wanted children five years later when economists John Donohue and Steven Levitt published their statistical argument that legal changes creating abortion on demand for pregnant women had reduced the probable crime rates of the post-*Roe v. Wade* birth cohorts by reducing the number and proportion of unwanted births. What had changed between 1995 and 2001 was that a national crime drop of approximately 40 percent that started in the early 1990s generated attention by the late 1990s, so that many of the same social scientists who had been trying to explain unexpected bad news in the early 1990s were now trying to explain unexpected good crime news in 2001. As I showed earlier, Donohue and Levitt noticed that the arrest rates of younger segments of the population had dropped more than among older age groups. And this was taken as the distinctive fingerprint of *Roe v. Wade* effect.

In less than a decade, future superpredators had become pioneer leaders in the great American crime decline. All during this transition, the kids born around 1985 were too young to have been a major feature in the crime rates projected for their futures during either the *Roe v. Wade* or superpredator fads. To be fair, Donohue and Levitt did have older cohorts of post-*Roe* kids to assess effects on arrest rates. But assuming that these arrest rate declines in the 1990s were *Roe* effects, and therefore also the legacy for the children born in 1990, was then and still is open to serious question.

But historians of science should take note of this episode. The criminological career of this cohort of US kids born in 1990 seems worthy of the *Guinness Book of World Records.* Before these kids turned seven, they were blamed for being a demographic time bomb certain to trouble our cities and fill our prisons. Yet before they turned 12, they were credited with leading a substantial reduction in American crime. The path from fatherless moral poverty to mother-loved wanted children was paved with crime statistics involving other age groups manipulated by creative theorists. Has there ever been a reversal of criminological fortune of this extremity?

IV. The Progeny of Moral Panic

Public and media attention were consistently focused on youth violence in the late 1980s and early in the 1990s when youth homicide arrests peaked, and the concern persisted in the middle of the 1990s after homicide rates started to fall back. The concern about youth violence provided the rationale for several layers of state laws designed to made transfers to criminal court processes and penalties easier and more frequent, as will be described in the next chapter.

If that was the legislative impact of the moral panic, what legislative effects—if any—came with the sharp decline in homicide rates of the middle and late 1990s? The only legislative impact was negative; the wave of transfer legislation abated. But none of the decades' earlier changes were reversed in the decade after 1995. The pressures for new legislation were substantively reversed, but there was little movement back in the late 1990s.

One of the reasons that declining crime rates did not produce an easing of public concerns was the string of school shootings in the middle and late 1990s that culminated in the Columbine disaster in 1999. In large part, then, the legislative outcomes of the ups and downs of the era were confined to the new laws provoked by the upswing.

APPENDIX A: ARTICLES CONCERNING JUVENILE CRIME AND JUSTICE IN *CRIME AND JUSTICE* BY YEAR

Zimring, Franklin E. 1979. "American Youth Violence: Issues and Trends." *Crime and Justice: A Review of Research* 1: 67–108.

Klein, Malcolm W. 1979. "Deinstitutionalization and Diversion of Juvenile Offenders: A Litany of Impediments." *Crime and Justice: A Review of Research* 1: 145–202.

Mennel, Robert M. 1983. "Attitudes and Policies Toward Juvenile Delinquency in the United States: A Historiographical Review." *Crime and Justice: A Review of Research* 4: 191–224.

Loeber, Rolf, and Magda Stouthamer-Loeber. 1986. "Family Factors as Correlates and Predictors of Juvenile Conduct Problems and Delinquency." *Crime and Justice: A Review of Research* 7: 29–150.

Greenwood, Peter W. 1986. "Differences in Criminal Behavior and Court Responses Among Juveniles and Young Adult Defendants." *Crime and Justice: A Review of Research* 7: 151–188.

Moffitt, Terrie E. 1990. "The Neuropsychology of Juvenile Delinquency: A Critical Review." *Crime and Justice: A Review of Research* 12: 99–170.

Spergel, Irving A. 1990. "Youth Gangs: Continuity and Change." *Crime and Justice: A Review of Research* 12: 171–276.

Feld, Barry C., 1993. "Criminalizing the American Juvenile Court." *Crime and Justice: A Review of Research* 17: 197–280.

Moore, Mark H., and Stewart Wakeling. 1997. "Juvenile Justice: Shoring Up the Foundations." *Crime and Justice: A Review of Research* 22: 253–302.

Pfeiffer, Christian. 1998. "Juvenile Crime and Violence in Europe." *Crime and Justice: A Review of Research* 23: 255–328.

Moore, Mark H., and Michael Tonry. 1998. "Youth Violence in America." *Crime and Justice: A Review of Research* 24: 1–26.
Cook, Philip J., and John H. Laub. 1998. "The Unprecedented Epidemic in Youth Violence." *Crime and Justice: A Review of Research* 24: 27–64.
Anderson, Elijah. 1998. "Social Ecology of Youth Violence." *Crime and Justice: A Review of Research* 24: 65–104.
Fagan, Jeffrey, and Deanna L. Wilkinson. 1998. "Guns, Youth Violence, and Social Identity in Inner Cities." *Crime and Justice: A Review of Research* 24: 105–188.
Feld, Barry C. 1998. "Juvenile and Criminal Systems' Response to Youth Violence." *Crime and Justice: A Review of Research* 24: 189–262.
Farrington, David P. 1998. "Predictors, Causes, and Correlates of Male Youth Violence." *Crime and Justice: A Review of Research* 24: 421–276.
Zimring, Franklin E. 1998. "Towards a Jurisprudence of Youth Violence." *Crime and Justice: A Review of Research* 24: 477–502.
Howell, James C., and David J. Hawkins. 1998. "Prevention of Youth Violence." *Crime and Justice: A Review of Research* 24: 263–316.
Bishop, Donna M. 2000. "Juvenile Offenders in the Adult Criminal System." *Crime and Justice: A Review of Research* 27: 81–168.
Cook, Philip J., and John H. Laub. 2002. "After the Epidemic: Recent Trends in Youth Violence in the United States." *Crime and Justice: A Review of Research* 29: 1–38.
Bottoms, Anthony, and James Dignan. 2004. "Youth Justice in Great Britain." *Crime and Justice: A Review of Research* 31: 21–184.
Doob, Anthony N., and Jane B. Sprott. 2004. "Youth Justice in Canada." *Crime and Justice: A Review of Research* 31: 185–242.
Morris, Allison. 2004. "Youth Justice in New Zealand." *Crime and Justice: A Review of Research* 31: 243–292.
Junger-Tas, Josine. 2004. "Youth Justice in the Neatherlands." *Crime and Justice: A Review of Research* 31: 293–348.
Kyvsgaard, Britta. 2004. "Youth Justice in Denmark." *Crime and Justice: A Review of Research* 31: 349–390.
Janson, Carl-Gunnar. 2004. "Youth Justice in Sweden." *Crime and Justice: A Review of Research* 31: 391–442.
Albrecht, Hans-Jorg. 2004. "Youth Justice in Germany." *Crime and Justice: A Review of Research* 31: 443–494.
Roberts, Julian V. 2004. "Public Opinion and Youth Justice." *Crime and Justice: A Review of Research* 31: 495-542.
Walgrave, Lode. 2004. "Restoration in Youth Justice." *Crime and Justice: A Review of Research* 31: 543–598.
Weerman, Frank M. 2007. "Juvenile Offending." *Crime and Justice: A Review of Research* 35: 261–318.
Loeber, Rolf and Wim Slot. 2007. "Serious and Violent Juvenile Delinquency: An Update." *Crime and Justice: A Review of Research* 35: 503–592.

APPENDIX B: YOUTH POPULATION AND POPULATION PROJECTIONS, US, 1980–2025

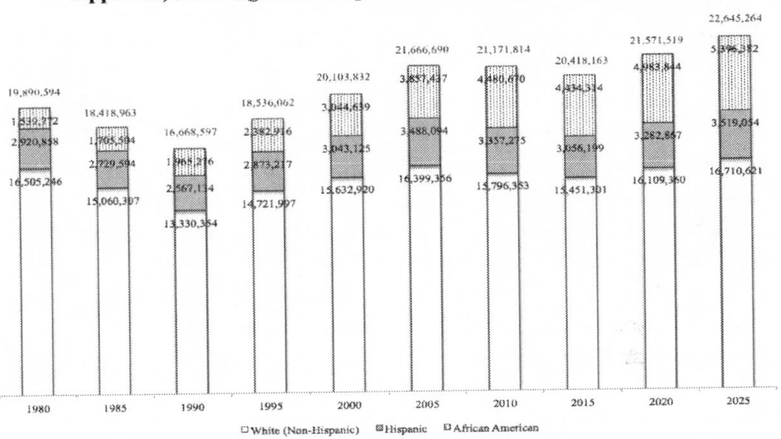

Figure 1.14. Youth Age 13–17 Populations and Projections, 1980–2025
Source: US Department of Commerce, Bureau of the Census and projections.

REFERENCES

Bennett, William J., John J. DiIulio, and John P. Walters. 1996. *Body Count: Moral Poverty . . . And How to Win America's War Against Crime and Drugs*. New York: Simon and Schuster.

Blumstein, Alfred, and Joel Wallman, eds. 2000. *The Crime Drop in America*. Cambridge: Cambridge University Press.

Center for Disease Control. 2004. *Health, United States 2004, with Chartbook on Trends in the Health of Americans*, National Center for Health Statistics, Table 45 (Death Rates for Homicide, According to Sex, Race, Hispanic Origin, and Age: United States, Selected Years 1950–2002), p. 194, www.cdc.gov/nchs/data/hus/hus04trend.pdf.

Cook, Philip J., and John H. Laub. 1998. "The Unprecedented Epidemic in Youth Violence." *Crime and Justice: A Review of Research* 24: 27–64.

Cook, Philip J., and John H. Laub. 2002. "After the Epidemic: Recent Trends in Youth Violence in the United States." *Crime and Justice: A Review of Research* 29: 1–38.

DiIulio, John. 1995. "The Coming of the Super-Predators." *Weekly Standard*, November 27, p. 1.

Donohue, John, and Steven Levitt. 2001. "The Impact of Legalized Abortion on Crime." *Quarterly Journal of Economics* 116(2): 379–420.

Fox, James Alan. 1996. *Trends in Juvenile Violence: A Report to the United States Attorney General on Current and Future Rates of Juvenile Offending.* Washington, DC: US Bureau of Justice Statistics.

McCollum, Bill. 1996. *Testimony Before the House Subcommittee on Early Childhood, Youth and Families.* April 30. (104th Con., 2d Sess.).

US Department of Commerce, Bureau of the Census, 1960–2010.

US Department of Justice, Bureau of Justice Statistics. 1991. *Criminal Victimization in the United States.* Washington, DC: US Government Printing Office.

US Department of Justice, Federal Bureau of Investigation. 1980–2010. *Uniform Crime Reports, Supplementary Homicide Reports.*

US National Center for Health Statistics. 1991. *Vital Statistics of the United States.* Washington, DC: US Government Printing Office.

US National Center for Health Statistics. 2005. *Health, United States, 2005.* Hyattsville, MD: US National Center for Health Statistics.

Wilson, James Q. 1995. "Crime and Public Policy." In James Q. Wilson and Joan Petersilia, eds., *Crime: Public Policies for Crime Control.* San Francisco, CA: Institute for Contemporary Studies.

Zimring, Franklin E. 1997. "Desperadoes in Diapers." *Los Angeles Times*, August 19.

Zimring, Franklin E. 1998. *American Youth Violence.* New York: Oxford University Press.

Zimring, Franklin E. 2005. *American Juvenile Justice.* New York: Oxford University Press. (Figure 1.13.) US Department of Commerce, Bureau of the Census, 1960–1994, 1995a.)

Zimring, Franklin E., and Jeffrey Fagan. 2005. "Two Patterns of Age Progression in Adolescent Crime." In Zimring, Franklin E., *American Juvenile Justice.* New York: Oxford University Press, chap. 7.

Zimring, Franklin E. and Gordon Hawkins. 1995. *Incapacitation: Penal Confinement and the Restraint of Crime.* New York: Oxford University Press.

Zimring, Franklin E. and Stephen Rushin. 2012. *Did Changes in Juvenile Sanctions Reduce Juvenile Crime Rates? A Natural Experiment.*

2

The Power Politics of Juvenile Court Transfer in the 1990s

FRANKLIN E. ZIMRING

The boundary between the juvenile court's delinquency jurisdiction and the criminal process should be one of those obvious fault lines between sharply different approaches to the same sort of problems that provoke analysis and debate in courts, in the academy, and in state legislatures. What are and what should be the differences in emphasis between a court for 17-year-old burglars and one that claims jurisdiction for those with identical charges but earlier dates of birth (Zimring 1998, ch. 5)? The discussion of what justifies separate treatment for adolescent offenders should be an important and jurisprudentially thick discourse, but it's not. Why?

Whatever the general age boundaries imposed by state legislation between juvenile and criminal court, there are always in the United States special proceedings that are available to facilitate the transfer of youth under the usual age threshold from the juvenile to the criminal court (Tanenhaus 2000, 13–35). Even if general rules such as maximum jurisdictional age are rarely informed by extensive analysis, surely these exceptional cases where a youth might be removed from juvenile court present the sort of high-stakes individual dramas that provoke deep thought and require the resort to the basics of legal philosophy, to a search for fundamentals.

Standards for transfer should inspire detailed legislative debate about the purposes and limits of juvenile courts. Judicial decisions about waiver from juvenile to criminal court should be thoughtful, meticulous, and ambivalent. Appellate review of judicial waiver decisions should be one of the major intellectual challenges of a state appeals court career. But transfer is a jurisprudential wasteland. The gap between theory and practice in transfer decision making is huge at every branch of state government, and the poverty of judicial performance in waiver decisions and appeals is a particular disappointment. Why? What is there about the jurisprudential issues raised by waiver that produces legislative and judicial underperformance?

Part of the problem was a disingenuous theory of waiver in the original juvenile court, and this has been exacerbated by political debates where transfer policy is a crude surrogate for support or opposition to juvenile courts generally. For the entire duration of the juvenile court, the waiver of some serious cases into a criminal court has been a practice in search of a theory. The problem from day one wasn't the absence of a prominent rationale for a separate juvenile court, but rather the embrace of an implausible cover story that only justified rejecting the delinquent if he "was not a fit subject for rehabilitation." So the task of the juvenile court judge was determining whether the subject of the petition was "amenable to treatment" (Zimring 1998, 162).

From day one an emphasis on amenability didn't sound plausible, because there were few or no treatment programs administered by early juvenile courts (Zimring 2005, 36–39). To be sure, repeated failure on probation and in custody was predictive of transfer to criminal court, but the tone of the discussion in such cases sounded much more like contempt of court that any more complex assessment of amenability. And two elements of cases that have no direct bearing on amenability to specialized treatment seem always to have been important in predicting transfer—the advanced age of the juvenile, and the seriousness of the charge. Joel Eigen found that juveniles accused of robbery homicide were 25 times as likely to be transferred in Philadelphia as those charged with robbery where no death occurred (Eigen 1981a; Eigen 1981b). Why were robbers so much more amenable to treatment?

This first great credibility gap in transfer jurisprudence was rich in potential for misrepresentation (Fagan & Zimring 2000, 4–6). The juvenile court judge was supposed to inquire about whether the subject of the hearing was "mature," but the reward for this status might be eligibility for capital punishment!

The problematic nature of nonamenability to treatment as a justification of waiver may help explain the lack of probing analysis in judicial opinions about transfer from juvenile to criminal court, because the obvious inconsistencies in the conceptual schema can generate feelings of insecurity about allowing deep inquiry into the foundations of transfer policy. If the underpinnings of transfer policy don't make sense, then covering transfer discussions with huge grants of discretion to the decision maker is one natural strategy to avoid confronting fundamental inconsistencies.

There is a second reason why discourse about transfer rarely displays depth or subtlety—and that is the crude preferences that animate the actions of most participants in the process. Attitudes toward transfer seem to come in only two conclusory varieties. Friends of the juvenile court believe all waiver is problematic and display zero tolerance for theories about its potential value (Zimring & Fagan 2000, 408–410). Critics of the juvenile court as soft on crime prefer maximum authority to transfer offenders into what is regarded as a more appropriately punitive criminal court (408–410). But this makes a debate about transfer into a referendum on the whole of the juvenile court rather than an exceptional outcome reserved for special cases.

The crude and mislabeled nature of discourse about transfer makes the identification of the reasons for policy changes difficult to identify. In this chapter, I try to determine the major reasons for legislative change on transfer in the last decade of the twentieth century. My argument is that identifying the central motives behind the 1990s shifts can help to create more effective strategies for protecting modern juvenile courts from the corruption of their mission. And misidentifying the real motives of legislative change can provoke well-intentioned people to make disastrous mistakes.

In the decade or so after 1990, there was a substantial trend in American states to pass legislation designed to increase the number of cases that could be transferred from juvenile court and to change the allocation of authority between judge and prosecutor in making transfer decisions (Zimring 1998, 11–15; Snyder & Sickmund 1995). The provocation for this legislative activity in the media was an increase in youth homicide in urban areas (Zimring 1998, 11–15 and ch. 3). To the extent that there was a mandate for change implied in this new legislation it was increasing punishment of youth violence, but it was far from clear how broad that mandate was or how much dissatisfaction with priorities and processes of juvenile courts was a major theme in the legislation. Was the legislative barrage of the 1990s the opening wave of an attempt to profoundly alter the power and jurisdiction of juvenile courts? If so, were some of the attempts to maintain the reach of juvenile courts by changing their policies either appropriate or successful in defending the juvenile court from diminished jurisdiction?

There were two important contrasts between juvenile and criminal courts in the United States of the 1990s. The first was a difference in the level of secure confinement imposed on offenders—with the criminal courts much more punitive than the juvenile courts. The second was a substantially different allocation of power between judges and prosecutors; criminal courts were run by a plea-bargaining dynamic which gave prosecutors much more power than judges, while juvenile courts conferred much more power on judges and probation staff.

I will argue in this chapter that the most important struggle during the 1990s wasn't about the jurisdiction of juvenile courts—or indeed even about the content of punishment policy for young offenders—but rather was an attempt to expand prosecutorial power in juvenile justice. I will also show that confusion among supporters of the juvenile court about the nature of the threat to juvenile justice produced one defensive strategy—so-called blended jurisdiction—that facilitated rather than deflected the major threat to the integrity and authority of the juvenile courts in the United States.

Dimensions of Difference

Figure 2.1 provides a rough estimate of different levels of secure confinement for the 13- to 17-year-old age groups at the end of juvenile court jurisdiction in most states and the 18- to 24-year-old age group where criminal courts provide exclusive jurisdiction.

The male incarceration rate for ages 18 to 24 is not available separately for jail and prison for each year in the age category. The aggregate rate for 18 to 24 is more than five times the confinement rate in ages 13 to seventeen. The confinement rate for the oldest groups under 18 is 946, so the comparison at the age boundary between 17- and 18-year-olds is probably much closer than five to one. But the 18 to 24 incarceration rate grew much more quickly in the last three decades of the twentieth century (Zimring 1998, ch. 4 at Fig. 4.1), so there was substantial

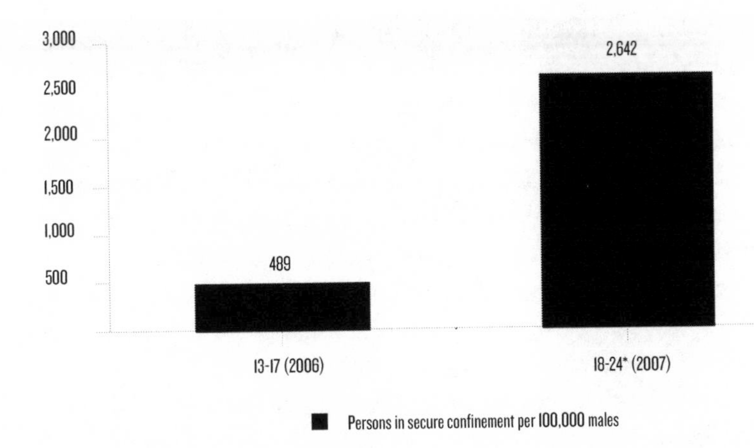

Figure 2.1. Secure Confinement per 100,000 Males for 13- to 17-Year-Olds and 18- to 24-Year-Olds, US, 2006–2007

* Based on 231,600 in prison, Bureau of Justice Statistics (BJS) prisoners in 2007, and assuming the same ratio of jail to prison for 18–24 as for all ages .42 times the 331,600 males or 100,199. For jail to prison ratios, compare BJS prisoners in 2007 with BJS jail inmates at mid-year 2007, both at www.ojp.usdoj.gov/bjs. The census population is estimated at 12,558 by taking two-fifths of the 15–19 total of 10,747,000 males and adding this to the 10,409,000 for ages 20–24. US Census Bureau, *Current Population Survey Annual Social and Economic Supplement, 2007*, Table 1. Sources: Melissa Sickmund, T.J. Sladky and Wei Kong (2008). "Census of Juveniles in Residential Placement Databook," http://ojjdp.ncjrs.org/ojstatbb/Cjrp/; "18 to 24, Bureau of Justice Statistics, Prisoners in 2007" and "Jail Inmates at mid-year 2007" in notes to 18–24 estimate.

reason to believe that juvenile courts were substantially less likely to greatly increase incarceration rates than criminal courts.

While the large gap between single-day incarceration rates might be a product of either smaller percentages of juveniles receiving custody or shorter custodial stays, the substantial front-loading of the juvenile system with detention suggests that much of the difference in aggregate incarceration populations is a result of shorter stays for the younger groups. If the ratio of prisoners to jail inmates on any given day is really more than 2 to 1 in the 18 to 24 group (as Figure 2.1 assumes), this would be *much* higher than the ratio of postadjudication confinement to detention in the juvenile system. The most probable contrast between juvenile and criminal courts is a large number of short stays at the front end of the juvenile court as opposed to much higher rates of post adjudication imprisonment in the criminal court.

There is no doubt that the juvenile court's reputation for relative leniency played a major role in the legislative politics of the 1990s, and that public fear of juvenile violence was a major element in legal change. But there are two quite different strategies for increasing severity that could be adapted to close any leniency gap between juvenile and criminal courts. One method would be to push cases that would otherwise be handled in juvenile courts into the criminal courts instead, where harsher policies are already in place. A second method, however, would be to increase the penalties and punishment priorities in the juvenile court to bring it closer to the values of criminal courts. These two separate threats to the traditional priorities of juvenile justice might both be pushed by the same actors at the same time. But to the extent that one threat is larger than the other, they call for different strategies of legal response in the juvenile court and among its traditional supporters.

The most visible form of legislative change in the 1990s was in changing the standards and procedures for transfer of serious crimes to criminal courts (Snyder & Sickmund 1995). The long-standing method of transfer was a hearing held before a juvenile court judge who had the power to waive the juvenile court's jurisdiction. This waiver would leave the prosecutor free to bring a charge in criminal court. Much of the legislation during the 1990s was designed to increase the number of charges and juveniles eligible for judicial waiver by reducing the minimum age for waiver, increasing the charges that could provide a threshold for transfer or by changing the burden of proof for judicial decision to waive. But two other methods of increasing transfers were also frequently proposed and passed. The first was legislation that provided original jurisdiction in criminal courts for particular charges brought against older juveniles. The second was an explicit grant of discretionary power to prosecutors to file in either juvenile or criminal court at their discretion.

The heavy emphasis on transfer legislation might have created the impression that a major priority of the legal change was reducing the jurisdiction and power of juvenile courts. In fact, the emphasis on murder cases as the source of public concern required a focus on waiver, because killings had always been the leading case for transfer to the much higher maximum penalties in the criminal system. Any set of juvenile court proposals driven by murder cases would emphasize transfer even if the proponents were not seeking to limit the jurisdiction of juvenile courts. Further, while the penal outcomes for murder in criminal courts are vastly higher than in juvenile court, the number of homicide cases—indeed the total number of transfers in most systems—is tiny. Only mass transfer structures such as those used in Florida and New York really cut into juvenile court jurisdiction in serious cases, and neither of these radical reforms came in the 1990s. For all the emphasis on transfer in the 1990s, there were none of the wholesale cutbacks that had been produced in the 1970s in New York and the 1980s in Florida (Zimring 1998, 15–16).

The Dog That Didn't Bark

Moreover, there was one other proposal significantly missing from the legislative record of the 1990s. The easiest way to alter the boundaries between juvenile and criminal courts is to alter the jurisdictional age that separates the two systems. There is wide variation already among the 50 states about the dividing line between juvenile and criminal court. Thirty-eight states extend the jurisdiction of juvenile courts to the eighteenth birthday, while two states make the age transition at sixteen.[1]

Because the rate of serious crime increases with each year in the midteens, there is a greater number of homicide, assault, burglary, and robbery arrests between these two birthdays than in the rest of the juvenile population (US Department of Justice 2009, Table 38). This means that a simple reduction of two years in the jurisdictional age would remove a majority of an age-18 state's serious juvenile cases to the criminal courts. Yet while 40 states made waiver or transfer easier in the early 1990s, no American state cut back the maximum age of delinquency by two years and only two states lowered the maximum age from 18 to seventeen. So the natural and simple method of expanding criminal court powers by reducing the caseload in juvenile court was never a part of the legislative agenda of the 1990s.

The absence of major emphasis on reduction of jurisdiction means that the 1990s should not be seen as a turf battle between juvenile and criminal courts. But why then the proliferation of transfer legislation and the extraordinary concentration of effort on the organization and boundaries of juvenile courts? Part of the emphasis on transfer might have been simply an attempt to do something punitive about youth violence without shifting resources or making major institutional alterations. But why multiple layers of legal change, and why were the laws so complex?

One plausible explanation for both the form and content of the 1990s brand of get-tough legislation is to regard it as an attempt to provide greater power to prosecutors within juvenile courts, to push the allocation of power in juvenile courts closer to the model of prosecutorial domination that has been characteristic of criminal courts in the United States for a generation.

The central mechanism of case disposition in criminal courts is plea bargaining, and the vast majority of the power to determine punishment rests with the prosecutor. The judge enters the legal process after the fact of punishment determination in negotiated cases, and this is the essence of what Morris and Hawkins (1977) called "an administrative law of crime." The contrast in juvenile court is substantial for institutional as well as historical reasons. Prosecutors are one of three powerful institutional presences inside the modern juvenile court. Juvenile court judges and referees, alone and in collaboration with probation staff, exercise power over detention decisions as well as whether a petition will be filed in a case, whether a juvenile will be diverted, and what type of postadjudication placement will be selected if the juvenile is adjudicated delinquent (Rosenheim 2002, 348–351). Both probation and judges are much more influential in juvenile than in criminal courts. While prosecutors are much more powerful in juvenile courts than they were a generation ago, they are much less powerful in juvenile than in criminal courts, and this is the comparison that carries the most contemporary meaning to the modern prosecutor.

Much of the complexity in 1990s-style transfer legislation, and certainly the shift from judicial waiver to "legislative direct file" and discretionary filing in juvenile or criminal court, creates more power or less work for juvenile court prosecutors, or both. The standard method of transfer in the twentieth-century juvenile court was a hearing in juvenile court, where the prosecutor attempted to persuade a juvenile court judge to transfer a juvenile within the court's jurisdiction. This type of waiver hearing is hard work for prosecutors, and while the success rate of such motions is about 80 percent, the risk of failure is nontrivial (Dawson 1992, 975).

Providing discretion to prosecutors to file in either juvenile or criminal courts is an obvious and direct shift of power from juvenile court judges to prosecutors. Providing exclusive jurisdiction for some charges in criminal court is a less obvious grant of power to prosecutors but no less direct, because it is the prosecutor who determines what charges to file. If murder charges go directly to criminal court but manslaughter may be tried in juvenile court, the selection of the charge becomes the selection of the court. So the proliferation of direct file provisions is really an enhancement of prosecutorial power as much as it is a legislative judgment about which juveniles should be transferred to criminal court, because it is contingent on prosecutorial charging discretions. And a shift from judicial waiver to direct file not only increases the power of prosecutors, it also decreases the workload necessary to produce a waiver outcome. All of this also might enhance the power of prosecutors to bargain with defense attorneys in the very early stages of cases that might end up in juvenile or criminal courts and to secure concessions in exchange for reduction of charges.

The Power Politics of California's Proposition 21

Searching for the true motives behind legislation is always something of a guessing game, and the incentives in the area of crime policy are always to represent public safety as the major reason for any proposed change in policy. This will mean that determining the real priorities in legal change is often difficult. But just at the end of the 1990s, a series of proposals drafted for Republican legislators by prosecutors[2] were packaged into a 34-part initiative put on the California ballot for March of 2000 as Proposition 21 and passed by the voters. This complex structure provides a fascinating window into the priorities of the most detailed get-tough agenda of the era.

The 17 separate changes in juvenile court legislation at the back end of Proposition 21 are a complicated attempt to leverage the powers of prosecutors at the expense of probation and judicial power (Gang Violence and Juvenile Crime Prevention Act of 1998, [Calif. Prop. 21]). The long list of changes include the usual candidates for juveniles in the 1990s—a new list of direct file categories and specific provisions making judicial waiver easier for prosecutors by expanding the list of crimes that generate a presumption of transfer and reducing the burden of proof in the judicial proceeding (Calif. Prop. 21, § 26).

But the complicated menu of changes includes two more obvious assaults on the power of other court offices. The first was phrased as a prohibition of release by probation staff if a juvenile over 14 has been charged with one of a series of felonies (Calif. Prop. 21, § 20). Typically, in California, initial detention decisions have been made by probation staff (as is intake screening), and a judicial officer then reviews the case when detention is elected after about 48 hours. Prior to Proposition 21, release by probation was not allowed only if a minor over 14 had personally used a gun. Section 20 expanded this ban to a long list of charges. What this unprincipled expansion did was shift the initial detention decision from probation to the prosecutor in a large number of cases, because the prosecutor can often select a charge that removes the probation staff's authority under the new statutory provision.

An even more visible power play was the two separate sections of Proposition 21 that deal with pretrial diversion programs of juveniles. One provision in Proposition 21 (§22) abolishes eligibility for a diversion program previously authorized by law that was administered by probation and the judiciary if a minor over 14 is charged with any felony. But a second section of Proposition 21 (§ 29), without mentioning the diversion program that Proposition 21 has just trivialized, creates a new pretrial diversion program to be administered in the juvenile court by—you guessed it—the prosecutor. Here is the smoking gun of the proposition's real agenda. There is no theory of diversion that can explain why the Gang Violence and Juvenile Crime Prevention Act of 1998 both abolishes and introduces a pretrial diversion program. The only principle that accommodates both these results is the positive value of prosecutorial power. What emerges from a careful reading of Proposition 21 is a zero-sum contest between prosecutors and other court personnel for the power to determine juvenile court policy.

And Proposition 21 is representative of much—if not most—of the legislative legacy of the 1990s. The most parsimonious explanation of why so little jurisdiction was shifted from juvenile to criminal court is that those pushing the new laws were not committed to reducing the importance or power of the juvenile court; they were instead interested in changing the power relations inside the juvenile court and the punitive priorities of the court. Both increased prosecutorial power and harsher sanctions were desired, and there was an assumption that larger prosecutorial power would achieve more punitive outcomes. But which was the more important objective? For those who drafted specifics of legislation (prosecutors themselves), it is hard to resist the conclusion that prosecutorial power was the higher priority.

Critics of the 1990s legislative frenzy, including this one, were about half right in their diagnosis of what was happening. My conclusion in 1998 was this:

> If the reforms of the past decade are typical of future trends, it is the mission of the juvenile court rather than its jurisdiction that is at risk. The goal of punitive reforms has been to reorient the juvenile court rather than to cut back on its size, its influence, or its power. For those who support the traditional mission of juvenile justice, the biggest worry will be not the decline in power of the juvenile court but the new policies that a powerful juvenile justice system may soon serve! (Zimring 1998, 16).

Why only half right? While much of the rhetoric of this paragraph wears pretty well, it also displays a regrettable failure to identify the growth of prosecutorial power as central to the threat. It was not impossible that the traditional focus of juvenile courts on limiting punishment and serving youth development could be undone by a punitive turn in the outlook of all the powerful actors in juvenile justice, but this was always unlikely. We probably won't soon live in a world in which juvenile court judges and probation officers place their faith in unqualified crime suppression and distrust most juvenile offenders. The greater danger is the shift of power within the juvenile court from the judges and probation staff who have been the bulwark of the juvenile court tradition to a regime of prosecutorial hegemony.

With the wisdom of hindsight, let me now suggest that the largest threat to enlightened delinquency policy has always been a shift of power rather than a change of heart. Prosecutors are already a powerful presence in juvenile justice, but they are not the sole determinants of juvenile justice sanctions. The danger of shifts like Proposition 21 is the transfer of sentencing powers—the power to detain, the power to divert, and the power to transfer—to prosecutors alone. And attention to these allocation of power issues should be the most prominent part of analyses of law reform throughout the domains of juvenile court policy.

In the section that follows, I revisit one set of law reform activities during the 1990s where both the problem addressed and the solutions adopted were dangerously innocent of this perspective.

The Strategic Folly of Blended Jurisdiction

One response to the pressure for new approaches to juvenile violence was the creation of a special new unit within juvenile courts that would have the power to impose much longer-than-usual sentences, and frequently would also provide more procedural protections when conducting trials. Redding and Howell (2000) describe the appeal of what is called the "blended" model in the following terms:

> Blended sentencing is an extension of the ideals of the juvenile court, allowing the court to maintain its jurisdiction over serious and violent offenders rather than having them transferred to criminal court and incarcerated in adult facilities. Blended sentencing is appealing to many juvenile justice officials, prosecutors, and defense attorneys because it preserves juvenile court jurisdiction and discretionary control . . . while providing a stronger accountability sanction and greater community protection (147).

I have long believed that the basic assumptions of blended jurisdiction were wrong and that extreme versions of the system (such as Texas) are monstrous (Zimring 1998, 169–174), but the merits of blended jurisdiction are not my point here. Instead, the 1990s adventures with blended jurisdiction will illustrate rather clearly why it is dangerous to design responses to assaults on American juvenile courts without a clear notion of what is motivating the attack.

What made blended sentencing appealing to many juvenile justice officials was the notion that expanding the punishment powers available in juvenile courts would mollify critics who were attempting to cut back on the jurisdiction and influence of the juvenile court. The problem here is that nobody was really trying to cut back on the court's jurisdiction—there were no crusades to transfer older juveniles out of the court.

There was only the attempt to make transfer easier in a few cases when huge penalties were available as a consequence. So the blended system was designed to respond to a nonexistent threat and in those cases where prosecutors wanted the huge adult system penalties, there were usually no provisions in the blended sentencing laws to make transfer unavailable.

But what if the real agenda was to reorient the juvenile court's sanctions and priorities? What if "it is the mission of the juvenile court rather than its jurisdiction that is at risk" (Zimring 1998, 16)? If the enhancement of prosecutorial power was sought and the creation of a structure of outcomes where plea bargaining was encouraged, then blended sentencing is just what the district attorney ordered. Once blended sentences become an alternative to transfer for the same juvenile (a standard condition), the district attorney offers a reduction to the blended jurisdiction if the juvenile will plead guilty in that setting. Where the blended alternative is also used as a step up from the punishment grade in regular delinquency cases, the juvenile will be choosing between a plea in the regular court or a trial in the blended tribunal. In each case, the punishment will often be determined before a judge arrives on scene. Sound a bit like criminal court?

The strategic choice argument I am making is that misreading the real agenda of the 1990s created a catastrophic error in response from many in juvenile justice. If the real danger had been the decline of court jurisdiction, then blended sentencing's expansion of punishment power might have been a remedy worth discussion. But if prosecutorial power and punitive priority were the goals of the struggle in the 1990s, then blended sentencing was nothing short of surrender. Those who hoped to hold on to a few cases otherwise headed for criminal court by sacrificing judicial power and limited punishment system-wide would celebrate a victory only General Pyrrhus could fully appreciate.

NOTES

1. Current 2009 distribution of states by maximum age for delinquency: age 15, Connecticut, New York, North Carolina; age 16, Georgia, Illinois, Louisiana, Massachusetts, Michigan, Missouri, New Hampshire, South Carolina, Texas, Wisconsin; age 17, Alabama, Alaska, Arizona, Arkansas, California, Colorado, Delaware, District of Columbia, Florida, Hawaii, Idaho, Indiana, Iowa, Kansas, Kentucky, Maine, Maryland, Minnesota, Mississippi, Montana, Nebraska,

Nevada, New Jersey, New Mexico, North Dakota, Ohio, Oklahoma, Oregon, Pennsylvania, Rhode Island, South Dakota, Tennessee, Utah, Vermont, Virginia, Washington, West Virginia, Wyoming. See US Department of Justice, Office of Juvenile Justice and Delinquency Prevention, Statistical Briefing Book (2004), http://ojjdp.ncjrs.gov/ojstatbb/structure_process/qa04101.asp?qaDate=2004.

2. There is some controversy as to which prosecutor's offices had the major role. Lisa Green, then of the Los Angeles Public Defenders Office, attributed most of the juvenile sections to the Los Angeles D.A., while other oral historians implicated Riverside.

REFERENCES

Dawson, Robert. 1992. An Empirical Study of Kent Style Juvenile Transfers to Criminal Court. *St. Mary's Law Journal* 23: 975–1054.

Eigen, Joel. 1981a. The Determinants and Impact of Jurisdictional Transfer in Philadelphia. In *Major Issues in Juvenile Justice Information and Training: Readings in Public Policy*, eds. John C. Hall, et al., 333–350. Columbus, OH: Academy for Contemporary Problems.

_____. 1981b. Punishing Youth Homicide Offenders in Philadelphia. *Journal of Criminal Law and Criminology* 72: 1072–1093.

Fagan, Jeffrey, and Franklin E. Zimring, eds. 2000. *The Changing Borders of Juvenile Justice: Transfers of Adolescents to the Criminal Court*. Chicago: University of Chicago Press.

California Proposition 21, Gang Violence and Juvenile Crime Prevention Act of 1998.

Morris, Norval, and Gordon Hawkins. 1977. *Letter to the President on Crime Control*. Chicago: University of Chicago Press.

Redding, Richard. E., and James C. Howell. 2000. Blended Sentencing in American Juvenile Courts. In *The Changing Borders of Juvenile Justice: Transfers of Adolescents to the Criminal Court*, eds. Jeffrey Fagan and Franklin E. Zimring, 145–180. Chicago: University of Chicago Press.

Rosenheim, Margaret K. 2002. The Modern American Juvenile Court. In *A Century of Juvenile Justice*, eds. Margaret K. Rosenheim, Franklin E. Zimring, David S. Tanenhaus, Bernardine Dohrn, 341–359. Chicago: University of Chicago Press.

Sickmund, Melissa, T. J. Sladky, and Wei Kong. 2008. Census of Juveniles in Residential Placement Databook. http://ojjdp.ncjrs.org/ojstatbb/Cjrp/.

Snyder, Howard N. and Melissa Sickmund. 1995. *Juvenile Offenders and Victims: A National Report*. Washington, DC: Office of Juvenile Justice and Delinquency Prevention.

Tanenhaus, David S. 2000. The Evolution of Transfer Out of Juvenile Court. In *The Changing Borders of Juvenile Justice: Transfer of Adolescents to the Criminal Court*, eds. Jeffrey Fagan and Franklin E. Zimring, 13–44. Chicago: University of Chicago Press.

US Bureau of the Census. 2007. Table 1. *Current Population Survey, Annual Social and Economic Supplement*. Washington, DC: US Department of Commerce. www.census.gov/prod/techdoc/cps/cpsmar07.pdf.

US Department of Justice, Bureau of Justice Statistics. 2007. *Prisoners in 2007.* Washington, DC: US Department of Justice. www.ojp.usdoj.gov/bjs.

US Department of Justice, Office of Juvenile Justice and Delinquency Prevention. 2004. *Statistical Briefing Book.* Washington, DC: US Department of Justice. http://ojjdp.ncjrs.gov/ojstatbb/structure_process/qa04101.asp?qaDate=2004.

US Department of Justice. 2009. Crime in the United States 2008, Table 38. www2.fbi.gov/ucr/cius2008/data/table_38.html.

Zimring, Franklin E. 1998. *American Youth Violence.* New York: Oxford University Press.

_____. 2005. *American Juvenile Justice.* New York: Oxford University Press.

_____. 2007. *The Great American Crime Decline.* New York: Oxford University Press.

Zimring, Franklin E. and Jeffrey Fagan. 2000. Transfer Policy and Law Reform. In *The Changing Borders of Juvenile Justice,* eds. Jeffrey Fagan and Franklin E. Zimring, 407–424. Chicago: University of Chicago Press.

PART II

New Borderlands for Juvenile Justice

An important part of a twenty-first-century agenda for reform in the legal world of adolescence is reversing the negative impact of the legal changes discussed in Part I of this book, but there are also several emerging issues that affect kids and the juvenile court that require sustained attention. Michael Caldwell provides a comprehensive test of the assumptions made in federal and state law on juvenile sex offenses and outlines some steps away from the destructive silliness of current policy. School failure was always an important risk factor in adolescent development, but Aaron Kupchik shows that school discipline has now become a pathological process that demands independent reforms. James Forman Jr. profiles the short but exciting history of the Maya Angelou Academy, and argues that quality education for incarcerated youth must become a priority for juvenile justice. David Thronson shows how immigration enforcement can threaten both the mission of the juvenile court and the prospects of youth without lawful status who come before it. James Jacobs addresses the important and complicated balance of policies governing the existence and use of information about youth misconduct.

The final focus issue in this collection of priority concerns—minority overrepresentation—is a problem as old as the juvenile court, but no less critical because it lacks novelty.

3

Juvenile Sexual Offenders

MICHAEL F. CALDWELL

The state interest in reducing sexual violence in society is both appropriate and honorable. The rate of violence in a society is arguably an appropriate proxy for the degree of civility in a society. However, to achieve the end of producing a more civil society, public policies must be effective at reducing the form of violence they target. When a society implements policies that infringe the civil liberties of a designated subgroup in exchange for a public good, this bargain can only produce a more civil society if the policies are effective at achieving that public good. If the policies are ineffective, the civil liberties of the subgroup are sacrificed for no benefit, resulting in a net loss of liberty and civility in society. To date, this simple and self-evident logic does not appear to carry much weight in public policies regulating adolescent sexual misconduct.

Several assumptions serve as the foundation for recent legislation designed to incapacitate or provide closer supervision of sexual offenders. This chapter first analyzes the empirical evidence behind these assumptions, and offers a preliminary model of the development of adolescent sexual behavior based on the convergence of research from several fields. Arrest statistics pertaining to sexual violence, it should be noted, have consistently shown that juveniles account for approximately one in five sexual crimes in the United States (Federal Bureau of Investigation, 2012; Finkelhor, Ormrod, & Chaffin, 2009). In an effort to reduce sexual violence in their communities, states have adopted sex offender registration and notification statutes and passed civil commitment laws that target sexual offenders. As a result, juvenile offenders have been included in most sex offender registration and notification laws, and in several state laws that allow for civil commitment (Lave & McCrary, 2011).

The additional restrictions that are placed on juvenile sexual offenders are grounded in a common belief that juvenile sexual offenders are unlike other delinquents. An adjudication for a sexual offense as an adolescent is assumed to indicate that the person has certain internal characteristics that other juvenile delinquents do not have, and that those internal characteristics make them much more likely to persist in sexual offending behavior than other delinquents are.

The exact nature of these internal characteristics remains somewhat unclear. However, special and sustained restrictions on juvenile sex offenders, and specialized sex offender treatment services, all rest on basic assumptions about what these characteristics are, and that they produce a stable propensity for sexual offending.

Yet as this chapter shows, the notion that juvenile sexual offenders typically have a distinct and specialized proclivity for sexual offending runs counter to a widespread acknowledgment that juvenile sexual offenders constitute a heterogeneous group (Garfinkle, 2003; Letourneau & Miner, 2005). A variety of typologies have been developed in an effort to describe the various constellations of characteristics that may contribute to sexual misconduct (Aebi, Vogt, Plattner, Steinhausen, & Bessler, 2012; Atcheson & Williams, 1954; Faniff & Kolko, 2012; Hunter, Figueredo, Malamuth, & Becker, 2003; Richardson, Kelly, Graham, & Bhate, 2004; Worling, 2001). These typologies have attempted to categorize juvenile sexual offenders on the basis of their recent behavioral histories or personality traits at the beginning of treatment. None have been used to identify juvenile sexual offenders that will persist in sexual offending into adulthood. Other studies have attempted to identify specific factors that may serve as proxies for putative internal traits. For practical reasons, these studies nearly always use samples of convenience of juvenile sexual offenders that have been referred to a treatment program or detention facility. However, the types of adolescents referred to a treatment program may say more about the decision process of the referral source than it does about the nature of sexual misconduct in adolescents as a group. In other words, these typologies may describe the types of adolescents the referral source selects to send to, or exclude from, the treatment program. Juvenile sexual offenders as a group may differ from these preselected samples, and these samples may differ significantly from each other. Indeed, the variation in findings across studies may be due in part to differences in sample characteristics.

The search to identify characteristics in juvenile sexual offenders that constitute a propensity to sexually offend over time is more complex than may be initially apparent. To begin with, characteristics that produce the onset of sexual misconduct may not be the same as the characteristics that produce a stable and persistent propensity for sexual offending over time.

For this reason, studies that review the histories of juvenile sexual offenders may have difficulty identifying factors that predict future risk. Secondly, decades of research into adolescent development has improved our understanding that significant development forces affect adolescents' ability to modulate emotions (Cauffman, Shulman, Steinberg, Claus, Banich, Graham, et al., 2010; Steinberg, Albert, Cauffman, Banich, Graham, & Woolard, 2008), moderate appetites and risk-taking behaviors (Steinberg, 2007; Steinberg, Albert, Cauffman, Banich, Graham, & Woolard, 2008), and resist a variety of external influences (Monahan, Steinberg, & Cauffman, 2009; Steinberg & Monahan, 2007). This body of research has documented that the capacity to modulate and direct the behavioral expression of internal drives and impulses changes considerably through the adolescent years. As a result, attempting to identify characteristics that will be persistently expressed through sexual offending behavior is complicated by the moving target of adolescents developing capacity for self-control.

Third, it remains unclear to what extent juvenile sexual misconduct reflects a delinquent expression of otherwise conventional sexual interests, rather than a more basic disturbance in the sexual interests and drives of juvenile sexual offenders. In short, it is possible that the sexual behavior of juvenile sexual offenders differs from the sexual behavior of nondelinquents in its delinquent characteristics rather than its sexual characteristics. Delinquent youth may act more impulsively, with more high-risk behaviors, employ less discretion, and act with less concern about the potential negative consequences of detection. In addition, delinquent youth tend to associate with other impulsive and risk-taking youth, providing them with more opportunities for sexual misconduct, more scrutiny by authorities, and more aggressive intervention by authorities when they are detected. In this case, the proclivity for delinquent behavior may be more strongly associated with adult sexual offending than juvenile sexual offending alone.

Research into many of these issues is limited. The available research provides little that would allow a reliable assessment of the probability that a specific adolescent will engage in adult sexual offending. However, the accumulating research is beginning to illuminate the most common features of juvenile sexual offenders as a group and how they relate to other delinquents and persistent adult sexual offenders. Although information regarding what is typical for juvenile sexual offenders as a group may have limited utility for the clinical understanding of a specific youth, its value in the formulation of public policies is much greater.

The next sections of this chapter analyze closely the research findings about the core assumptions underlying current policies aimed at combating juvenile sexual violence. Are juvenile sexual offenders a distinct subgroup? Are they more dangerous than other delinquents? Are they sexual deviants similar to adult sexual offenders? The empirical answers to these questions demonstrate that adolescent sexual offenders are distinct from adult sexual offenders in many important respects. Further, the extant research provides virtually no reason to believe that sex offender registration and notifications laws or civil commitment policies can be effectively applied to adolescents. The chapter concludes that many of these policies were adopted at a time when little empirical information was available to inform the debate. However, empirical information has now accumulated that can inform and help shape new public policies that will be more effective in reducing sexual violence and improving community safety.

Are Juvenile Sexual Offenders a Distinct Subgroup of Delinquents?

If juvenile sexual offenders have distinct characteristics that propel them toward sexual offending, it follows that they should be apt to specialize in sexual offending. Specifically, they should persist in sexual offending to a significantly greater degree than other juvenile delinquents do, and they should be somewhat more apt to recidivate with sexual offenses than with other types of offenses.

Arrest data from the National Incident Based Reporting System (Finkelhor, Ormrod, & Chaffin, 2009; Snyder, 2000), and the Canadian Uniform Crime Report (Brennan & Taylor-Butts, 2008), have consistently indicated that juveniles are disproportionately represented in the offense reporting and arrest data for sexual assault. These data have shown that between 15 and 20 percent of all sexual assaults are committed by adolescents. In sexual assaults of children, the most prevalent age of the offender is between 13 and 15 with a decline in prevalence by approximately half by age eighteen. If the factors that impel sexual violence in adolescents were stable, one would expect that the sexual recidivism rate of adolescent offenders would be significantly higher than that of adult sex offenders. In fact, the opposite appears to be the case.

Perhaps the largest meta-analysis of adult sexual offense recidivism was conducted by Hanson and Morton-Bourgon (2004). In a review of 82 studies including 29,450 adult sexual offenders they found a mean sexual recidivism rate of 13.7 percent, with several studies reporting sexual recidivism rates above 30 percent (Hanson & Bussiere, 1998). In addition, general recidivism rates were approximately three times the rates of sexual recidivism in these studies. By contrast, Caldwell (2010) conducted a meta-analysis of 63 studies that reported sexual recidivism data on samples of juvenile sexual offenders that were not prescreened on the basis of risk. The meta-analysis included 11,219 juvenile sex offenders, and found the mean sexual recidivism rate of 7.08 percent. The mean rate of general recidivism in these studies was 43.4 percent, or six times the sexual recidivism rate. In addition, only one study of 50 juvenile sexual offenders reported adult sexual recidivism rates over 15 percent, while 22 studies reported rates of less than 5 percent. The follow-up time of these studies added to the sexual recidivism rate only over the first five years of follow-up. Studies with follow-up times that exceeded 10 years reported sexual recidivism rates below 10 percent.

These data provide indirect evidence that juvenile sexual offending is apt to be driven by less specific and stable characteristics than adult sex offending is. More direct information about whether juvenile sexual offenders are a distinct subset of juvenile delinquents can be drawn from recidivism studies of cohorts of delinquents that include juvenile sexual offenders and non–sex offending delinquents. There are seven such studies in the extant literature (Caldwell, 2007; Caldwell, Ziemke, & Vitacco, 2008; Driessen,

2002; Milloy, 1994; Mulder, Vermunt, Brand, Bullens, & Van Marle, 2012; Zimring, Jennings, Piquero, & Hayes, 2007; Zimring, Piquero, & Jennings, 2007). These studies use different statistical analytic techniques to compare groups, making them difficult to compare as written. To overcome this limitation, effect sizes were calculated from the 2 X 2 tables that could be derived from the available information. The effect size statistic is a measure of the difference between two groups, divided by the pooled standard deviation (Cohen, 1988). As used here, it is a measure of how much of an effect having a juvenile sexual adjudication has on adult sexual recidivism. One advantage of this method is that effect sizes from different studies can be combined to produce a weighted mean effect size. To do this, the effect size for each study is weighted by the inverse of its variance. This has the effect of giving greater weight to studies with larger samples and more distinct differences between groups. Cohen (1988) has recommended a common frame of reference in which effect sizes less than 0.30 are considered "small" and may reflect uncontrollable extraneous variables rather than a true relationship between the variables being studied.

Table 3.1 shows the effect sizes of the seven studies that have examined the effect of having a juvenile sexual offense arrest or adjudication on adult sexual recidivism as compared to a nonsexual arrest or adjudication.

Table 3.1. Studies of Risk Factors Predicting Persistent Sexual Offending among Adolescent Sexual Offenders (N = 9017)

Factor	Number of studies	Number of studies showing increased risk	Number of studies showing decreased risk
Assaulting a younger victim	9	2	2
Age at admission to treatment	11	0	0
History of being physically or sexually abused, or neglected	13	2	1
Substance abuse history	8	0	0
Having a stranger victim	8	2	0
Having a male child victim	16	0	2
Force used in the offense	5	0	1
Total number of victims	7	1	0
Prior arrests for any offense	8	0	0
Prior sexual assault charges	14	3	0

As can be seen, the individual effect sizes are typically small and the weighted mean effect size is quite small, indicating that having a juvenile sexual offense arrest or adjudication had very little effect on adult sexual recidivism, over and above having a nonsexual adjudication or arrest. The exception to this pattern is seen in the results in Mulder, Vermunt, Brand, Bullens, & Van Marle (2012), where the effect size was moderate but negative. This last finding means that juveniles with a sexual offense adjudication were actually *less* likely to have an adult sexual offense arrest than non–sex offending delinquents were. Effects of this size may well be unrelated to any internal traits of juvenile sexual offenders, or indeed any differences between the behavior of juvenile sexual offenders and individuals who have no juvenile sexual offense record. For example, it is reasonable to assume that in marginal cases, law enforcement officials may be more apt to arrest or charge an individual with a previous record of juvenile sexual offending than an individual without that history. Thus the small effects seen here may be due to greater vigilance or responsiveness of law enforcement, or to many other unidentified factors. However, these data must be considered with the caution that four of the seven studies drew their samples from the same state (Caldwell, 2007; Caldwell, Ziemke, Vitacco, 2008; Driessen, 2002; Zimring, Piquero, & Jennings, 2007).

Looking at these seven studies in more detail reveals additional information about the broader criminal propensities of juvenile sexual offenders as compared to other delinquents. In brief, juvenile sexual offenders as a group appear to be no more likely to engage in sexual violence than similar non–sex offending delinquents. For example, Zimring, Piquero & Jennings (2007) found that although juveniles who had an adolescent police contact related to a sex offense had a slightly higher rate of adult police contacts for a sexual offense, the best predictor of adult sex offending was having a large number of juvenile police contacts for any reason.

The evidence that a general delinquent propensity predicts adult sexual offending approximately as well as having a juvenile sexual offense intervention does not entirely settle the question of whether a juvenile sexual offender adjudication may be a reliable proxy for latent traits that predisposes the youth to persistent sexual offending. It is possible that highly delinquent youth engage in sexual misconduct as a part of their poor self-management skills.

Those self-management skills tend to improve with age, accounting for the tendency for the prevalence of offending to decline dramatically with age from mid-adolescence through early adulthood. This segment of the juvenile sexual offender population may dominate and conceal a more dangerous and persistent sex offender whose offending does not arise from generalized adolescent risk-taking or poor self-management. If this were the case, youth whose sexual offending is driven by more persistent and specific traits would be expected to "specialize" in sexual offending, and juvenile sexual offender specialists should present a more specific and persistent risk for adult sexual offending.

Here again, the extant research does not support the hypothesis that sexual misconduct among juvenile sexual offender specialists is a manifestation of more stable and specific traits that predispose the youth to sexual offending. For example, a smaller number of arrests for general, nonsexual offending may indicate that the individual's sexual offenses were not a manifestation of a general criminal propensity, but instead were driven by a specific propensity for sexual misconduct. Nine studies have examined this issue by analyzing whether the number of prior arrests for any reason serves as a reliable predictor of adult sexual recidivism (Auslander, 1998; Boyd, 1994; Hecker, Scoular, Righthand, & Nangle, 2002; Miner, 2002a; Nisbett, Wilson, & Smallbone, 2004; Prentky, Harris, Frizzell, & Righthand, 2000; Smith & Monastersky, 1986; Worling & Curwen, 2000; Zimring, Piquero & Jennings, 2007). None of these studies have found that fewer prior nonsexual offense arrests predict a higher rate of sexual recidivism.

In a more specific study of this issue, Rajlic and Gretton (2007) compared adult recidivism rates between a group of 140 juvenile sexual offenders with a history of other offenses and 128 juvenile sexual offender specialists who had no history of nonsexual offense arrests, followed for an average of 6.6 years. They found that the specialists had lower rates of sexual recidivism (7% compared to 12.9% for the more delinquent juvenile sexual offenders) that did not differ significantly from the "generalists" ($C^2(1, N = 268) = 1.98, p = .16$). The juvenile sexual offender specialists reoffended with general offenses at a rate that was less than half that of the more generally delinquent juvenile sexual offenders (26.6% for the specialists compared to 64.3 percent for the generalists; $C^2(1, \mathrm{N} = 268) = 40.39, \mathrm{p} < .001$). In short, there appears to be no evidence that juveniles whose only adolescent delinquency involves sexual misconduct are driven to offend by more stable and specific sex offending traits. These data also indicate that a general criminal propensity is likely to be a part of persistent sexual offending among the small subgroup of adolescents that continue to sexually offend in adulthood.

Are Juvenile Sexual Offenders More Dangerous Than Other Delinquents?

One potential area of concern about juvenile sexual offenders involves the perception of sexual offenses as being a particularly callous and harmful category of crime. Obviously, sexual offenses involve very personal, intrusive, and harmful acts. It is a reasonable belief that if an individual is capable of such a personal offense, particularly against a child, then they must be capable of almost any type of violent behavior.

Studies have consistently shown that juvenile sexual offenders are far more likely to reoffend with nonsexual offenses than sexual offenses. In his meta-analysis of 63 data sets, Caldwell (2010) found that on average, juvenile sexual offenders' general offense rate was six times that of their sexual reoffense rate. In addition, several studies that have compared recidivism rates of juvenile sexual offenders to non–sex offending delinquents have found that the two groups had similar general and violent reoffense rates, or offense rates that were significantly lower for the juvenile sexual offenders. For example, in a study comparing 91 juvenile sexual offenders to 174 non–sex offending delinquents, Caldwell, Ziemke, and Vitacco (2008) found no significant differences in the sexual or violent reoffense rates of juvenile sexual offenders and non–sex offending delinquents, but juvenile sexual offenders were less likely to be charged with offenses in general. The sample was drawn from a program designed for the most disruptive and aggressive youth held in the state's training schools, and therefore represented an unusually criminally prone group. Sixty-nine percent of the juvenile sexual offenders in this study were charged with a new offense of any kind over the 5.9-year follow-up, while 88 percent of the non–sex offending juveniles were charged with an offense of some kind (C^2 (1, N = 264) = 8.47, $p < .005$).

Similarly, in a study of all juveniles released from secured custody over a two-year time period, Caldwell (2007) compared reoffense rates of 249 juvenile sexual offenders and 1780 non–sex offending delinquents. He found that juvenile sexual offenders were no more likely to be charged with a sexual or other violent offense, but committed fewer general and felony offenses. Excluding sexual offenses, juvenile sexual offenders averaged 4.8 (SD = 6.9) charges per youth compared to 6.3 (SD = 7.6) offenses per non–sex offending juvenile ($t=2.56$, $p<.05$).

Similarly, in a Dutch study of 66 juvenile sexual offenders and 662 other delinquents, Mulder, Vermunt, Brand, Bullens, and Van Marle (2012) found that juvenile sexual offenders were significantly less apt to commit general, violent, or sexual offenses in the follow-up period (Mean follow-up = 5.8 years, SD = 2.4 years). Forty-seven percent of juvenile sexual offenders committed a new offense of any kind compared with 83 percent of the other delinquents. Similarly, 27 percent of juvenile sexual offenders committed new violent offenses compared to 67 percent of the other youth. Only 3 percent of the juvenile sexual offenders committed a new sexual offense compared to 5 percent of property offenders and 6 percent of violent offenders.

One of the main contributors to public concern about young sexual offenders who may be engaged in relatively minor sexual misconduct is the occasional high-profile and horrific sexual homicide case that makes the news. These cases are often listed in the preamble to laws that impose more restrictive or long-term measures on sexual offenders. Undoubtedly individuals can be identified who began their offending careers with relatively minor juvenile sexual misconduct and who eventually progressed to sadistic sexual homicides. However, this fact offers little of value to inform public policy. As an illustration, one could establish that the players in the National Basketball Association's All Star Game were significantly more likely to have played on an organized basketball team in seventh grade than the general population. However, as a practical matter, seventh-grade basketball players possess a miniscule risk of playing in the NBA, much less finding themselves in the All Star Game. More importantly, attempting to identify a specific seventh-grade player who will progress to the NBA would be a fool's errand. In the same way, a retrospective analysis of the developmental course of the most serious adult sexual offenders offers very little to our understanding of juvenile sexual offenders as a group, and the characteristics that lead from adolescent sexual misconduct to persistent sexual or other violent adult offending.

Studies that directly address the possibility of progression of juveniles' offending toward this type of more severe sexual violence are largely absent from the literature. However, in a study of a cohort of 2,029 juveniles consecutively released from secured custody over a two-year period and followed for five years, Caldwell (2007) found that none of the 54 homicides committed by the cohort in the follow-up was committed by a juvenile sex offender. Interestingly, there were three sexual homicides committed by participants who had no previous juvenile history of sexual misconduct of any kind, including school disciplinary measures for minor misbehavior such as using inappropriate sexual language.

Perhaps the most extensive study to address this issue was conducted by Sample (2006), using all adult offenders released from secured custody in Illinois between 1990 and 1997. This cohort included 16,948 sexual offenders among the 146,918 offenders followed for five years after release. Sex offenders were among the least likely to be rearrested for a homicide in the five-year follow-up. Only 2.9 percent of the sex offenders were rearrested for homicide during the follow-up period; about one-third the rate for robbers (8.2%), and lower than homicide offenders (5.7%), burglars (5.4%), larceny offenders (4.2%), and even property damage offenders (3.0%). Thus the available evidence, though limited, provides no indication that a progression from relatively less serious sexual offending to sexual homicide is characteristic of juvenile sexual offenders. In fact, the limited findings in Caldwell (2007) suggest that a proclivity for sexual homicide emerges in some nonsexual offending juvenile delinquents in adulthood, without any adolescent indications of sexual maladjustment.

Sexual Deviance and Juvenile Sexual Offenders

The extant research into persistent offending in adult sexual offenders has demonstrated that direct measures and indirect indicators of a dominant sexual arousal to deviant stimuli are reliable predictors of adult sexual offense recidivism. A small number of studies of juvenile sexual offenders have shown that these youth are apt to show arousal to children or situations that are similar to their prior offenses (Robinson, Rouleau, & Madrigano, 1997; Seto, Murphy, Page, & Ennis, 2003; Seto, Lalumiere, & Blanchard, 2000). While this suggests that clinicians may be well advised to focus treatment services on deviant sexual arousal, it says nothing about whether these indications of sexual deviance in adolescence are stable or predict future sexual misconduct.

It is important to note that in studies of adult sex offenders the relationship between deviant sexual preference and sexual recidivism is defined as a *primary* sexual arousal to criminal sexual conduct. Some level of arousal to underaged targets or scenarios involving force has been found commonly in studies of adult sexual offenders. However, the reliable relationship between deviant sexual arousal and recidivism is limited to a greater arousal to prepubescent children or scenarios involving force than to consenting adult sexual activity (Hanson & Bussiere, 1998).

The same precision cannot be found in the majority of research into deviant sexual arousal in juvenile sexual offenders. In perhaps the largest meta-analysis of persistent adult sexual offending, Hanson and his colleagues (Hanson & Bussiere, 1998; Hanson & Morton-Bourgon, 2004) reported that direct measures of deviant sexual preference for children assessed using phallometric methods was the strongest predictor of sexual recidivism. Other proxy variables believed to indicate sexual deviance, such as having a male child victim, have also proven to be reliable predictors of adult sexual recidivism. As a part of this meta-analysis the researchers examined sexual deviance of juvenile sexual offenders in 12 comparisons from seven studies. Those results provided a positive weighted mean effect size. However, the median effect size (the middle score in the series) was zero, and only three of the twelve effect sizes were positive while seven were negative or zero.[1] In addition, the three studies that relied on directly measured phallometric results to define sexually deviant arousal all failed to produce a positive effect size (Gretton et al., 2001), although a later study by Gretton and her colleagues found that a posttreatment inability to suppress a deviant sexual arousal was marginally related to sexual recidivism (Clift, Rajlic, & Gretton, 2009). At the same time, three of the four positive effect sizes relied on a definition of sexual deviance that involved a self-report measure that conflated repeated sexual *behavior* with children and a self-reported sexual *arousal* to children.

Perhaps the most serious problem in the juvenile sexual offender risk literature is the often vague and inconsistent definition of what constitutes deviant sexual arousal in an adolescent. A common strategy is to use the number of sexual offenses with underaged children as a proxy for deviant sexual arousal. However, which sexual behaviors involving children are subject to prosecution varies considerably across jurisdictions. The statutory age of consent for sexual intercourse ranges from 16 to 18 (Glosser, Gardiner, & Fishman, 2004). However, there is a great deal of variation in what constitutes criminal sexual conduct based on the relative ages of the victim and accused. For example, 24 states have no close-in-age exception that would allow underage teens who are nearly the same age to legally engage in sexual intercourse. The remaining states often have complex statutory schemes. For instance, in Maine it is illegal to engage in a "sexual act" with someone who is less than 14 years of age. However, "sexual contact" or "sexual touching" with someone who is less than 14 years of age is legal under certain circumstances. Furthermore, if the child is between 14 and 16 and their partner is within five years of their age, sexual intercourse is not illegal. In Utah "sexual conduct" with someone who is between the ages of 16 and 18 is only illegal if the partner is more than 10 years older than the teen. In North Dakota, under certain circumstances it is legal to engage in sexual penetration with someone who is as young as 10 years of age, while in California, Idaho, and Wisconsin sexual intercourse with someone under age 18 is always illegal (Glosser, Gardiner, & Fishman, 2004). As a result, the coding from official records of adolescent sexual offenses involving a child will have considerable jurisdictional variation.

In addition, public health surveys appear to indicate that illegal sexual behavior is quite common and may be normative. Published studies have found that 13 to 35 percent of young people initiate intercourse by the end of eighth grade, and by about age 16 to 17 between 50 and 70 percent of adolescents have experienced sexual intercourse (Centers for Disease Control and Prevention, 2002). It seems likely that in many states, the majority of adults have engaged in criminal sexual activity with a child, typically when they were also a child.

Of course, researchers can overcome these inconsistent definitions in state statutes by defining a child victim as a child under a specific age. If having victimized a child is a useful proxy for stable sexual deviance, then the age of the child victim should comport with the diagnostic criteria for pedophilia. However, the major diagnostic classification systems do not entirely agree about the age at which a child should be considered prepubescent. The Tenth Edition of the *International Classification of Disease* (World Health Organization, 1993) sets the age for prepubescent children at 11, while the Fifth Edition of the *Diagnostic and Statistical Manual of the American Psychiatric Association* (American Psychiatric Association, 2013) indicates that prepubescent children may be as old as thirteen. Typically, researchers who take this approach rate child victims as children under age twelve. However, this approach has also provided little support for the predictive utility of having a child victim. To date, at least ten studies have examined the utility of having a child victim in predicting persistent offending in juvenile sexual offenders (Auslander, 1998; Boyd, 1994; Caldwell, Ziemke, & Vitacco, 2008; Hecker, Scoular, Righthand, & Nangle, 2002; Nisbett, Wilson, & Smallbone, 2004; Rassmussen, 1999; Smith & Monastersky, 1986; Weibush, 1996; Wolk, 2005; Worling & Curwen, 2000). One unpublished dissertation (Boyd, 1994) found that having a child victim more than four years younger was predictive of sexual reoffense; one published study (Nisbett, Wilson, & Smallbone, 2004) found that having a child victim significantly lowered the risk of sexual recidivism, and the remaining eight studies found no significant relationship in either direction.

Similarly, the Hanson meta-analyses found that phallometrically measured sexual arousal to male children was one of the stronger predictors of sexual recidivism in adults (Hanson & Bussiere, 1998; Hanson & Morton-Bourgon, 2004). A common proxy for this factor is the presence of a male child victim in the individual's history of sexual misconduct. However, of the 16 studies of juvenile sexual offenders that have examined this factor (Auslander, 1998; Boyd, 1994; Caldwell, 2007; Caldwell, 2013; Caldwell, Ziemke, & Vitacco, 2008; Clift, Rajlic, & Gretton, 2009; Hecker, Scoular, Righthand, & Nangle, 2002; Miner, 2002a; Nisbett, Wilson, & Smallbone, 2004; Prentky, Harris, Frizzell, & Righthand, 2000; Rassmussen, 1999; Schram, Milloy, & Rowe, 1991; Skowron, 2004; Smith & Monastersky, 1986; Wolk, 2005; Williams, 2007), none found a significant relationship between having a male victim and persistent sexual offending in juvenile sexual offenders. However, two studies (Caldwell, Ziemke, & Vitacco, 2008; Miner, 2002a) found a significantly negative relationship with sexual recidivism; juvenile sexual offenders who had a male child victim were less likely to sexually recidivate as adults.

One group has examined phallometrically measured deviant sexual arousal as a predictor of sexual recidivism (Gretton, McBride, Hare, O'Shaughnessy, & Kumka, 2001; Clift, Rajlic, & Gretton, 2009). In the first of these studies, Gretton and her colleagues measured sexual deviance in 186 male juvenile sex offenders using three methods. They employed a common method of identifying a deviant sexual preference by calculating a "deviance index" measured as the average change in arousal from detumescence to arousal to "deviant" stimuli (e.g., children, coercive or manipulative sex as defined in the above categories) as a function of the average change in arousal to "nondeviant" stimuli (e.g., adults, consensual sex). However, they found that deviant arousal categorized in this way did not have a significant relationship with sexual recidivism, even when deviance was redefined as equal deviant and nondeviant arousal.

Several years later, these researchers published a study using participants from the same program, in which they reported the results of phallometric assessment of 112 juvenile sex offenders at the beginning of treatment and 83 that had completed sex offender treatment (Clift, Rajlic & Gretton, 2009). During the assessment, the youth were instructed to try to suppress their arousal to deviant stimuli (the "suppress" condition) in one trial, and to allow themselves to become aroused without interference in another trial (the "arousal" condition). In all, 40.2 percent of the original pretreatment sample and 22.0 percent of the posttreatment youth were eliminated from the study for various reasons. In addition, the stimulus set did not contain a consenting homosexual set. The authors attempted to accommodate this issue by eliminating a small number of youth that had self-identified as homosexual. However, this remains problematic in light of the research documenting the disconnect between self-reported sexual identity and arousal (Igartua, Thombs, Burgos, & Montoro, 2009; Pathela, Hajat, Schillinger, et al., 2006; Remafedi, 1992; Smith, Rissel, Richters, et al., 2003). It is quite possible that Clift and his colleagues included some participants that would have showed a dominant arousal to homosexual stimuli if it had been presented.

As a result, it cannot be determined how many "deviant" recidivists would have been "nondeviant" recidivists if a consenting homosexual stimulus set had been included. In addition, the results of this study varied depending on the statistical analysis method that was used. Posttreatment measures of deviance when the youth were given the "arousal" instructions were related sexual recidivism for stimuli involving children of both genders when analyzed with a Cox proportional hazard analysis. However, the same data analyzed with a Receiver Operating Characteristic (ROC) analysis found no relationship between sexual deviance and sexual recidivism in the "arousal" condition, but found a significant relationship between sexual deviance and sexual recidivism in the "suppress" condition for stimuli involving children in general, and female children specifically.

Considering the many limitations of this study, the results must be considered inconclusive. Specifically, a substantial part of the sample was eliminated—the nondeviant stimulus set that served as a reference point lacked a consenting homosexual stimulus—and the final results varied depending on the statistical analysis method used. If the excluded participants had been retained and a substantial portion of the youth who showed no deviant arousal had sexually reoffended, the relationships between deviant arousal and recidivism that were found may well have been erased, or even reversed.

In one of the few other studies of the relationship between phallometrically measured sexual deviance and sexual recidivism in juveniles, Rice et. al. (2012) compared the relationship between phallometrically measured deviance and recidivism among a group of 38 juveniles and 46 adults referred for assessment following a sexually motivated offense. They reported an uncommonly high rate of sexual recidivism among the juvenile offenders that exceeded the rate for adult offenders (41% for the juveniles compared to 21% for the adult offenders; the exact number of recidivists was not reported). They also reported that a child sexual preference predicted sexual recidivism for the juveniles, but not for the adult offenders.

These last two studies raise the possibility that there are some juveniles for whom sexually deviant arousal may play a role in persistent sexual offending. However, the characteristics of these last two studies render the results inconclusive. Within the context of the extant literature many of the findings of the latter study are outliers, and the meaning of these results remains unclear. The bulk of the empirical evidence provides no basis for policies that rest on the assumption that sexually deviant arousal is an important factor in persistent adolescent sexual offending.

The results of the extant research into sexual deviance in juvenile sexual offenders leave three possible explanations. First, the proxy variables for deviant sexual arousal may not be reliable in juvenile sexual offenders.

Second, measures of deviant sexual arousal in juvenile sexual offenders may be accurate, but adolescent sexual offenders' sexual deviance dissipates with age, and they develop more conventional arousal patterns and behavior in late adolescence or early adulthood. Third, measures of deviant arousal may be accurate, and sexual deviance may be static, but juvenile sexual offenders may develop better ways of controlling that arousal with age. In other words, the link between the arousal and the behavioral expression of that arousal may typically break as the adolescent ages. Considering that some of these variables are direct phallometric measures of arousal, the first of these options seems unlikely, but it is not impossible. None the less, taken at face value the extant research shows that sexual arousal in adolescents is not related to persistent sexual behavior in a static or predictable way. Rather, sexual arousal in adolescents appears to be fluid, and its link to sexual behavior is inconsistent.

This illustrates one of the issues that distinguish juvenile sexual offenders from their adult counterparts. The factors that are related to the onset of a behavior may be quite different from the factors that predict the persistence of that behavior. To illustrate, most children may start smoking cigarettes out of a desire to look mature or sophisticated. The 25-year-old who continues to smoke probably does so out of habit and addiction. The glamour and peer approval of smoking cigarettes has long since stopped being a relevant motivator.

By the same token, factors in the adult histories of adult sexual offenders may be useful predictors of persistence in part because they occur in the stream of a continuing behavior. Individuals who were influenced to initiate, but not continue, the behavior have largely dropped out of the samples used to study persistent offending in adults. By contrast, the shorter history of a juvenile sex offender may only contain factors that triggered the onset of the behavior. In any event, to date no static risk factors have proven to be consistently reliable predictors of long-term sexual reoffense risk in adolescents.

Whatever factors may be important in the transition from the initiation of the behavior to sustained sexual misconduct over time may not be evident in adolescence. The fact that the factors that reliably predict persistence of sexual misconduct in adult offenders appear to have little relationship to persistent offending in adolescence suggests that some third factor influences the dynamics of persistent sexual offending in adolescents. This third factor either activates or otherwise alters the dynamics of offending in the vast majority of juvenile sexual offenders. Over the past two decades, research from several disciplines has been converging to suggest that the normal sociobiological development of adolescents is that third factor.

Developmental Dynamics of Juvenile Sexual Offending

Bolstered by the scientific findings described above, there appears to be an emerging consensus that adolescent sexual interests and behavior are multidetermined and dynamic. To date there is relatively little research into the changing developmental dynamics that may shape adolescent sexual misconduct. However, research into the neurological and social development of appropriate mating behavior in primates offers several suggestive parallels to the development of human adolescents. In addition, closely related research into the development of sexual characteristics and social behavior in adolescence has been emerging from the field of developmental neuroscience.

One of the unique features of sexual behavior in primates is the fact that the capacity to reproduce is decoupled from the motivation to engage in sexual behavior. In most animals, the capacity and the motivation to copulate are both determined by hormones. The separation of mating ability from hormonally modulated sexual interest in primates permits social experiences and context to influence sexual behavior (Wallen & Zehr, 2004). Research has established that the development of socially appropriate sexual behavior in humans and other primates is a complex process involving hormonal mechanisms, neural structures and their development, and social experiences. The physical ability to engage in sexual behavior and the development of mature and reproductively appropriate sexual behavior appear to occur on separate timelines, and through distinct and separate but interactive mechanisms (Sisk & Foster, 2004).

Research with primates has demonstrated that the physical ability to copulate matures through a genetic and neurobiological mechanism that is separate from the actions of the gonadal hormones that influence sexual motivation (Wallen, 2001; Wallen & Zehr, 2004). In some primate species, immature development in these areas affects the ability of pubescent males to accurately appraise the sexual salience of social stimuli, thus affecting the social or reproductive appropriateness of sexual behaviors (Wallen, 2001). In primates, pubescent males often make a variety of "mating errors," including selecting inappropriate targets of sexual behavior (e.g., sexually immature targets), showing sexual arousal to nonsexual stimuli (e.g., food), and displaying sexual behavior at socially inappropriate times (Wallen & Zehr, 2004). The social context of mating behavior affects future mating behavior by altering the hormonal activity that affects sexual motivation, and through the social reactions to sexual behavior that in effect enforce the social restrictions on sexual behavior (Wallen, 2001, 2005; Wallen & Tannenbaum, 1997; Wallen & Zehr, 2004; Zehr, Maestripieri, & Wallen, 1998). These mating errors in primates typically dissipate as the individual matures through this combination of developmental maturity of the hormonally driven sexual motivation mechanisms and learning of group sexual norms through social interactions.

In this way, the ability to process and understand social information is an important foundation for the development of mature and socially appropriate sexual behavior. Research into the developmental maturity of the brains of primates has shown changes in synaptic density (Bourgeois & Rakic, 1993), neural circuitry in the prefrontal cortex (Woo, Pucak, Kye, Matus, & Lewis, 1997), and changes in dopaminergic fibers that mirrors the reorganization of the frontal lobe that occurs in human adolescents (Benes, Taylor, & Cunningham, 2000; Huttenlocher & Dabholkar, 1997; Mrzljak, Uylings, Van Eden, & Judas, 1990). Recent advances in neuroscience have begun to elaborate the neural substrate and neurodevelopmental changes in humans involved in social reasoning and sexual maturation.

In humans, adolescence marks a period of extensive maturational changes in areas of the brain that mirror functional changes in adolescents emotional, appetitive, risk-taking, and social behaviors (Blakemore, 2008; Monahan, Steinberg & Cauffman, 2009; Steinberg, 2007). Human adolescence is marked by an increase in emotional and appetitive behaviors that are innervated by the limbic system in the brain. Maturational changes in the areas of the limbic system that control sexual impulses and emotions are triggered by an increase in sexual hormones, and mature differently in males and females.

It has been well established that changes in testosterone levels have a direct and fairly rapid effect on sexual behavior in human males

(Davidson, Camargo, & Smith, 1979; Luisi & Franchi, 1980; Salmimies, Kockott, Pirke, et al., 1982; Skakkebaek, Bancroft, Davidson, et al., 1981). Prepubertal males have relatively low serum testosterone levels that increase 10 to 20 times in about a year as the individual goes through puberty (Faiman & Winter, 1974; Knorr, Bidlingmaier, Butenandt, et al., 1974; Lee, Jaffe, & Midgley, 1974; Udry, Billy, Morris, et al., 1985). Udry and his colleagues have demonstrated that nearly half of the variance in an index of sexual behavior and fantasies in adolescent boys was determined by testosterone levels (Udry, 1988; Halpern, Udry, Campbell, & Suchindran, 1993). Higher testosterone levels have also been related to aggression, social dominance, and hyperreactivity to status threats in males (Archer, 2006; Archer, Birring, &Wu, 1998; Finkelstein, Susman, Chinchilli, Kunselman, D'Arcangelo, Schwab, et al., 1997; Josephs, Sellers, Newman, & Mehta, 2006; Mazur & Booth, 1998; Mehta, Jones, & Josephs, 2008; Newman, Sellers, & Josephs, 2005; O'Connor, Archer, &Wu, 2004; Pope, Kouri, & Hudson, 2000).

Thus, at puberty, adolescent boys typically experience a relatively rapid onset of sexual impulses and fantasies, accompanied by an increase in dominance and aggressive impulses. Depending on the timing of the onset of puberty, these unfamiliar impulses can occur well before, somewhat after, or at about the same time that adolescents experience an increased reward sensitivity contributing to increased risk-taking and impulsiveness, and an increase in susceptibility to peer influences (Cauffman, Shulman, Steinberg, Claus, Banich, Graham, et al., 2010; Cauffman & Steinberg, 2000; Steinberg, 2004; 2007; Steinberg, Albert, Cauffman, Banich, Graham, & Woolard, 2008; Steinberg & Monahan, 2007). As these hormonally influenced and neurologically based behavioral activation mechanisms are developing rapidly, the cognitive areas involved with behavioral control mechanisms are developing more slowly.

Recent research in the developmental neuroscience of adolescence has documented that the frontal lobes of the adolescent brain mature in a linear fashion through early adulthood. These areas serve as the neural substrate for planning, decision making, impulse control, and other executive functions that allow impulses to be moderated and expressed in socially appropriate ways (Gogtay, Giedd, Lusk, Hayashi, Greenstein, Vaituzis, et al., 2004; Giedd, 2004; Lenroot & Giedd, 2006). Although these areas are maturing throughout the time as the hormonally driven increase in sexual and aggressive impulses, and the increase in reward sensitivity, risk-taking, and susceptibility to peer influence related to the development of limbic and other mid-brain structures, the relative influence of these mechanisms on sexual behavior depends on the particular mix of developmental capabilities and external social contingencies at a given moment.

However, the global trend is clear. Throughout adolescence, the neurological and hormonal mechanisms that tend to increase impulsive, aggressive, sexual, and risk-taking behaviors develop rapidly, while the maturity of the mechanisms that control modulated impulses and socially appropriate behaviors lag behind, catching up at full adult maturity in the early twenties (Steinberg, 2010).

Most importantly, each of these developmental dynamics change as the individual matures into young adulthood. In many areas, the individual's ability to exercise fully mature control over their impulses and engage in mature and socially appropriate intimate interactions improves through a process of biological maturity and social learning. Although social norms and influences vary tremendously across settings, many of these developmental forces are universal, affecting all adolescents to some degree. Given the fluid nature of these developmental forces, it should not be surprising that a specific subgroup of a type of behavior (e.g., sexually criminal behavior) would also be highly unstable over time.

Public Policy and the Regulation of Adolescent Sexual Behavior

Sex Offender Registration and Notification Laws

Despite the common misconceptions about the persistence of juvenile sexual offender violence (Letourneau & Miner, 2005), the concern about adolescent sexual violence is not groundless. Federal Bureau of Investigation arrest statistics have consistently shown that approximately 1 in 5 sexual assault arrests involve an adolescent (Federal Bureau of Investigation, 2012). In recent decades there has been a growing appreciation of the prevalence and harm of sexual violence in society. Jurisdictions have responded by adopting a variety of statutes intended to reduce sexual violence in the community. Among the most common of these measures have been sex offender registration and community notification statutes, and laws that allow for the civil commitment of sex offenders after their criminal sentence is complete. The majority of these statutes apply to juvenile offenders in some situations (Garfinkle, 2003; Lave & McCrary, 2011).

One of the stated goals of statutes that establish sex offender registries is to improve public safety by reducing sexual violence in the community. The rational is that if members of the community exercise greater vigilance with individuals who are at the greatest risk of sexual violence, fewer people will be vulnerable to victimization. However, professionals working in the field of juvenile justice have questioned the potential effectiveness of sex offender registration statutes (Chaffin, 2008; Garfinkle, 2003; Letourneau & Miner, 2005; Trivits & Reppucci, 2002; Zimring, 2004). Recent research has examined the potential for these statutes to be effective at identifying truly high-risk juvenile sexual offenders and at achieving their stated goal of improving community safety.

Recent studies have cast doubt on whether offense-based statutory schemes are an effective way to identify higher-risk juvenile offenders. In a study of 91 juvenile sex offenders, Caldwell and his colleagues (Caldwell, Ziemke & Vitacco, 2008) found that the Sex Offender Registration and Notification Act (SORNA) criteria embedded in Title 1 of the 2006 Adam Walsh Child Protection and Safety Act did not identify juveniles that were at greater risk for general or sexual offending. The majority of the participants (70.3%) met the criteria for Tier 3 registration, the most restrictive level. Contrary to expectations, SORNA criteria identified youth that were at significantly lower risk for violent offending over a six-year follow-up. Among the SORNA eligible youth, 46.9 percent were charged with a violent offense in the follow-up period, while the comparable rate for the youth that did not qualify for registration under SORNA was 70.4 percent. Sex offenders and non–sex offending youth were charged with new sex offenses at similar rates (12.1% for the sex offenders compared to 11.6% for the non–sex offending youth). Similarly, three risk measures that were used to determine the level of restrictiveness of registry requirements did not predict sexual recidivism. In addition, the study found that characteristics of the adjudicated sex offenses failed to predict any type of recidivism.

These results were extended and replicated in an independent study by Batastini and her colleagues (Batastini, Hunt, Present-Koller, & DeMatteo,

Table 3.2. Recidivism Rates for Sex Offender Registration and Notification Act (SORNA) Eligible and Not Eligible Youth, and Non–Sex Offending Juveniles (Non-JSO)

Caldwell, Ziemke, Vitacco (2008)			Batistini, Hunt, Present-Koller, DeMatteo (2011)		
Group	Any recidivism	Sexual recidivism	Group	Any recidivism	Sexual recidivism
SORNA tier 3	65.6%	10.9%	SORNA tier 3	15.0%	1.5%
Not SORNA eligible	77.8%	14.8%	Not SORNA eligible	19.5%	2.4%
Non-JSO	88.4%	11.6%			

2011), who examined the rearrest rates of a group of 112 adjudicated juvenile sexual offenders over a two-year period post treatment. This sample was made up of youth who were treated in the community, while the Caldwell et al. (2008) sample was made up of high-risk violent offenders held in secured custody. Table 3.2 summarizes the results of these two studies that sampled youth at opposite ends of the intervention spectrum.

Sixty-seven of Batastini's participants (62%) met the criteria for Tier 3 registration under SORNA. Only one of the 67 juveniles who qualified for registration sexually reoffended in the two-year follow-up period, and only one of the 41 juvenile sexual offenders who did not qualify for registration sexually reoffended. There were no significant differences in the rates of general offending between the SORNA designated groups.

The Adam Walsh Act SORNA criteria, like most registration statutes, rely on the characteristics of an adjudicated offense (e.g., age of the victim, age of the perpetrator, nature of the charge). As noted above and elsewhere (Caldwell, Ziemke, & Vitacco, 2008), many of these offense characteristics appear to have no more than a weak relationship with persistent sexual offending in juvenile sexual offenders. It is not surprising, then, that registration criteria have not been found to accurately identify high-risk juvenile sexual offenders. In a multistate study, Zgoba and her colleagues examined the Adam Walsh Act SORNA tier assignment system, applied retrospectively to adult offenders released between 1990 and 2004 (Zgoba, Miner, Knight, Letourneau, Levenson, & Thornton, 2012). The researchers found a significant inverse relationship between Adam Walsh Act tier designation and 10-year sexual recidivism rates. That is, individuals who were classified as higher risk and placed on more restrictive tiers using the Adam Walsh Act criteria had lower sexual recidivism rates. In contrast, individualized assessments of high risk on the registration tiers that individual states used were associated with higher sexual recidivism rates. The results indicate that the Adam Walsh Act SORNA criteria are unreliable, and that jurisdiction specific variables may make it extremely difficult to formulate a uniform national sex offender registration policy.

To date, there is little scientific evidence that registration actually protects children by decreasing offender recidivism. At least 15 studies have examined the effects of sex offender registration and community notification statutes on recidivism or the rate of sexual offending in a community. The majority of these have studied adult sexual offenders. Nine studies compared recidivism rates among samples of adult sexual offenders before and after the adoption of registration statutes. A complicating variable in this type of time series analysis is the steady decline in the rate of sexual offending in the United States over the last several decades (Federal Bureau of Investigation, 2012; Finkelhor & Jones, 2004). Because the rate of sexual violence has been declining nationwide, any study that uses an earlier time frame as a baseline and compares it to a later time frame (i.e., after adoption of a new policy) is likely to find a lower rate of sexual violence in the more recent time frame regardless of any intervening policy change. Of the studies on adult sexual offenders constructed in this way, two studies found a significantly lower rate of sexual recidivism among registered offenders or offenders subject to broader notification, compared to unregistered or offenders subject to less extensive notification who were processed at an earlier time (Duwe & Donnay, 2008; Washington State Institute for Public Policy, 2005). However, neither study controlled for the general trend of declining sexual offending over time. The remaining six studies found no significant relationship between the adoption of registration statutes and rates of sexual violence (Sandler, Freeman, & Socia, 2008; Schram & Milloy, 1995; Vasquez, Maddan, & Walker, 2008; Veysey, Zgoba, & Dalessandro, 2008; Zevitz, 2006; Zgoba, Witt, Dalessandro, & Veysey, 2008).

Among the studies of adult sex offenders, only two studies have compared registered to unregistered sex offenders processed at similar times (Adkins, Huff, & Stageberg, 2000; Freeman, 2012). Both found that registration was not associated with significantly different sexual or general reoffense rates between the registered and unregistered sex offenders.

While sex offender registration appears to provide no benefit to public safety, community notification appears to significantly decrease community safety. In a study comparing registration and notification laws across several states in a time series study using economic data analytic techniques, Prescott and Rockoff (2008) reported mixed evidence for the effectiveness of registration and notification statutes. Some analyses indicated that large registries may reduce the incidence of sexual recidivism. However, their most significant finding was that the adoption of community notification laws was associated with a significant increase in sexual recidivism among individuals subject to these laws. The data suggested that any benefit derived from having a sex offender registry was eliminated by adopting community notification provisions.

In a large study of adult sex offenders in New York State, Freeman (2012) compared 10,592 adult offenders subject to community notification laws to 6,573 sex offenders who were not subject to community notification. The results showed that the group subject to notification had lower nonsexual rearrest rates (40.5% versus 49.8% for the no-notification comparison group), and lower sexual rearrest rates (6.3% versus 8.0% for the comparison group). However, after controlling for a variety of potentially confounding factors, Freeman found that offenders subject to notification were arrested significantly faster than those not subject to notification.

The author noted the fact that a smaller proportion of the notification group was ultimately rearrested, and that individuals who were on a higher registration tier were rearrested significantly faster than their lower tiered counterparts (although both were subject to the same community notification procedures), indicating that the accumulated stress and stigma of community notification may have generated earlier failure rates in the notification group.

Only four studies have examined the effects of sex offender registration and notification among juvenile sexual offenders. Letourneau and her colleagues examined the arrest data for 26,574 youth adjudicated in South Carolina between 1991 and 2004 (Letourneau, Bandyopadhyay, Sinha, & Armstrong, 2010). After controlling for several other policy issues, they found that applying registration and notification laws to adolescent offenders had no significant deterrent effect on juvenile sexual offending. In a subsequent study, Letourneau and Armstrong (2008) found no significant differences in rates of new convictions between a group of 111 registered juvenile sex offenders and a matched group of 111 nonregistered delinquents.

In a similar study, Letourneau and her colleagues found no significant differences in new arrests for crimes against persons in a group of 574 registered juvenile sex offenders compared to 701 nonregistered juveniles (Letourneau, Bandyopadhyay, Sinha, & Armstrong, 2009). Similarly, Caldwell and Dickinson (2009) examined risk measures and recidivism rates between samples of 106 registered and 66 unregistered juvenile sex offenders followed for an average of 49.2 months after being released from secured custody. They found that the youth that were required to register had significantly lower-risk scores on scales that most accurately predicted recidivism, but registered youth were charged with new crimes at rates similar to those of unregistered youth. Thus registration appeared to be applied to lower-risk youth, but those youth then reoffended at rates that were similar to higher-risk youth. At a minimum, the findings indicate that the statutory criteria that trigger registration fail to identify higher-risk youth. The results also suggest that registration may increase recidivism rates of relatively low-risk youth, to that of relatively higher-risk youth.

While research has not established that sex offender registration and notification laws produce a substantial benefit to community safety, that does not mean that they are inconsequential. Recent research with adult sex offenders has documented that registration has unintended negative effects on sex offenders, such as mental distress, harassment, and social isolation (Levenson & Cotter, 2005; Levenson, D'Amora, & Hern, 2007; Robbers, 2009; Schiavone & Jeglic, 2009; Tewksbury, 2005; Tewksbury & Lees, 2006), which might make these offenders more likely to reoffend (Letourneau & Miner, 2005). Indeed, the results of the studies by Caldwell and Dickenson (2009) and Freeman (2012) provide preliminary but compelling evidence that registration and notification has the effect of impeding community reintegration of less resilient offenders, who are then rearrested more rapidly. In addition, it is often overlooked that the sex offender's employer, cohabitants, and school are typically listed on the registration web page with the sex offender. The collateral harm to those who associate with registered sex offenders has only recently begun to be studied (Human Rights Watch, 2013).

Civil Commitment of Sexual Offenders

For many reasons, it is difficult to assess the effectiveness of statutes that allow for the civil commitment of sexual offenders through sexually violent persons laws. Perhaps the greatest difficulty relates to the fact that these individuals are rarely released, and then only after years of treatment that has putatively reduced their risk. Thus, the accuracy of the judgments as to who should be committed cannot normally be evaluated. Although there is an active debate about risk assessment methods in the community of expert witnesses (Doren, 2006; Janus, 2004; Janus & Meehl, 1997; Vrieze & Grove, 2008; Wollert, 2006; Wollert & Waggoner, 2009), the effectiveness of these statutes as applied has been evaluated in only one study of juvenile sexual offenders (Caldwell, 2013).

In a study of 198 juvenile sexual offenders who were eligible for civil commitment, Caldwell (2013) examined the accuracy of the initial determination of which youth met the commitment criteria. The studied civil commitment process followed a two-stage review protocol. In the first stage, 54 of the youth were determined to meet the criteria for commitment and were confined until a final hearing. The remaining 144 youth who were reviewed were determined not to meet the criteria and were released. In the second stage, the 54 confined youth were reviewed a second time for a final commitment hearing. Fifty-one of the 54 youth were released at this stage and three remained confined. Caldwell compared the recidivism rates of the 51 juveniles who were originally determined to meet the commitment criteria and confined with 144 juvenile sexual offenders who were eligible for commitment but were not subject to a petition. Over a five-year follow-up, the two groups had similar rates of felony sexual offending. Among the 51 youth that were petitioned for commitment 9.8 percent were charged with a new sexual felony while 13.2 percent of the 144 released youth were so charged, a nonsignificant difference. Assuming that the three youth that had remained confined would have sexually recidivated did not significantly alter the results.

Further analysis revealed several factors that predicted which youth were subject to a petition. Petitioned youth were significantly more likely to be Caucasian, had significantly more infractions involving sexual behavior in the juvenile corrections institution, and were significantly more apt to have multiple male victims. Although this provides very preliminary information, the overestimate of the risk posed by the youth that were initially committed, combined with the low base rates of juvenile sexual offenders in general and the lack of reliable indicators of sexual recidivism risk, raise questions about the appropriateness of applying these statutes to adolescent offenders.

Research Evidence and Public Policies

As this chapter has demonstrated, the extant research provides almost no basis for believing that sex offender registration and notification laws or civil commitment policies can be generally applied to adolescents effectively. To date, no static risk factors have emerged that reliably predict persistent sexual offending in adolescent offenders. This outcome is not due to lack of effort. Table 3.3 shows the factors that have been studied at least five times.

Many other factors have been studied fewer times, and with less consistent results. The dominant picture is one of consistently null findings. On those occasions when a significant relationship has been found, other studies have often found the opposite result or no relationship. Although the problem is compounded by a lack of consistency in the operational

Table 3.3. Studies of Risk Factors Predicting Persistent Sexual Offending among Adolescent Sexual Offenders

Factor	Number of studies	Number of studies showing increased risk	Number of studies showing decreased risk
Assaulting a younger victim	9	2	2
Age at admission to treatment	11	0	0
History of being physically or sexually abused, or neglected	13	2	1
Substance abuse history	8	0	0
Having a stranger victim	8	2	0
Having a male child victim	16	0	2
Force used in the offense	5	0	1
Total number of victims	7	1	0
Prior arrests for any offense	8	0	0
Prior sexual assault charges	14	3	0

definition of risk factors, that uncertainty itself mirrors the lack of understanding of the dynamics that produce adolescent sexual misconduct. Although there is little doubt that future studies will alter the specifics of this picture, the trend at the current time is clear: the diversity of juvenile sexual offenders and the fluidity of sexual misconduct in adolescence makes identifying reliable stable predictors of continuing sexual offending a daunting task. Further, risk scales that are made up of items that have not proven to be reliable predictors in their own right are unlikely to prove reliable.

Part of the difficulty in identifying the small group of juvenile sex offenders that will persist in offending may be the prevailing approach to sex offender risk research. Juvenile sex offenders are widely acknowledged to be a very heterogeneous group, made up of individuals who offend for a wide range of reasons and through a variety of dynamics. The diversity of juvenile sex offenders notwithstanding, actuarial risk methods look for a set of risk factors that can tap into a putative universal trait that predicts persistent sexual violence in all juvenile sexual offenders. These methods attempt to tailor a single risk scale to a diverse group of offenders with the hope that it will fit individuals within and outside of that group. In many ways, this is analogous to tailoring a suit to the "average" adolescent male in the hope that it will "fit" all adolescent males. The more probable outcome would be that the average suit would actually be a poor fit for all but a small minority of adolescents. This problem is inevitable when attempting to fit a nomothetic (group) measure from a diverse population to an idiographic (individual) situation. Basic psychological measurement principles would indicate that it is unlikely that this approach can ever yield highly reliable results (Caldwell, 2002). Nevertheless, most sex offender registration statutes rely on a short list of offense characteristics that make a particular juvenile eligible for registration. Others rely on risk scales that have been developed with a similar methodology, for the specific purpose of informing a level of registration (Caldwell, Ziemke, & Vitacco, 2008).

Enacted in 1994, the Jacob Wetterling Crimes Against Children and Sexually Violent Offenders Registration Act was the first national effort to include adolescents on state sex offender registries and to encourage community notification (Garfinkle, 2003). At the time, research that would indicate that juvenile sex offenders differed significantly from adult offenders could only be inferred from general information about delinquency and adult crime.

However, by the time Adam Walsh Child Protection and Safety Act was enacted in 2006, research evidence was accumulating. Certainly, sympathy for the victims of sexual violence and the urge to act to improve community safety are commendable motives. Unfortunately, when the movement to enact these measures began, the lack of empirical information provided little foundation for a rational discussion of the issues, and may have contributed to the moral panic that drove these statutes forward. Concerned about horrific individual cases, distorted information suggesting extremely high recidivism rates, and misleading estimates that sex offenders "typically" had hundreds of victims and scores of undetected offenses (Abel, Becker, Mittleman, Cunningham-Rather, Rouleau, & Murphy, 1987; Groth, Longo, & McFadin, 1982) led legislatures to enacted statutes that seemed to reflect common sense. As empirical information accumulates, the public policy debate must now shift to focus on what measures can be shown to effectively improve community safety.

NOTE

1. Due to an error, 21 cases were omitted from the original calculation of the effect size for the Schram, Milloy, & Rowe (1991) study, producing an erroneous effect size of .89. The actual effect size for the full sample is - .14.

REFERENCES

Abel, G., Becker, J., Mittleman, M., Cunningham-Rather, J., Rouleau, J., & Murphy, W. (1987). Self-reported sex crimes of nonincarcerated paraphiliacs. *Journal of Interpersonal Violence, 2*, 3–25.

Adkins, G., Huff, D., & Stageberg, P. (2000). *The Iowa sex offender registry and recidivism.* Des Moines: Iowa Department of Human Rights.

Aebi, M., Vogt, G., Plattner, B., Steinhausen, H-C., & Bessler, C. (2012). Offender types and criminality dimensions in male juveniles convicted of sexual offenses. *Sexual Abuse: A Journal of Research and Treatment, (24)3*, 265–288.

American Psychiatric Association. (2013). *Diagnostic and Statistical Manual–5th Edition.* Washington, DC: American Psychiatric Association Press.

Archer, J. (2006). Testosterone and human aggression: An evaluation of the challenge hypothesis. *Neuroscience and Biobehavioral Reviews, 30*, 319–345.

Archer, J., Birring, S. S., & Wu, F.C.W. (1998). The association between testosterone and aggression in young men: Empirical findings and a meta-analysis. *Aggressive Behavior, 24*, 411–420.

Atcheson, J. D., & Williams, D. C. (1954). A study of juvenile sex offenders. *American Journal of Psychiatry, 111*, 366–370.

Auslander, B. (1998). *An Exploratory Study Investigating Variables in Relation to Juvenile Sexual Re-offending*. Unpublished doctoral dissertation, Florida State University.

Batastini, A. B., Hunt, E., Present-Koller, J., & DeMatteo, D. (2011). Federal standards for community registration of juvenile sex offenders: An evaluation of risk prediction and future implications. *Psychology, Public Policy and Law, 17*, 451–474.

Becker, J. V., Kaplan, M. S., & Tenke, C. E. (1992). The relationship of abuse history, denial and erectile response: profiles of adolescent sexual perpetrators. *Behavior Therapy, 23*, 87–97.

Benes, F. M., Taylor, J. B. & Cunningham, M. C. (2000). Convergence and plasticity of monoaminergic systems in the medial prefrontal cortex during the postnatal period: Implications for the development of psychopathology. *Cerebral Cortex, 10*, 1014–1027.

Blakemore, S. J. (2008). Development of the social brain during adolescence. *Quarterly Journal of Experimental Psychology, 61*, 40–49.

Bourgeois, J. P. & Rakic, P. (1993). Changes of synaptic density in the primary visual cortex of the macaque monkey from fetal to adult stage. *Journal of Neuroscience, 13*, 2801–2820.

Boyd, N. (1994). *Predictors of Recidivism in an Adolescent Sexual Offenders' Population*. Unpublished doctoral dissertation, University of Wisconsin–Madison.

Brennan, S., & Taylor-Butts, A. (2008). *Sexual Assault in Canada 2004 and 2007*. Ottawa: Canadian Centre for Justice Statistics.

Caldwell, M. (2002). What we do not know about juvenile sexual reoffense risk. *Child Maltreatment, 7*, 291–302.

Caldwell, M. F. (2007). Sexual offense adjudication and sexual recidivism among juvenile offenders. *Sexual Abuse: A Journal of Research and Treatment, 19*, 107–113.

Caldwell, M. (2010). Study characteristics and recidivism base rates in juvenile sex offender recidivism. *International Journal of Offender Therapy and Comparative Criminology, 54*, 197–212.

Caldwell, M., (2013). Accuracy of sexually violent person assessments of juveniles adjudicated for sexual offenses. *Sexual Abuse: A Journal of Research and Treatment*. http://sax.sagepub.com/content/early/2013/03/15/1079063213480818.full.pdf.

Caldwell, M., & Dickenson, C. (2009). Sex offender registration and recidivism risk in juvenile sexual offenders. *Criminal Justice and Behavior, 27*, 1–17.

Caldwell, M., Ziemke, M., & Vitacco, M. (2008). An examination of the sex offender registration and notification act as applied to juveniles: evaluating the ability to predict sexual recidivism. *Psychology, Public Policy, and Law, 14(2)*, 89–114.

Cauffman, E., Shulman, E., Steinberg, L., Claus, E., Banich, M., Graham, S., et al. (2010). Age differences in affective decision making as indexed by performance on the Iowa Gambling Task. *Developmental Psychology, 46*, 193–207.

Cauffman, E., & Steinberg, L. (2000). Researching adolescents' judgment and culpability. In T. Grisso & R. Schwartz (eds.), *Youth on trial* (pp. 325–343). Chicago: University of Chicago Press.

Centers for Disease Control and Prevention. (2002). Youth risk behavior surveillance—United States, 2001. *Morbidity and Mortality Weekly Report, 51*, 1–64.
Chaffin, M. (2008). Our minds are made up—Don't confuse us with the facts: Commentary on policies concerning children with sexual behavior problems and juvenile sex offenders. *Child Maltreatment, 13*, 110–121.
Clift, R.J.W., Gretton, H. M., & Rajlic, G. (2007). The relationship between deviant arousal and sexual recidivism in adolescent sex offenders. In M. C. Calder (ed.), *Children and young people who sexually abuse* (pp. 96–102). Dorset, UK: Russell House.
Clift, R., Rajlic, G., & Gretton, H. (2009). Discriminative and predictive validity of the penile plethysmograph in adolescent sex offenders. *Sexual Abuse: A Journal of Research and Treatment, 21*, 335–362.
Cohen, J. (1988). *Statistical power analysis for the behavioral sciences*. Hillsdale, New Jeresy: Lawrence Erlbaum.
Davidson, J., Camargo, C., & Smith, E. (1979). Effects of androgen on sexual behavior of hypogonadal men. *Journal of Clinical Endocrinology and Metabolism, 48*, 955–958.
Doren, D. (2006). Recidivism risk assessments: Making sense of controversies. In Marshall, Fernandez, Marshall, Serran (eds.), *Sexual offender treatment: Controversial issues* (pp. 3–15). New York: John Wiley & Sons.
Driessen, E., (2002). *Characteristics of Youth Referred for Sexual Offenses*. Unpublished doctoral dissertation, University of Wisconsin–Milwaukee.
Duwe, G., & Donnay, W. (2008). The impact of Megan's Law on sex offender recidivism: The Minnesota experience. *Criminology, 46*, 411–446.
Faiman C, Winter J. (1974). Gonadotropins and sex hormone patterns in puberty: Clinical data. In Grumbach, M. M., Grave, G. D., & Mayer, F. F. (eds), *Control of the Onset of Puberty* (pp. 32–61). New York: John Wiley & Sons.
Faniff, A. M., & Kolko, D. J. (2012). Victim age based subtypes for juveniles adjudicated for sexual offenses: comparisons across domains in an outpatient sample. *Sexual Abuse: A Journal of Research and Treatment, (24)3*, 224–264.
Federal Bureau of Investigation. (2012). Crime in the United States 2012. www.fbi.gov/about-us/cjis/ucr/crime-in-tFros*sexual abuse cases*. Washington, DC: Office of Juvenile Justice and Delinquency Prevention.
Finkelhor, D., Ormrod, R. & Chaffin, M. (2009). *Juveniles who commit sex offences against minors*. Washington, DC: Office of Juvenile Justice and Delinquency Prevention.
Finkelstein, J. W., Susman, E. J., Chinchilli, V. M., Kunselman, S. J., D'Arcangelo, M. R., Schwab, J., et al. (1997). Estrogen or testosterone increases self-reported aggressive behaviors in hypogonadal adolescents. *Journal of Clinical Endocrinology and Metabolism, 82*, 2433–2438.
Freeman, N. J. (2012). The public safety impact of community notification laws: Rearrest of convicted sex offenders. *Crime and Delinquency, 58*(4), 539–564.
Freeman, N. J., Sandler, J. C., & Socia, K. M. (2009). A time-series analysis on the impact of sex offender registration and community notification laws on plea bargaining rates. *Criminal Justice Studies, 22*, 153–165.

Garfinkle, E. (2003). Coming of age in America: The misapplication of sex-offender registration and community notification laws to juveniles. *California Law Review, 163*, 163–208.

Giedd, J. (2004). Structural magnetic resonance imaging of the adolescent brain. *Annals of the New York Academy of Sciences, 1021*, 77–85.

Glosser, A., Gardiner, K., & Fishman, M. (2004). *Statutory rape: A guide to state laws and reporting requirements.* Washington, DC: Department of Health and Human Services.

Gogtay, N., Giedd, J.N., Lusk, L., Hayashi, K.M., Greenstein, D., Vaituzis, A.C., et al. (2004). Dynamic mapping of human cortical development during childhood through early adulthood. *Proceedings of the National Academy of Sciences USA, 101*, 8174–8179.

Gretton, H. M., McBride, M., Hare, R. D., O'Shaughnessy, R., & Kumka, G. (2001). Psychopathy and recidivism in adolescent sex offenders. *Criminal Justice and Behavior, 28*, 427–499.

Groth, N., Longo, R., & McFadin, J.B. (1982). Undetected recidivism among rapists and child molesters. *Crime & Delinquency*, 28, 450–458.

Halpern, C., Udry, R., Campbell, B., & Suchindran, C. (1993). Testosterone and pubertal development as predictors of sexual activity: A panel analysis of adolescent males. *Psychosomatic Medicine, 55*, 436–447.

Hanson, K. & Bussiere, M. (1998). Predicting relapse: A meta-analysis of sexual offender recidivism studies. *Journal of Consulting and Clinical Psychology, (66)*, 348–362.

Hanson, K., & Morton-Bourgon, K. (2004). *Predictors of Sexual Recidivism: An Updated Meta-Analysis.* Public Safety and Emergency Preparedness of Canada. www.publicsafety.gc.ca/res/cor/rep/_fl/2004-02-pred-se-eng.pdf.

Hecker, J., Scoular, J., Righthand, S., & Nangle, D. (2002). *Predictive Validity of the J-SOAP over 10-plus years: Implications for risk assessment.* Poster presented at the 21st annual conference of the Association for the Treatment of Sexual Abusers, Montreal, Quebec, Canada, October.

Human Rights Watch (2013). *Raised on the Registry: The Irreparable Harm of Placing Children on Sex Offender Registries in the US.* Human Rights Watch: Washington, DC. www.hrw.org/sites/default/files/reports/us0513_ForUpload_1.pdf.

Hunter, J. A., Figueredo, A. J., Malamuth, N. M., and Becker, J. V. (2003). Juvenile sex offenders: Toward the development of a typology. *Sexual Abuse:A Journal of Research and Treatment, (15)1*, 27–48.

Huttenlocher, P. R. & Dabholkar, A. S. (1997). Regional differences in synaptogenesis in human cerebral cortex. *Journal of Comparative Neurology, 387*, 167–178.

Igartuna, K., Thombs, B., Burgos, G., & Montoro, R. (2009). Concordance and discrepancy in sexual identity, attraction, and behavior among adolescents. *Journal of Adolescent Health, 45*, 602–608.

Janus, E. S. (2004). Closing Pandora's box: Sexual predators and the politics of sexual violence. *Seton Hall Law Review, 34*, 1233–1253.

Janus, E. S., & Meehl, P. E. (1997). Assessing the legal standard for predictions of dangerousness in sex offender commitment proceedings. *Psychology, Public Policy, and the Law*, 3, 33–64.

Josephs, R. A., Sellers, J. G., Newman, M. L., & Mehta, P. H. (2006). The mismatch effect: When testosterone and status are at odds. *Journal of Personality and Social Psychology, 90*, 999–1013.

Koss, M. P., Gidycz, C. A., & Wisniewski, N. (1987). The scope of rape: Incidence and prevalence of sexual aggression and victimization in a national sample of higher education students. *Journal of Consulting and Clinical Psychology, 55*, 162–170.

Knorr, D., Bidlingmaier, F., Butenandt, O., et al. (1974). Plasma testosterone in male puberty. *Acta Endocrinol 75*, 181–194.

Lave, T. R., & McCrary, J. (2011). *Assessing the Crime Impact of Sexually Violent Predator Laws*. http://ssrn.com/abstract=1884772.

Lee, P. A., Jaffe, R. B., & Midgley, A. R. Jr. (1974). Serum gonadotropin, testosterone, and prolactin concentrations throughout puberty in boys: A longitudinal study. *Journal of Clinical Endocrinological Metabolism, 39*, 664–672.

Lenroot, R., & Giedd, J. (2006). Brain development in children and adolescents: Insights from anatomical magnetic resonance imaging. *Neuroscience and Biobehavioral Reviews, 30*, 718–729.

Letourneau, E. J., & Armstrong, K. S. (2008). Recidivism rates for registered and nonregistered juvenile sexual offenders. *Sexual Abuse: A Journal of Research and Treatment, 20*, 393–408.

Letourneau, E. J., Bandyopadhyay, D., Armstrong, K., & Sinha, D. (2010). Do sex offender registration and notification requirements deter juvenile sex crimes? *Criminal Justice and Behavior, 37*, 553–569.

Letourneau, E. J., Bandyopadhyay, D., Sinha, D., & Armstrong, K. S. (2009). The influence of sex offender registration on juvenile sexual recidivism. *Criminal Justice Policy Review, 20*, 136–153.

Letourneau, E. J., & Miner, M. H. (2005). Juvenile sex offenders: A case against the legal and clinical status quo. *Sexual Abuse: Journal of Research and Treatment, 17(3)*, 293–312.

Levenson, J. S., & Cotter, L. (2005). The impact of Megan's Law on sex offender reintegration. *Journal of Contemporary Criminal Justice, 21(1)*, 49–66.

Levenson, J. S., & D'Amora, D. A. (2007). Social policies designed to prevent sexual violence: The emperor's new clothes? *Criminal Justice Policy Review, 18*, 168–199.

Lewis, D. A., Cruz, D., Eggan, S., & Erickson, S. (2004). Postnatal development of prefrontal inhibitory circuits and the pathophysiology of cognitive dysfunction in schizophrenia. *Annals of the New York Academy of Sciences, 1021*, 64–76.

Mazur, A., & Booth, A. (1998). Testosterone and dominance in men. *Behavioral and Brain Sciences, 21*, 353–397.

Mehta, P. H., Jones, A. C., & Josephs, R. A. (2008). The social endocrinology of dominance: Basal testosterone predicts cortisol changes and behavior following victory and defeat. *Journal of Personality and Social Psychology, 94*, 1078–1093.

Milloy, C. (1994). *A Comparative Study of Juvenile Sex Offenders and Non-Sex Offenders*. Olympia, WA: Washington State Institute for Public Policy.

Miner, M. (2002a). Factors associated with recidivism in juveniles: An analysis of serious juvenile sex offenders. *Journal of Research in Crime and Delinquency, 39(4)*, 421–436.

Miner, M. H. (2002b). Factors associated with recidivism among 129 juvenile sex offenders released from Minnesota Corrections. Unpublished raw data.

Miner, M. H., Robinson, B. E., Knight, R. A., Berg, D., Swinburne Romine, R., & Netland, J. (2010). Understanding sexual perpetration against children: Effects of attachment style, interpersonal involvement, and hypersexuality. *Sexual Abuse: A Journal of Research and Treatment, (20)3*, 58–77.

Monahan, K., Steinberg, L., & Cauffman, E. (2009). Affiliation with antisocial peers, susceptibility to peer influence and antisocial behavior during the transition to adulthood. *Developmental Psychology, (45)*, 1520–1530.

Mrzljak, L., Uylings, H. B., Van Eden, C. G., & Judas, M. (1990). Neuronal development in human prefrontal cortex in prenatal and postnatal stages, Pr*ogress in Brain Research, 85*, 185–222.

Mulder, E., Vermunt, J., Brand, E., Bullens, R., & Van Marle, H. (2012). Recidivism in subgroups of serious juvenile offenders: Different profiles, different risks? *Criminal Behavior and Mental Health, 22*, 122–135.

Newman, M. L., Sellers, J. G., & Josephs, R. A. (2005). Testosterone, cognition, and social status. *Hormones and Behavior, 47*, 205–211.

Nisbett, I., Wilson, P., & Smallbone, S. (2004). A prospective longitudinal study of sexual recidivism among adolescent sex offenders. *Sexual Abuse: A Journal of Research and Treatment, 16(3)*, 223–234.

O'Connor, D. B., Archer, J., & Wu, F. C. (2004). Effects of testosterone on mood, aggression, and sexual behavior in young men: A double-blind, placebo-controlled, cross-over study. *Journal of Clinical Endocrinology and Metabolism, 89*, 2837–2845.

Pathela P, Hajat A, Schillinger J, et al. (2006). Discordance between sexual behavior and self-reported sexual identity: A population-based survey of New York City men. *Annals of Internal Medicine, 145*, 416–425.

Pope, H. G. Jr., Kouri, E. M., & Hudson, J. I. (2000). Effects of supraphysiologic doses of testosterone on mood and aggression in normal men: A randomized controlled trial. *Archives of General Psychiatry, 57*, 133–140.

Prentky, R., Harris, B., Frizzell, K., & Righthand, S. (2000). An actuarial procedure for assessing risk with juvenile sex offenders. *Sexual Abuse: A Journal of Research and Treatment, 12(2)*, 71–93.

Prescott, J. J., & Rockoff, J. E. (2008). Do sex offender registration and notification laws affect criminal behavior? *Journal of Law and Economics, 54*, 161–206.

Rajlic, G., & Gretton, H. (2007). An examination of two sexual recidivism risk measures in adolescent offenders: The moderating effect of offender type. *Criminal Justice and Behavior, 37*, 1066–1085.

Rassmussen, L. (1999). Factors related to recidivism among juvenile sexual offenders. *Sexual Abuse: A Journal of Research and Treatment, 11(1)*, 69–85.

Remafedi, G., (1992). Demography of sexual orientation in adolescents. *Pediatrics, 89*, 714–721.

Rice, M., Harris, G., Lang, C., Chaplin, T. (2012). Adolescents who have sexually offended: Is phallometry valid? *Sexual Abuse: A Journal of Research and Treatment, 24*,133–152.

Richardson, G., Kelly, T., Graham, F., & Bhate, S. (2004). Personality-based classification derived from the personality pattern scales from the Millon Adolescent Clinical Inventory (MACI). *British Journal of Clinical Psychology, 43*, 258–298.

Robbers, M. (2009). Lifers on the outside: Sex offenders and disintegrative shaming. *International Journal of Offender Therapy and Comparative Criminology, 53*, 5–28.

Robinson, M.-C., Rouleau, J. L., & Madrigano, G. (1997). Validation de la ple´thysmographie pe´nienne comme mesure psychophysiologique des inte´re^ts sexuels des agresseurs adolescents [Validation of penile plethysmography as a psychophysiological measure of the sexual interests of adolescent sex offenders]. *Revue Que´be´coise de Psychologie, 18*, 111–124.

Salmimies, P., Kockott, K., Pirke, K., Vogt, J., & Schill, W. (1982). Effects of testosterone replacement on sexual behavior in hypogonadal men. *Archives of Sexual Behavior, 11*, 345–353.

Sample, L. (2006). An examination of the degree to which sex offenders kill. *Criminal Justice Review, 31*, 230–250.

Sandler, J. C., Freeman, N. J., & Socia, K. M. (2008). Does a watched pot boil? A time-series analysis of New York State's sex offender registration and notification law. *Psychology, Public Policy, and Law, 14*, 284–302.

Schiavone, S., & Jeglic, E. (2009). Public perception of sex offender social policies and the impact on sex offenders. *International Journal of Offender Therapy and Comparative Criminology, 53*, 679–695.

Schram, D., & Milloy, C. D. (1995). *Community notification: A study of offender characteristics and recidivism*. Olympia, WA: Washington Institute for Public Policy.

Schram, D. D., Milloy, C. D., Rowe, W. E. (1991). *Juvenile Sex Offenders: A Follow-Up Study of Re-offense Behavior*. Olympia, WA: Washington State Institute for Public Policy.

Seto, M. C., Lalumiere, M. L., & Blanchard, R. (2000). The discriminative validity of a phallometric test for pedophilic interests among adolescent sex offenders against children. *Psychological Assessment, 12*, 319–327.

Seto, M. C., Murphy, W. D., Page, J., & Ennis, L. (2003). Detecting anomalous sexual interests among juvenile sex offenders. *Annals of the New York Academy of Sciences, 989*, 118–130.

Sisk, C. L., & Foster, D. L. (2004). The neural basis of puberty and adolescence. *Nature Neuroscience, 7*, 1040–1047.

Skakkeback, N., Bancroft, J., Davidson, D., & Warner, P. (1981). Androgen replacement with oral testosterone unecanoate in hypogonadal men: A double-blind controlled study. *Clinical Endocrinology, 14*, 49–67.

Skowron, K. (2004). *Differentiation and predictive factors in adolescent sexual offending*. Unpublished Thesis, Carleton University, Ottawa, Canada.

Smith, W., & Monastersky, C. (1986). Assessing juvenile sexual offenders' risk for reoffending. *Criminal Justice and Behavior, 13*, 115–140.

Smith, A. M., Rissel, C. E., Richters, J., et al. (2003). Sex in Australia: sexual identity, sexual attraction and sexual experience among a representative sample of adults. *Australia and New Zealand Journal of Public Health, 27*, 138–145.

Snyder, H. (2000). *Sexual Assault of Young Children as Reported to Law Enforcement: Victim, Incident, and Offender Characteristics* (Bureau of Justice Statistics Bulletin NCJ 182990). Washington, DC.

Steinberg, L. (2004). Risk-taking in adolescence: What changes and why? *Annals of the New York Academy of Sciences, 1021*, 51–58.

Steinberg, L. (2007). Risk taking in adolescence: New perspectives from brain and behavioral science. *Current Directions in Psychological Science, 16*(2), 55–59.

Steinberg, L., (2010). A dual systems model of adolescent risk-taking. *Developmental Psychobiology, 52*, 216–224.

Steinberg, L., Albert, D., Cauffman, E., Banich, M., Graham, S., & Woolard, J. (2008). Age differences in sensation seeking and impulsivity as indexed by behavior and self-report: Evidence for a dual systems model. *Developmental Psychology, 44*, 1764–1778.

Steinberg, L., & Monahan, K. C. (2007). Age differences in resistance to peer influence. *Developmental Psychology, 43*, 1531–1543.

Tewksbury, R. (2005). Collateral consequences of sex offender registration. *Journal of Contemporary Criminal Justice, 21(1)*, 67–81.

Tewksbury, R. & Lees, M. (2006). Perceptions of sex offender registration: Collateral consequences and community experiences. *Sociological Spectrum, 26(3)*, 309–334.

Trivits, L. C., & Reppucci, N. D. (2002). Application of Megan's Law to juveniles. *American Psychologist, 57*, 690–704.

Udry R. (1988). Biological predispositions and social control in adolescent sexual behavior. *American Sociological Review, 53*, 709–722.

Udry R., Billy J., Morris N., et al. (9185). Serum androgenic hormones motivate sexual behavior in adolescent boys. *Fertility and Sterility, 43*, 90–94.

Vasquez, B. E., Maddan, S., & Walker, J. T. (2008). The influence of sex offender registration and notification laws in the United States: A time series analysis. *Crime & Delinquency, 54*, 175–192.

Veysey, B., Zgoba, K., & Dalessandro, M. (2008). A preliminary step towards evaluating the impact of Megan's Law: Trend analysis of sexual offenses in New Jersey from 1985 to 2005. *Justice Research and Policy, 10*, 1–18.

Vrieze, S., & Grove, W. (2008). Predicting sex offender recidivism. I. Correcting for item overselection and accuracy overestimation in scale development. II. Sampling error-induced attenuation of predictive validity over base rate information. *Law and Human Behavior, 3*, 266–278.

Waite, D., Keller, A., McGarvey, E., Wieckowski, E., Pinkerton, R., & Brown, G. (2005). Juvenile sex offender re-arrest rates for sexual, violent nonsexual and property crimes: A 10-year follow-up. *Sexual Abuse: A Journal of Research and Treatment, 17(3)*, 313–331.

Wallen, K. (2001). Sex and context: Hormones and primate sexual motivation. *Hormones and Behavior, 40*, 339–357.
Wallen, K. (2005). Hormonal influences on sexually differentiated behavior in nonhuman primates. *Frontiers in Neuroendocrinology, 26*, 7–26.
Wallen, K., and Tannenbaum, P. L. (1997). Hormonal modulation of sexual behavior and affiliation in rhesus monkeys. *Annals of the New York Academy of Sciences, 807*, 185–202.
Wallen, K., & Zehr, J. (2004). Hormones and history: The evolution and development of primate female sexuality. *Journal of Sex Research, 41*, 101–112.
Washington State Institute for Public Policy (2005). *Sex offender sentencing in Washington State: Has community notification reduced recidivism?* (Document No. 05-12-1202). Olympia. www.wsipp.wa.gov.
Weibush, R. G. (1996). *Juvenile Sex Offenders: Characteristics, System Response, and Recidivism.* Washington, DC: National Criminal Justice Reference Service.
Welchans, S. (2005). Megan's Law: Evaluations of sexual offender registries. *Criminal Justice Policy Review, 16*, 123–140.
Williams, J. (2007). *Juvenile sex offenders: Predictors of recidivism.* Unpublished doctoral dissertation, Auburn University.
Wolk, N. (2005). *Predictors Associated With Recidivism Among Juvenile Sexual Offenders.* Unpublished doctoral dissertation, University of Houston.
Wollert, R. (2006). Low base rates limit expert certainty when current actuarial tests are used to identify sexually violent predators. *Psychology, Public Policy, and Law, 12*, 56–85.
Wollert, R., & Waggoner, J. (2009). Bayesian computations protect sexually violent predator evaluations from the degrading effects of confirmatory bias and illusions of certainty: A reply to Doren and Levenson (2009). *Sexual Offender Treatment, 4*, 1–23.
Woo, T. U., Pucak, M. L., Kye, C. H., Matus, C. V., & Lewis, D. A. (1997). Peripubertal refinement of the intrinsic and associational circuitry in monkey prefrontal cortex. *Neuroscience, 80*, 1149–1158.
World Health Organization (1992) *International Classification of Disease–10th edition.* www.who.int/classifications/icd/en/.
Worling, J. R. (2001). Personality-based typology of adolescent male sexual offenders: Differences in recidivism rates, victim selection characteristics, and personal victimization histories. *Sexual Abuse: A Journal of Research and Treatment, 13(3)*, 149–166.
Worling, J., & Curwen, T. (2000). Adolescent sexual offender recidivism: success of specialized treatment and implications for risk prediction. *Child Abuse & Neglect, 24(7)*, 965–982.
Zehr, J., Maestripieri, D., & Wallen, K. (1998). Estradiol increases female sexual initiation independent of male responsiveness in rhesus monkeys. *Hormones and Behavior, 33*, 95–103.
Zevitz, R. G. (2006). Sex offender community notification: Its role in recidivism and offender reintegration. *Criminal Justice Studies, 19(2)*, 193–208.

Zgoba, K., Miner, M., Knight, R., Letourneau, E., Levenson, J., & Thornton, D. (2012). A Multi-State Recidivism Study Using Static-99R and Static-2002 Risk Scores and Tier Guidelines from the Adam Walsh Act. Washington, DC: National Institute of Justice. www.ncjrs.gov/pdffiles1/nij/grants/240099.pdf.

Zgoba, K., Witt, P., Dalessandro, M., & Veysey, B. (2008). *Megan's Law: Assessing the practical and monetary efficacy.* Washington, DC: US Department of Justice, Office of Justice Programs. www.ncjrs.gov/pdffiles1/nij/grants/225370.pdf.

Zimring, F. E. (2004). *An American travesty: Legal responses to adolescent sexual offending.* Chicago: University of Chicago Press.

Zimring, F., Jennings, W., Piquero, A., & Hays, S. (2009). Investigating the continuity of sex offending: Evidence from the second Philadelphia birth cohort. *Justice Quarterly, 26*, 58–76.

Zimring, F., Piquero, A., & Jennings, W. (2007). Sexual delinquency in Racine: Does early sex offending predict later sex offending in youth and young adulthood? *Criminology and Public Policy, 6(3)*, 507–534.

4

The School-to-Prison Pipeline

Rhetoric and Reality

AARON KUPCHIK

Schools are an important and often overlooked site for studying children's introductions to the juvenile justice system. Schools teach behavioral norms and expectations, and they establish credentials for future academic and professional endeavors, both of which can shape the likelihood that youth become involved with the justice system. Schools are the first social institution outside of the family in which the vast majority of youth spend significant time, and the first institution in which most youth have an opportunity to be marked as failures, criminals, or deviants.

There are at least three ways in which a child's introduction to the juvenile or criminal justice system can be shaped by his or her school experiences. First, since the school offers the first public exposure for most youth, it is where children's social, emotional, behavioral, cognitive, and other deficits become apparent; these deficits result in increased risk of both school failure and future incarceration. Second, youth who do poorly in school may become frustrated, fail to advance academically, and eventually pursue illegal activity rather than graduate and pursue legitimate career paths. Third, the ways that schools perceive children's behavior to be problematic, as well as how they prevent and respond to misbehavior, can increase their risk of future punishment, including involvement in the justice system. In this chapter I focus on this last mechanism by discussing the significance of school discipline for our understanding of contemporary juvenile justice.

The chapter proceeds by first describing contemporary school discipline, and particularly what is often referred to as the "school-to-prison pipeline." I then discuss risk factors for entering the pipeline, and potential strategies for attenuating the connection between schools and the justice system. As I describe below, unhealthy changes in the assumptions and processes of school discipline have accumulated over the past generation—and correcting this aspect of the school-to-prison pipeline should be a priority concern.

Describing the School-to-Prison Pipeline

Discipline, or behavioral modification through the use of rules and punishment, has been a central mission of public schools since the spread of compulsory education throughout the United States. Early American schools were in large part designed to "Americanize" immigrant and lower-class youth and their families by teaching lessons about expected behaviors that would help these youth obtain work and assimilate into American society (e.g., Tyack 1974). Ensuring that these children learned to be punctual, respectful to authorities, and docile was possibly as—if not more—important to nineteenth-century teachers as teaching reading, writing, and arithmetic. While some scholars have viewed school systems as instilling the behaviors demanded by an industrial society (e.g., Bowles and Gintis 1977), others, like Durkheim (2011), have taken a broader view, arguing that schools establish a baseline for "moral education" by instilling respect for moral authority or democratic participation (Dewey 1916).

Though discipline has always been central to American schools, there have been substantial changes to schools' disciplinary practices and policies over the past two decades. Beginning in the 1990s, schools across the United States began to change how they conceptualize, detect, and respond to student misbehavior in significant ways; collectively, these changes are often known as elements of the school-to-prison pipeline (Kim, Losen, and Hewitt 2010). One important change was the introduction of surveillance and security technologies—such as surveillance cameras, metal detectors, drug-sniffing police dogs, and locked gates at the school's perimeter—that are traditionally found in criminal justice systems, not schools (see Monahan and Torres 2010). Another is the increasing reliance on exclusionary punishments that remove students from school or classrooms, such as expulsion, out-of-school suspension, or in-school suspension (serving a short suspension in the school, away from instruction and in a separate "punishment" room) (Skiba et al.

2006). A third important change is a growing link between formal criminal justice systems and schools. The most prominent shift here has been the expansion of police in schools, often called school resource officers, who are trained, uniformed officers that report to a commanding officer at the police department, not the school, though they are stationed at the school on a regular, often full-time basis. As Feld (2011) illustrates, the influence of police is substantially heightened by the weaker protections from searches students face at school, compared to anywhere else.

Schools are more likely now than in years past to rely on formal punishment, and to have close ties to criminal justice agencies. Students today often face suspension, expulsion, or arrest for behaviors that at one time led to detention or a verbal reprimand at the principal's office. Fistfights between students, for example, have traditionally been seen as an unfortunate but expected part of growing up, and were ignored or dealt with informally; they now lead to formal arrest as well as school suspension in many schools (Kupchik 2010).

The emergence of contemporary school discipline and security practices were in part a response to high rates of community and school crime in the late 1980s and the early 1990s. But these strategies have only expanded in the past twenty years, despite continually decreasing school crime rates (Robers et al. 2012), and have spread beyond high-crime areas to schools in all sectors of society (Simon 2007). Moreover, according to the evidence, increasing punishment and links to the criminal justice system are a relatively ineffective means of preventing school crime (see Gottfredson 2001), and yet this approach has come to eclipse other strategies that have a higher chance of success (Kupchik 2010).

In response to these changes, advocates, scholars, and educational professionals have begun paying more attention to the school-to-prison pipeline. The pipeline metaphor highlights the way that schools fail many youth by setting them on the path to prison rather than productive professional and social futures; this occurs as they are excluded from schools, denied necessary educational and social services, and referred to law enforcement for what are often minor infractions. The metaphor takes on different meanings at different times. Its most basic meaning suggests that schools communicate with police about student misconduct in a way that leads students to develop arrest records and eventually serve time in prison. But the term is also used to refer to a more subtle and more common chain of events: students are repeatedly suspended, fail academically, and have their social, emotional, and educational needs unmet by the school; they withdraw from school or are expelled; and this school failure or withdrawal substantially increases the risk that they become ensnared in the criminal justice system (Fabelo et al. 2011). As schools have grown more hostile to youth misbehavior, they have set more youth on the path to educational and social exclusion, and in the process increased the chances that these youth end up in prison.

The risks of being entrapped by such a pipeline to prison are unequally distributed among youth. Students of color, particularly low-income black youth, are far more likely to be punished in school, suspended, expelled, and eventually arrested than others. Studies find racially disproportionate disciplinary responses, even when statistically controlling for self-reported rates of misbehavior (e.g., Skiba et al. 2000). Black youth are singled out for punishment because they are perceived to be more threatening, more loud and disruptive, their style of dress and manners of speaking viewed as "thug-like," and they are seen as more disrespectful than others to teachers (Bowditch 1993; Ferguson 2000; Lewis 2003; McCarthy and Hoge 1987; Skiba et al. 2000). Furthermore, a small but growing body of research finds that school policies and practices vary in ways that correlate with aggregate student body race and socioeconomic status, with schools serving larger populations of poor youth and youth of color more likely to rely on harsh discipline and less likely to use restorative discipline approaches (Payne and Welch 2010; Welch and Payne 2010, 2012), and less likely to respect students' rights (Bracy 2010; Kupchik 2009).

As a result of these practices, school discipline undermines a primary goal of public education, or at least the version of public education outlined by Dewey (1916); rather than allowing a platform from which all youth can achieve success, students who arrive at school with the fewest social and academic opportunities for success are unfairly targeted and further marginalized.

After a brief discussion of the accuracy and helpfulness of the pipeline metaphor to describe the problem of school discipline and its effects on youth, I consider what factors put youth at risk of school discipline, as well as strategies that schools, school districts, and policy makers could pursue to dismantle this pipeline. Much of my discussion stems from my recent ethnographic research investigating school discipline in four schools, located in two states (see Kupchik 2010).

Helpfulness of a Metaphor

Metaphors are useful rhetorical devices; they draw comparisons between dissimilar objects in a way that helps an audience grasp and identify with what might be a complex idea. In a case like the school-to-prison pipeline, a metaphor can distill wordy, obtuse academic language into a concept that the public can easily understand and remember: that excessive school punishment, rigid security, and the neglect of students' needs can increase the chances that youth go to prison.

The pipeline metaphor certainly succeeds at illuminating an important problem for a wider audience than would otherwise be reached. Consider, for example, that in December 2012 the US Senate Judiciary Committee's Subcommittee on the Constitution, Civil Rights, and Human Rights held hearings on ending the school-to-prison pipeline. This was the first time (of which I am aware) that the issue of harmful school discipline was discussed before Congress, and it was framed entirely using the pipeline metaphor. Conferences, books (e.g., Kim, Losen, and Hewitt, 2010), and State Legislative Task Forces (one of which is in my home state of Delaware), among other actions, were formed specifically to address this pipeline. The pipeline metaphor clearly resonates with the public.

In terms of visibility, the metaphor is a huge success. This is a crucial victory, given how harmful school discipline can be. Above I refer to some of the most visible harms, including increases in arrests for minor school misconduct and growing racial inequality. Excessive school discipline also causes other, more subtle problems. Ironically, it might actually increase school crime. Research consistently shows that schools with positive, inclusive school climates have less crime and disorder than others, while controlling for relevant characteristics (e.g., Gottfredson 2001). This means that misbehavior problems are lower in schools where students feel respected and listened to, and where students feel close bonds to teachers and other staff; when schools are a place of caring, respect, and inclusion, students behave better. But the harsh punishments, rigid security, and denial of services that make up the school-to-prison pipeline undermine efforts to build such a school social climate (Kupchik 2010). Furthermore, because excessive discipline usually entails removal from class or school, students miss instructional time and might do worse on the all-important standardized exams by which schools are measured.

Contemporary school discipline and security also teaches a number of undesirable lessons to today's youth. Based on their experiences at the hands of police, zero-tolerance policies, and other security and disciplinary practices, some students become alienated from school and develop a sense of powerlessness (Fine et al. 2004; Nolan 2011), which may result in an apathetic stance toward future civic participation or other interactions with authorities. Indeed, students who are suspended while in school are less likely to vote or volunteer their time years later, while young adults (Kupchik and Catlaw 2013a).

There is thus a substantial problem in how schools discipline students, but one that received little public or political attention—that is, until the metaphor of the pipeline began to gain recognition. From an advocacy or political action perspective, the school-to-prison pipeline is a very helpful metaphor indeed.

Yet the metaphor has its limitations. It is somewhat inaccurate, and oversimplifies a very complicated process. The connection between schools and prisons is far more circuitous and less certain than the pipeline metaphor suggests. Relatively few youth are arrested in schools (albeit too many); instead most are given out-of-school suspension, in-school suspension, or other school punishment. Most youth who are arrested in general have their cases dismissed or not petitioned, receive a suspended sentence, or receive supervision such as probation;[1] since school-based arrests tend to be for minor offenses (see Wolf 2012), one can presume that even fewer students receive incarceration than average for the juvenile justice system.

Instead of directly going to prison, as the pipeline metaphor suggests, students who get caught up in school punishment suffer a myriad of consequences that adversely affect their futures but that don't directly lead to prison. They miss instructional time and become less likely to graduate, they are denied potentially helpful mentoring and psychological counseling in favor of punishment, while serving suspension or expulsion they have more time and opportunity for deviance, their records and limited academic backgrounds handicap employment possibilities, and so on. Figure 4.1 reproduces Hirschfield's (2012) depiction of this complex chain of events.

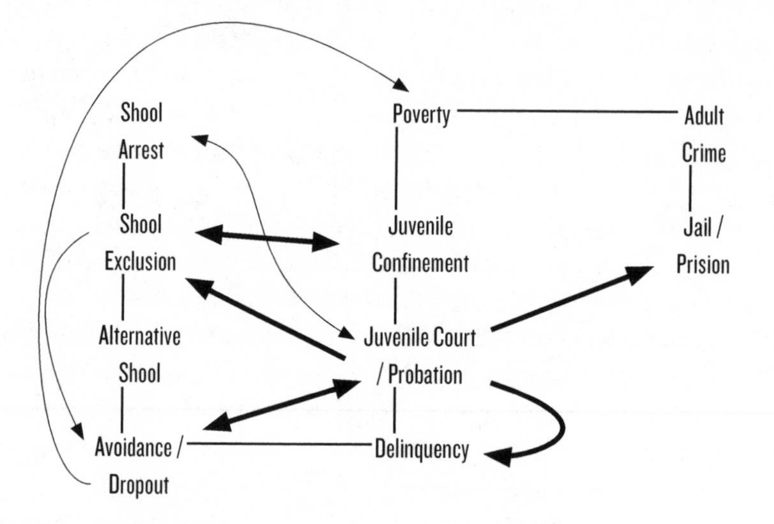

Figure 4.1. A Model of the School-to-Prison Pipeline
Model is probabalistic, multidirectional, and often multilevel.
Source: Hirschfield (2012).

As Hirschfield illustrates, the pipeline metaphor oversimplifies a very complex process. It also suggests the intentional delivery of a "product" (in this case, youth) through the pipeline to its destination (prison), which is not the case with schools. And it prioritizes the role of schools in shaping the risk of incarceration at the expense of—and in a way that overlooks—the role of social welfare, child welfare, and mental health systems (Hirschfield 2012). Further, it overlooks structural inequality, which may fuel the pipeline (see Irwin et al. 2013; Payne and Welch 2010; Welch and Payne 2010, 2012), as well as racial disproportionality in who enters the pipeline (see Skiba et al. 2000).

Thus the school-to-prison pipeline is somewhat misleading in terms of conceptual clarity. Nonetheless, it effectively catalyzes public attention to a serious problem. In the following sections I discuss the underlying problem behind the pipeline: contemporary school discipline and security practices that often result in school exclusion, dropping out, diminished social and professional life chances, and arrest. After discussing characteristics of individual youth, schools, and communities that put them at greater risk of these negative events, I then consider promising strategies for undoing these harms, or dismantling the pipeline.

Risk Factors for Entering the Pipeline

Rather than trying to isolate the risk factors for entering the school-to-prison pipeline at any of the many junctures of which it is composed, it seems more helpful to discuss the factors that put youth at risk of involvement in school discipline. Certainly, youth who commit criminal acts in school are at greatest risk of entering the pipeline. But many other individual characteristics, as well as school and community factors, shape both the likelihood of a youth's involvement with school discipline and how harmful that discipline will be to him or her.

Individual-Level Risk Factors

Above I discuss the impact of race and ethnicity on school discipline. Several studies have now demonstrated how teachers' and other school staff members' biased perceptions of threat and disorder can result in youth of color being perceived as unruly or dangerous (e.g., Lewis 2003; Skiba et al. 2000). When one considers that most school disciplinary incidents are low-level, subjectively defined behaviors—such as disorderly conduct, disrespect, or defiance, which are largely dependent on teachers' perceptions of youth—the importance of racialized perceptions of youth in shaping school discipline becomes even clearer (see Kupchik 2010).

Another individual-level risk factor is school failure. Students who earn bad grades, score poorly on tests, and drop out of school are at greater risk of school discipline than others. Yet the available evidence offers only a murky view of why this occurs. We know little about temporal order, for example; do students who get punished miss class time and as a consequence do poorly in school, or do school disciplinarians unfairly target failing students for punishment? In my research, I found that according to teachers, students often misbehave in class because they are struggling academically, and want to distract the class from their academic failure; if this is true, broadly, then school failure causes misbehavior, which in turn causes discipline.

Some speculate that given the pressure brought upon schools under No Child Left Behind to demonstrate high mean standardized test scores, low-performing students are intentionally suspended and pushed out of school for minor misbehaviors so that they will not be there on exam day (see Simmons 2007). But there is little evidence to confirm such a causal relationship. When one considers the pressure put on schools to raise test scores or face funding cuts and possibly even closure, it's easy to believe this occurs. Yet it is questionable whether disciplinarians know which students are likely to do well on standardized exams and which will do poorly, or that the concerns of central administration (test scores) shape the work done by those on the front lines of discipline (deans of discipline or teachers).

We also know that students who fail to graduate are at greater risk than others of incarceration (see Fabelo et al. 2011; Western 2006). But again it isn't clear if this is because of individual attributes such as their level of self-control, residual effects of being labeled as a criminal while in school, denial of career opportunities, or other factors.

Prior disciplinary involvement is another important risk factor for the school-to-prison pipeline. Students who develop a reputation as troublemakers or "frequent flyers," as I often heard them called by school staff during my fieldwork (Kupchik 2010), are likely to receive punishment in response to less serious offending or with less justification relative to other youth. Again, it's important to keep in mind that most school discipline is for subjectively defined misbehavior, such as disrespect to teachers, which depends almost entirely on the school staff member's perception of a juvenile's intentions and the level of threat posed to their authority.

School-Level Risk Factors

The entire discussion of a school-to-prison pipeline has surfaced in recognition of the harms that occur when schools increase their connections to criminal justice institutions. This occurs directly, though police officers in schools, but also indirectly by incorporating criminal justice-oriented logics, strategies, and technologies. According to the National Center for Education Statistics, during the 2009–2010 school year 22.9 percent of public schools, but 60.1 percent of public high schools, used random searches with drug-sniffing dogs; 61.1 percent of all schools, and 84.3 percent of high schools, used electronic surveillance cameras (Robers et al. 2012). Furthermore, 68.1 percent of surveyed 12- to 18-year-old public school students reported a security guard or assigned police officer at their schools. The pipeline is fueled not only by students being arrested for misbehavior at school, but also because schools have increasingly adopted criminal justice-oriented logics whereby students are viewed as threats to be policed rather than youth to be taught (Kupchik 2010).

Advocates for students' rights often assume that the presence of police officers in schools, usually called school resource officers, or SROs, leads to greater numbers of arrests at school (e.g., Petteruti 2012). Certainly this makes sense intuitively, since it removes a key barrier; schools no longer need to call 911 in response to minor criminal behavior or in response to behavior that may or may not be criminal. It also places officers in a position where they might respond to student misconduct in a way that escalates a situation, so that a student having a bad day can easily turn into a student pushing an SRO, which would not have been a criminal offense had no officer been present (see Nolan 2011). Yet the population of SROs has been growing at the same time that juvenile arrests have been decreasing nationally, making a causal relationship more difficult to establish (see James 2012).

Recently, however, research has begun to empirically validate the assumption that more police means more school-based arrests. These studies find that schools with SROs have higher rates of arrests for minor criminal behaviors (Na and Gottfredson 2011), such as disorderly conduct (Theriot 2009), than similar schools which do not have SROs or that have fewer SROs.

Other school discipline and security practices, such as implementation of zero-tolerance policies, use of surveillance cameras and drug-sniffing dogs, and metal detectors, contribute significantly to the pipeline, as does the weak protection from searches that students face at school (Feld 2011). As I find in my research, with the constellation of policies and practices that make up the school disciplinary regime, schools can be rigid environments in which rules and rule enforcement are prioritized over other goals, often including even academics (Kupchik 2010). The focus on enforcing rules can mean that students' social, emotional, and academic needs take a backseat to school punishment, resulting in high suspension rates.

An additional important and related school-level risk factor is poor school social climate. The concept of school social climate is difficult to define because it is used in so many ways and so broadly, but it usually refers to the relationships among students and school staff, to students' level of integration into the school community, and to the rules governing student and staff behaviors (see Williams and Guerra 2011). As I state above, a large volume of research finds that establishing a strong, supportive, and cohesive social climate is one of the best ways to reduce student misbehavior and school punishment rates. This means that in schools where students feel a part of the school community, where they feel cared for and respected by school staff, and where they believe that rules are fair and fairly enforced, there is less student misbehavior and school punishment. Since the school social climate is adversely affected by rigid rules, unfair punishments, excessive security, and the presence of police officers (see Kupchik 2010; Mukherjee 2007; Nolan 2011), the impact of school social climate on the school-to-prison pipeline means that the buildup of school policing and discipline indirectly fuels the pipeline as well.

Another important school-level risk factor is the neoliberal agenda on which No Child Left Behind, Race to the Top, and other accountability measures are based. Regardless of whether school officials intentionally remove academically struggling students so as to raise test scores, it's very clear that the neoliberal mandate to which accountability regimes respond is a pipeline risk factor. The school disciplinary regime and high-stakes school accountability stem from a similar view of how public institutions ought to be managed. Both are aspects of neoliberal management, where accountability is at the level of student or school rather than larger social system (e.g., disciplinary policies or school funding, respectively), and market-based logics encourage institutions to hone their "client base" by excluding those who do not fit.

Schools that adopt more of an instrumental, neoliberal perspective are more likely to pursue punishment as a response to individual transgression, thus the extent to which schools have incorporated neoliberal government can shape the extent to which their students are at risk for the pipeline (Kupchik and Catlaw 2013b).

Community-Level Risk Factors

Several community-level factors expose youth to elevated risk of the school-to-prison pipeline. Certainly, schools in crime-ridden neighborhoods may need to (or feel the need to) impose greater security mechanisms and hire more SROs. Beyond responses to real or perceived crime, however, risk of being caught in the pipeline can vary based on community-level disadvantage and social marginalization, and the conditions that often arise in racially segregated, high-poverty communities.

As Jonathan Kozol vividly illustrates (1991; 2005), conditions in high-poverty schools, especially those in segregated urban communities attended primarily by youth of color, tend to be inferior to those in more advantaged communities. This applies to the building infrastructure as well as funding for academics, extracurricular activities, and teacher training. Schools are primarily funded by local property taxes, which are far higher in wealthier areas due to both their higher property values and their lower proportions of tax-exempt businesses; thus funding is far greater in wealthy areas. Moreover, schools in such communities have better ability than those in poorer communities to raise other funds, both public and private.

Funding inequality impacts the pipeline in several indirect ways. Schools with constrained budgets may have larger classes, and thus teachers can give less attention to each student, which allows more opportunity for student misbehavior. They are less able to provide counseling or other therapeutic services for students that could help keep them on track to graduate. And teachers and administrators in them tend to be overwhelmed and stressed, which can result in greater reliance on rigid discipline as a way to try to impart order on what is perceived as chaos (Kupchik 2010).

Some research also finds that schools in disadvantaged urban communities with mostly students of color discipline and teach students differently than do other schools, in ways that subject them to greater risk of entering the pipeline. Kozol (2005), for example, finds that schools in urban areas use rote instruction based on standardized curricula and rigid discipline, in contrast to wealthier suburban schools that allow students greater flexibility and less rigid restrictions. Similarly, Rile-Hayward (2000) finds that teachers in low-income urban areas teach young children in very rigid ways that deemphasize critical thinking while prioritizing rule following; she describes how this is an intentional effort to keep youth safe in dangerous neighborhoods, by training them to follow laws rather than succumbing to the dangers of street life. These youth receive less of the benefits of education given to wealthier youth and receive harsher discipline.

In his recent ethnographic study *Punished*, Victor Rios (2011) builds on these assessments by describing the troubles faced by black and Latino boys in Oakland, California. Rios studies the lives of several youth and illustrates what he calls the "youth control complex," a system of controlling and punishing them that permeates school, family, and community life whereby teachers, police, and parents work together to criminalize youth behaviors. He shows how youth who live in communities like Oakland, with an aggressive police force that dominates disadvantaged populations, are at heightened risk of entering the pipeline. This is because their actions are rigorously monitored and policed under the assumption that they will engage in crime, while few opportunities for legitimate success are made available to them.

Strategies for Reform

The fact that a growing number of academics and youth advocates, and even the US Senate, have begun to recognize the school-to-prison pipeline as an important problem facing youth today suggests an opportunity for intervention. The waning of the get-tough era in juvenile justice, as discussed elsewhere in this volume, also suggests that there is hope for replacing punitive policies with practices that will help children while more effectively maintaining school safety. Hopefully these developments translate into action to reduce the extent of the pipeline, and that uses the existing evidence about effective strategies for school discipline rather than assumptions about what might work. This evidence suggests several promising strategies that can be implemented for individual students, schools, and entire communities.

Student Supports

Though much of the problem of the school-to-prison pipeline is that school policy and practice overreacts to typical youth behavior, students have some share of the blame, too. Reducing student misbehavior would help schools learn restraint, and the pipeline would shrink. The criminological literature on causes of youth crime and deviance is thorough, and includes many suggestions for how to prevent youth misbehavior. Rather than summarizing these many criminological theories and their resulting policy suggestions, I wish to discuss just a few interventions that could be directed at individual youth; each of these seeks to support students' needs and reduce their rates of misbehavior.

Tutoring is an important student support that could go a long way toward reducing student misbehavior. As I mention above, teachers with whom I spoke in my research almost unanimously told me that most students misbehave in class because they don't understand the course material; by being the class clown they can distract the class from the object of their discomfort, and gain popularity rather than feel embarrassed. But the most common response to students who act up in class—including the responses of the teachers who shared with me this insight—is to kick these children out of class, sending them to a disciplinarian's office or to in-school suspension for a "time out." This might help the teacher in the short term, but it hurts both the student, who only falls further behind by missing more class time, and the teacher, who then has to deal with a student who is even more likely to act up in the future.

It is understandable for teachers to want to remove distracting, difficult students from class so they can more effectively teach to those students who behave. But why on earth do schools not couple punishment with tutoring, to stem the problem? Such a problem-solving approach contradicts contemporary school discipline's narrow focus on rule enforcement (Kupchik 2010), but could go a long way toward preventing future misbehavior. Moreover, since school failure and prior school punishment both predict future school discipline and entrance to the pipeline, a strategy like tutoring could prevent small problems (acting up in class) from growing into larger ones (long-term suspension, expulsion, arrest).

Another intervention directed at individual students is to hire additional counselors and mentors for youth. Mentoring and serving as role models is a primary goal of SRO programs (see Kupchik 2010), but in my research I find that SROs are poorly equipped for this role. The SROs I met during my research in schools were well-intentioned, caring adults. But the fact that they must act on information of any crime means that they can't hold a student's confidence if the student's problems include any illegal activity such as underage drinking or drug use. SROs are police officers, who are trained in conflict and security—not in how to talk to an upset adolescent, as they typically have no training in adolescent development or counseling skills. As caring as SROs may be, they are much worse equipped for this portion of their job than a trained counselor would be. Were schools to add counselors or to replace SROs with counselors, they would be better able to help individual youth suffering from personal trauma or hardship, and help prevent students' personal problems from causing misbehavior and placing them at risk of the pipeline.

A third intervention directed at helping individual students is to invest more resources in schools as sites of student care. Greater attention to the needs of the most disadvantaged students, particularly those who come to school hungry, with inadequate clothing, or other basic needs unmet, would help them to focus on schoolwork rather than their suffering. Many schools try to fulfill this role through health centers—these efforts should be applauded, expanded, and focused on the neediest students.

School Policies

To most effectively address the school-to-prison pipeline, reform must be addressed at the source of so much of the problem: school policies. A first step—and perhaps the most important step that schools could take—might be to undo some of the buildup in punishment and school security that has come about since the 1990s. That is, regardless of how effective reform may be, at a minimum schools ought to strive to do less harm than is currently done by the excessive, counterproductive practices seen across the United States. Schools could begin by dismantling zero-tolerance policies, so long as federal rules requiring them are dropped. This would mean that students are not excluded from school categorically, but instead receive punishments as determined by a school administrator after careful evaluation of each case.

While the end of zero-tolerance policies would be a step forward, it's not clear how much such reform would really shape the reality of school discipline. Stories of elementary school students suspended, expelled, or arrested for pointing their fingers at someone in the shape of a pretend gun, bringing in a cake knife along with their birthday cake, or wearing the wrong color shoes (e.g., Advancement Project et al. 2013) illustrate the absurdity of zero tolerance but not the breadth of its reach. Since prior research finds that most suspensions and other school punishments are for discretionary offenses, not behavior for which any zero-tolerance policy prescribes mandatory punishment (e.g., Kupchik 2010; Reyes 2006), it seems reasonable to question just how many students are affected directly by zero-tolerance policies.

Their indirect effects may be large, however. The importance of zero-tolerance policies is largely as symbolism of school priorities and operating logics (Kupchik 2010). These policies boldly declare that the solutions to behavior problems should be seen in black-and-white terms. Moreover, because they explicitly forbid consideration of the context of misbehavior or any mitigating factors, they are fundamentally undemocratic (Lyons and Drew 2006). To the extent that these policies influence the rationale underlying broader disciplinary practices, they may be very harmful to students.

Another straightforward policy shift aimed at undoing much of the buildup in security and discipline would be to reduce the numbers of SROs in the nation's schools. Certainly a police presence is necessary in some schools: those with serious problems of violence where students may be too frightened to learn and teachers too intimidated to teach. Yet this characterizes few schools in the United States, especially since school crime and violence have been declining consistently for the past twenty years (see Robers et al. 2012). In other schools, the presence of SROs has been shown to lead to arrests for minor offenses, such as disorderly conduct (Na and Gottfredson 2011; Theriot 2009). Some studies show that SROs can occasionally be the cause of student misbehavior by asserting their authority in ways students may perceive to be unfair and oppressive, and to which they respond by acting out (Mukherjee 2007; Nolan 2011). Arrests of students for minor offenses is a primary gateway to the pipeline; based on the available evidence, it seems very clear that reducing police presence wherever possible in schools across the United States would therefore reduce this flow into the pipeline.

A final correction to the contemporary school discipline binge I wish to discuss is to reduce suspensions through greater reliance on alternative punishments. As any parent knows, it is important to punish children when they misbehave, so that they can learn from their mistakes. Yet effective parents also understand that the punishments they give to their children should allow their children opportunities for redemption and learning, and should not be too damaging to their children. The goal is to bring about the desired behavior, not to hurt the child. Yet school punishments tend to do just that: they hurt children by excluding them from school for a fixed period of time, meaning that they go without instruction and often without adult supervision, while failing to teach appropriate behavior, solve the underlying problem, or allow for redemption. Alternatives to suspension and expulsion that seek to repair students' deficits while avoiding stigmatizing punishment, such as conflict mediation or remedial education, would help reduce a primary entrée to the pipeline, suspension, both directly (by reducing the number of suspensions given out) and indirectly (by helping students to improve their behavior).

Schools can also look to the growing body of evaluation research focusing on school disciplinary policy to implement new school policies that will reduce the flow of students into the pipeline. Several strategies, including school-wide positive behavioral intervention and support (PBIS) and restorative justice practices, are supported by multiple evaluations showing effectiveness at reducing student misbehavior and school suspension, expulsion, and arrest (e.g., Sugai and Horner 2002). These and other similar strategies have several elements in common: they seek to replace punitive discipline with prosocial education, build relationships between students and school staff, better integrate students who misbehave into the school environment, and create a climate of inclusiveness where students perceive the school's authority to be fairly imposed. These strategies also help to strengthen the school social climate, which we know is an important factor in preventing student crime and misbehavior (see Gottfredson 2001).

Another way to improve the school social climate would be to more thoroughly involve students in school governance. This means more than simply having a student council that plans school events—it means that schools listen to youth and take their concerns and perspectives seriously. It also requires schools to solicit feedback from all youth, not only those who are elected to student council. A more democratic, inclusive governance structure could equip schools to more fluidly respond to students' concerns while providing students with more of a stake in conformity and empowering students to act as trustworthy citizens.

Of course, efforts to reduce the school-to-prison pipeline must reach out to teachers and school disciplinarians as well. These school staff members are particularly important because they are first responders to the problems of minor student misbehavior, which can easily turn into major misbehavior if the school responds inappropriately. And yet in my research I found very little training in effective classroom management or child development among them. Typically, teachers are so focused on lesson plans and preparing students for exams that they pay too little attention to student behavior. Most of the disciplinarians I met have backgrounds in coaching or the military, not training in child development or evidence-based responses to youthful misbehavior, and take a no-nonsense approach to student discipline that can often run contrary to inclusive behavior management strategies.

I did meet a number of teachers who seem very skilled in classroom management; these teachers excel at integrating all students into their classrooms, while eliciting respectful behavior from their students. When students do misbehave in their classes (which is rare), they take a few minutes to deal constructively with the problem, often by taking the student outside to check in with him or her and see if something is wrong. Though this takes time, it ends up saving much more time by preventing future misconduct. Were schools to allow these skilled teachers a forum for teaching other teachers—and disciplinarians—how to deal with misbehaving youth in a productive, respectful, and caring way, others may learn more effective strategies as well.

When students do require interventions, it would make more sense to have them consult trained professionals rather than former coaches, who may have good intentions but little training in effective responses to student crises. In my research I found no connection between schools' disciplinary apparatuses and their counseling or mental health resources. This makes little sense to me, since a student who repeatedly gets in trouble ought to see a trained professional who may be able to assess underlying reasons for misbehavior. Yet contemporary school discipline is so focused on rules and rule enforcement that mental health is rarely a consideration when the school's behavior code is broken, even when the same students repeatedly demonstrate cause for concern.

Schools should also make greater efforts to diversify their staff. Having more staff who are members of racial and ethnic minorities may help ameliorate the racial gap in school discipline, if they are less inclined to view youth of color as menacing and dangerous. Though school staff who are members of racial and ethnic minority groups may still use punitive strategies, research on attitudes among juvenile justice system workers does suggest that concerns, particularly about disproportionate minority confinement, vary by race and ethnicity (Ward et al. 2011). Thus diversity in schools might lead to greater attention paid to the problem of race and ethnicity and school punishment, which could result in reductions of punitive discipline.

The final strategy schools could pursue involves building connections between schools and families. The relationship between schools and students' families is very complex, and fraught with miscommunication and misunderstanding. Teachers often complain about students' families in ways that suggest class-based judgments about parenting practices (Kupchik 2010; see Lareau 2003). Yet some teachers are effective at building bridges with parents; they enlist the parents as allies rather than adversaries or onlookers, and demonstrate to students that they care. If teachers were better able to facilitate the type of parental participation in school affairs that they seek, and parents better able to support schools' efforts while effectively communicating their needs and concerns, then students would be better off. Such bridges could limit student behavior by establishing better-rounded support systems, all while reducing schools' reliance on exclusionary punishments.

Community Interventions

A third terrain for dismantling the school-to-prison pipeline is at the community level. In particular, policy makers need to address the link between the juvenile justice system and the school. Though the metaphor of a pipeline oversimplifies the connection between school and incarceration, the fact that this metaphor has any meaning suggests that too many youth travel too easily from one institution to the other.

Recently, some high profile judges have begun to recognize the harms of punitive school discipline and overly aggressive policing in schools; this includes the harm to students, but also the difficulty to courtroom workgroups posed by inflated caseloads consisting mostly of minor offenses. These judges, such as Judge Steven Teske of Clayton County, Georgia, have taken it upon themselves to address the situation. Teske brokered an agreement between the schools and police that set forth guidelines for when students should be arrested, and also gave options to SROs, such as referral to conflict management classes, that allow them to respond in ways short of arresting students. It resulted in fewer misdemeanor cases in juvenile court stemming from school misbehavior; Teske is now a well-known speaker at conferences and workshops across the country and in Congress, and has helped other jurisdictions to adopt similar agreements to reduce school-based arrests (see Teske 2012).

Another intervention that would reduce the pipeline is to decouple justice systems and schools in other ways as well. In my home state of Delaware, collaboration between the attorney general's office and schools leads to long-term school exclusion for alleged behavior that may have no connection to the school. When students are arrested in their communities at night or during weekends for certain felony offenses, the attorney general's office lets schools know; the school then may decide to remove the student from school. While I understand the desire to prevent a student accused of selling drugs or committing serious violence from entering the school, this practice excludes students from schools when they haven't broken a school rule or committed a crime within its walls—all before a juvenile court adjudication. As a result, youth who are already involved in the justice system receive less adult supervision, fewer educational opportunities, and greater stigma.

When all else fails and youth are incarcerated, the justice system needs to work more effectively with schools to facilitate reintegration upon release. This requires that juvenile correctional facilities maintain adequate curricula, so that facility residents keep pace with their grade levels. It is also crucial for the justice system to work with the school to ease the transition back to being in the community school. Youth who are readjusting to community schools are likely to need help with many issues, including coursework, potential social conflicts, and even scheduling classes. If this transition can be made any easier for them, some youth may be diverted from the pipeline.

Other community-level efforts in addition to juvenile justice system interventions may help stem the pipeline as well. Recent evidence in support of wraparound services as a response to serious emotional and behavioral problems among youth (see Pullmann et al. 2006) suggests that this approach may be helpful as a response to student misbehavior. Wraparound is a form of therapy where youth receive services from counselors who also help connect them to community organizations and supports, and who coordinate care within the family and school, in an effort to work holistically with youth in support of their social and emotional needs. Applying such an approach to school misbehavior would mean greater coordination among schools, communities, therapists, and families to recognize and respond to students' problems in a way that supports them rather than excludes them from school or forces them into the school-to-prison pipeline. This strategy could help diagnose students' needs and deficits early, connect youth to necessary services, and expand the school's options for responding to unruly students beyond suspension or expulsion.

Discussion: Are Policies Enough?

The array of disciplinary and security practices that comprise what is known as the school-to-prison pipeline poses a serious threat to the current status and future opportunities of today's youth. Unlike topics traditionally studied within the field of juvenile justice, which apply only to the minority of youth who are arrested, the harms posed by counterproductive school policies affect almost all young people: all who attend public schools (and possibly private schools, too, though research has not shown the problem to exist there).

Defenders of punitive school discipline assume that rigid rules and exclusionary punishments best protect students from harm and enable learning (e.g., Arum 2003). Of course they are correct about the importance of consistent rule enforcement for school safety, but they miss the point. Critics (including myself) of contemporary school security and discipline don't argue that we should fail to impose discipline or maintain security in schools, but that we need to do so more intelligently. As I describe above, current practices and policies subject students to constant surveillance, denial of necessary services, suspension for minor misbehavior, and arrest for offenses that could better be dealt with informally. Students' needs go unmet, the causes of their behaviors go unaddressed, and they bear the brunt of excessive punishment for years to come. The point is not that we should have *less* security or discipline in public schools, but that we should impose security and discipline policies that are supported as sound practice by evidence, and we should do so thoughtfully rather than reactively.

In the preceding sections I have described what such responses might look like, and how policy makers and school administrators might go about deconstructing the pipeline through intervention at the individual student, school, and community levels. Whether the political will exists to engage in true reform is questionable, especially considering the financial costs of hiring counselors and tutors. Moreover, though each of the above policy suggestions is supported by evidence on constructive interventions for youth, it's not clear how effective policy reform would prove to be in this context.

One reason why policy changes may alter little school practice is because the treatment of children in schools is, to some extent, a product of broadly shared social pressures, views, and anxieties. In my research I found that efforts by schools to institute effective discipline policies, or of individuals to work constructively with individual students despite bad policies, were uphill battles (Kupchik 2010). Attitudes supporting punitive, reactionary discipline are so ingrained among school staff that policy revisions are unlikely to do much alone. Until schools experience a sea change in how teachers and administrators think, whereby they begin to trust and respect youth more and fear them less, new policies will have little impact.

Such a change seems extremely unlikely any time soon when one realizes that most educational professionals seek to work in public schools because they care about children—yet their mistrust and hostility toward children is fueling the school-to-prison pipeline. As well-intentioned as they may be, they are products of a culture that demonizes and fears children under the mantra of complaining about "Kids these days," while waxing nostalgically about their own childhood years (see Sternheimer 2006). Punitive practices and rigid security are the embodiment of these broadly shared negative views toward children, and are likely to persist as long as these views remain ineffectively addressed in teacher training.

A second reason why I am skeptical about the potential impact of policy changes is that the current climate of education policy leaves little room for effective reform. Schools today are so overburdened by new and ever-changing mandates. The granddaddy of these is the pressure to improve standardized test scores due to the requirements of No Child Left Behind. But there are others as well. Schools are also under pressure to reduce bullying, and almost every state has recently created legislation requiring schools to report bullying or adopt bullying prevention programs;[2] they are instructed to adopt new curricula as school district administrators alter their preferred approach to education; and so on. Schools and school staff are asked to do so much already, and with ever shrinking resources. It seems unlikely that additional requests to shift their approach to discipline and security will get much traction, especially if these new policies ask them to take more time to get to know students and invest more energy in caring for these students' welfare.

Though it is unlikely that any single policy change will have large effects, it is crucial that schools make efforts to limit the number of youth who are unnecessarily punished at school and arrested. The long-term harms to them, their families, and their communities necessitates a new approach that seeks to prevent these harms of the school-to-prison pipeline for so many youth.

NOTES

1. See www.ojjdp.gov/ojstatbb/court/JCSCF_Display.asp.
2. See www.stopbullying.gov/index.html.

REFERENCES

Advancement Project, American Civil Liberties Union of Mississippi, Mississippi State Conference of the NAACP, and Mississippi Coalition for the Prevention of Schoolhouse to Jailhouse. (2013) *Handcuffs on Success: The Extreme School Discipline Crisis in Mississippi Public Schools*. www.aclu-ms.org/files/5713/5843/3850/Handcuffs_on_sucess.pdf.

Arum, Richard. (2003) *Judging School Discipline: The Crisis of Moral Authority*. Cambridge, MA: Harvard University Press.

Bowditch, Christine. (1993) "Getting Rid of Troublemakers: High school disciplinary procedures and the production of discipline." *Social Problems* 40: 493–507.

Bowles, Samuel, and Herbert Gintis. (1977) *Schooling in Capitalist America: Educational Reform and the Contradictions of Economic Life*. New York: Basic Books.

Bracy, Nicole L. (2010) "Circumventing the Law: Students' rights in schools with police." *Journal of Contemporary Criminal Justice* 26: 294–315.

Dewey, John. (1916) *Democracy and Education: An Introduction to the Philosophy of Education*. New York: Macmillan.

Durkheim, Emile. (2011[1961]) *Moral Education*, Everett K. Wilson and Herman Schnurer (trans.). New York: Dover Publications.

Fabelo, Tony, Michael Thompson, Martha Plotkin, Dottie Carmichal, Miner Marchbanks, and Eric Booth. (2011) *Breaking Schools' Rules: A Statewide Study of How School Discipline Relates to Students' Success and Juvenile Justice Involvement*. New York: Council of State Governments Justice Center and Public Policy Research Institute.

Feld, Barry C. (2011) "*T.L.O.* and *Redding*'s unanswered (misanswered) fourth amendment questions: Few rights and fewer remedies." *Mississippi Law Journal* 80: 847–954.

Ferguson, Ann A. (2000) *Bad Boys: Public Schools in the Making of Black Masculinity*. Ann Arbor: University of Michigan Press.

Fine, Michelle, April Burns, Yasser A. Payne, and Maria E. Torre. (2004) "Civics Lessons: The color and class of betrayal." *Teachers College Record* 106, 2193–2223.

Gottfredson, Denise C. (2001) *Schools and Delinquency*. New York: Cambridge University Press.

Hirschfield, Paul. (2012) "A Critical Assessment of Theory and Research on the 'School to Prison Pipeline.'" Paper presented at the American Society of Criminology Annual Conference, Chicago, IL, Nov. 14–17, 2012.

Irwin, Katherine, Janet Davidson, and Amanda Hall-Sanchez. (2013) "The race to punish in American schools: Class and race predictors of punitive school-crime control." *Critical Criminology* 21: 47–71.

James, Bernard. (2012) "The Truth: Behind the school-to-pipeline dispute." *School Safety*, Winter 2012, pp. 12–17.

Kim, Catherine Y., Daniel J. Losen, and Damon T. Hewitt. (2010) *The School-to-Prison Pipeline: Structuring Legal Reform*. New York: NYU Press.

Kozol, Jonathan. (1991) *Savage Inequalities: Children in America's Schools*. New York: Harper Collins.

Kozol, Jonathan. (2005) *The Shame of the Nation: The Restoration of Apartheid Schooling in America*. New York: Random House.

Kupchik, Aaron. (2009) "Things are Tough All Over: Race, ethnicity, class and school discipline." *Punishment & Society* 11: 291–317.

Kupchik, Aaron. (2010) *Homeroom Security: School Discipline in an Age of Fear*. New York: NYU Press.

Kupchik, Aaron and Thomas Catlaw. (2013a) "Discipline and Participation: The long-term effects of suspension and school security on the political and civic engagement of youth." Paper presented at the 2013 Conference on Closing the School Discipline Gap, The Civil Rights Project at UCLA, Washington, DC, January 10, 2013.

Kupchik, Aaron and Thomas Catlaw. (2013b) "The Dynamics of School Discipline in a Neoliberal Era." In Glenn W. Muschert, Stuart Henry, Nicole L. Bracy and Anthony Peguero (eds.) *Responding to School Violence: Confronting the Columbine Effect.* Boulder, CO: Lynne Rienner Publishers.

Lareau, Annette. (2003) *Unequal Childhoods: Class, race, and family life*. Berkeley: University of California Press.

Lewis, Amanda E. (2003) *Race in the Schoolyard: Negotiating the Color Line in Classrooms and Communities.* New Brunswick, NJ: Rutgers University Press.

Lyons, William, and Julie Drew. (2006) *Punishing Schools: Fear and Citizenship in American Public Education.* Ann Arbor: University of Michigan Press.

McCarthy, John D., and Dean R. Hoge. (1987) "The Social Construction of School Punishment: Racial disadvantage out of universalistic process." *Social Forces* 65: 1101–1120.

Monahan, Torin, and Rodolfo D. Torres. (2010) *Schools Under Surveillance: Cultures of Control in Public Education*. New Brunswick, NJ: Rutgers University Press.

Mukherjee, Elora. (2007) *Criminalizing the Classroom: The Over-Policing of New York City Schools.* New York: New York Civil Liberties Union.

Na, Chongmin., and Gottfredson Denise C. (2013) "Police Officers in Schools: Effects on school crime and the processing of offending behaviors." *Justice Quarterly* 30: 619–650.

Nolan, Kathleen. (2011) *Police in the Hallway: Discipline in an Urban High School.* Minneapolis: University of Minnesota Press.

Payne, Allison Ann, and Kelly Welch. (2010) "Modeling the Effects of Racial Threat on Punitive and Restorative School Discipline Practices." *Criminology* 48: 1019–1062.

Petteruti, Amanda. (2012) *Education Under Arrest: The Case Against Police in Schools.* Washington, DC: Justice Policy Institute.

Pullmann, Michael D., Jodi Kerbs, Nancy Koroloff, Ernie Veach-White, Rita Gaylor, and Dede Sieler. (2006) "Juvenile Offenders with Mental Health Needs: Reducing Recidivism using Wraparound." *Crime & Delinquency* 52: 375–397.

Reyes, Augustina H. (2006) *Discipline, Achievement, and Race: Is Zero Tolerance the Answer?* Lanham, MD: Rowman and Littlefield.

Rile-Hayward, Clarissa. (2000) *De-Facing Power*. New York: Cambridge University Press.

Rios, Victor M. (2011) *Punished: Policing in the Lives of Black and Latino Boys.* New York: NYU Press.

Robers, Simone, Jijun Zhang, Jennifer Truman, and Thomas D. Snyder. (2012) *Indicators of School Crime and Safety: 2011.* Washington, DC: US Department of Education, National Center for Education Statistics, and US Department of Justice, Bureau of Justice Statistics.

Simmons, Lizbet. (2007) "The Public School, the Prison, and the Bottom Line: Expenditure and expediency." Paper presented at the American Sociological Association annual conference, New York, NY, August 11–14, 2007.

Simon, Jonathan. (2007) *Governing through Crime: How the War on Crime Transformed American Democracy and Created a Culture of Fear.* New York: Oxford University Press.

Skiba, Russell J., Robert S. Michael, Abra Carroll Nardo, and Reece Peterson. (2000) *The Color of Discipline: Sources of Racial and Gender Disproportionality in School Punishment.* Indiana Education Policy Center, Research Report SRS1.

Skiba, Russell, Cecil R. Reynolds, Sandra Graham, Peter Sheras, Jane Close Conoley, and Enedina Garcia-Vazquez. (2006) *Are Zero Tolerance Policies Effective in the Schools? An Evidentiary Review and Recommendations.* Report by the American Psychological Association Zero Tolerance Task Force. Washington, DC: American Psychological Association.

Sternheimer, Karen. (2006) *Kids These Days: Fact and Fiction About Yoday's Youth.* Lanham, MD: Rowman and Littlefield.

Sugai, George, and Robert Horner. (2002) "The Evolution of Discipline Practices: School-wide positive behavior supports." *Child and Family Behavior Therapy* 24: 23–50.

Teske, Steven C. (2012) Testimony before the Senate Subcomittee on the Constitution, Civil Rights, and Human Rights; Subcommittee Hearing on "Ending the School to Prison Pipeline," December 12, www.judiciary.senate.gov/pdf/12-12-12TeskeTestimony.pdf.

Theriot, Matthew T. (2009) "School Resource Officers and the Criminalization of Student Behavior." *Journal of Criminal Justice* 37: 280–287.

Tyack, David B. (1974) *The One Best System: A History of American Urban Education.* Cambridge, MA: Harvard University Press.

Ward, Geoff, Aaron Kupchik, Laurin Parker, and Brian Chad Starks. (2011) "Racial Politics of Juvenile Justice Policy Support: Juvenile court worker orientations toward disproportionate minority confinement." *Race and Justice* 1: 154–184.

Welch, Kelly, and Allison Ann Payne. (2010) "Racial Threat and Punitive School Discipline." *Social Problems* 57:25–48.

Welch, Kelly, and Allison Ann Payne. (2012) "Exclusionary School Punishment: The Effect of Racial Threat on Expulsion and Suspension." *Youth Violence and Juvenile Justice* 10: 155–171.

Western, Bruce. 2006. *Punishment and Inequality in America.* New York: Russell Sage Foundation.

Williams, Kirk R. and Nancy G. Guerra. (2011) "Perceptions of Collective Efficacy and Bullying Perpetration in Schools." *Social Problems* 28: 126–143.

Wolf, Kerrin. (2012) *An Exploration of School Resource Officer Arrests in Delaware.* Ph.D. Dissertation, University of Delaware; unpublished.

5

Education behind Bars?

The Promise of the Maya Angelou Academy

JAMES FORMAN JR.

Editors' Note: the pages that follow are a lightly edited version of the keynote address given on April 12, 2013, by James Forman Jr. at the Choosing the Future for Juvenile Justice conference at the William S. Boyd School of Law, University of Nevada, Las Vegas, which we organized around the topics in this volume. The young persons subject to secure confinement in the juvenile justice system are a population of very high-risk students who suffer almost universal educational disadvantage. While the need for education for these kids is obvious, there is almost no literature or programmatic emphasis on creating quality education in correctional facilities. Why? Is there no hope for educationally low achieving youth in correctional facilities? Or is the opportunity to create a "prison-to-schools pipeline" one of the most important reform imperatives of twenty-first-century juvenile justice?

The theme of our conference is choosing the future of juvenile justice. In my talk I will argue that as we choose that future, education must be at the center of our efforts. I believe this is the only way we will create a juvenile justice system that serves the needs of young people and ensures safe, vibrant communities.

I should begin with some good news. We stand at a moment of positive change in American juvenile justice. Overall crime is declining, juvenile crime is going down, and the number of youth held in custody is also dropping fast.

States are adopting less punitive policies as well. A recent report by the National Conference of State Legislatures documents a variety of changes.[1] For example, many states have raised the age of juvenile court jurisdiction, which means that more young people will be tried as juveniles rather than as adults. Other states have improved access to counsel, fortified various procedural rights, and improved access to mental health treatment. One of the most important trends has been the adoption of improved assessment tools, so that juvenile justice officials can distinguish the few young people who need secure detention from the many more who can be safely released into community supervision.

These are all positive trends. But here's my concern. There is one area where we have seen little progress. And it is an area that is rarely mentioned in reports on the juvenile justice system or, typically, at conferences such as this one.

The topic we overlook is education—specifically, the quality of education that we provide to kids who are in the juvenile justice system, and in particular, to those who are in juvenile facilities. Why should the juvenile justice reform community focus on education? Let me offer three reasons.

First, young people who are locked up in juvenile facilities are among our nation's most vulnerable. Nearly all of them are poor, almost 50 percent have special needs, and the majority have failed, quit, or been kicked out of school at some point. Most are high school age, but function academically at the middle school level, and have only have a handful of high school credits. Given these deficits, unless we take steps to radically alter their educational trajectories, most young people who spend time in juvenile facilities will never earn a high school diploma or GED. And today, dropping out of high school relegates you to the margins of society.

Second, we have a chance to reach them while they are locked up. Incarceration is not a good thing, and we should all hope for a world with less of it. But as long as we have some young people behind bars, we must face this question: can anything good come out of the experience? I would argue that the answer is yes, and that one possible good is a quality educational experience.

Teens are in school for six to seven hours a day. And this is typically true even for kids in facilities. So if we are serious about improving the life prospects of incarcerated teens, how can we avoid tackling the institution—the school—that is responsible for half of their waking hours?

Here's the final reason we should focus on schools. Education, many have argued, is the civil rights issue of our time. A similar case can be made for the juvenile and criminal justice systems. Today, blacks are about eight times more likely to go to prison as whites, and a black man born in my generation is twice as likely to go to prison as one born in my father's generation. In the juvenile justice arena, disproportionate minority contact remains a grave concern. So we should wonder: if education is one of the great civil rights issues of our time, and if criminal and juvenile justice are two others, then shouldn't we be talking about the places where those issues meet? And they meet at schools inside our juvenile facilities.

But if what I have said so far is true, we must confront the next question: why don't schools feature more prominently when we talk about reforming the juvenile justice system? Let me offer three reasons. The first two we can admit, and the third we can't.

The first reason is that much juvenile justice reform has been driven by lawyers, and lawyers are good at many things (or so my profession likes to believe), but education is one area where we lack special expertise. We don't know schools. They remain a bit of a black box. Lawyers might be able to influence the inputs (such as money), but we lack a clear sense of how to achieve things such as quality instruction.

The second reason—and we can admit this one too—is that juvenile justice reformers have been focused on reducing the number of young people who are incarcerated. In this effort, the reform community has come to see juvenile facilities as inherently toxic and largely beyond reform. If the goal is to shut them down, what is the point of working to make these places better? Such efforts might even backfire, because improving schools inside juvenile prisons arguably reinforces a system that some reformers would like to abolish.

I respect these views. But I would argue that we cannot afford to give up on the 70,000 or more teens still behind bars today. Unless anyone can make the case that juvenile facilities will all be emptied out sometime soon, I would argue that we have a moral obligation to improve the schools these young people are compelled to attend.

This brings me to the third reason we have failed to put education at the center of juvenile justice reform. Few of us will admit this one—not even to ourselves. But I think it is pervasive and powerful. I believe that many who work in the juvenile justice field, including some of the most well-intentioned, have come to accept a reduced set of expectations for young people in the juvenile system. Too many of us believe that for kids who are incarcerated, our highest and only hope should be that they don't commit another crime after they are released.

Now, there is nothing wrong with having this as one of our goals. But avoiding rearrest shouldn't become our only goal for young people in the system.

* * *

I believe that we can do better, that we can have higher expectations for the young people in this system, and that we can demand more from our institutions. What explains my faith?

I've seen it. Almost twenty years ago I became a public defender, working in juvenile court in Washington DC. It was the greatest job I ever had, but it was also filled with frustration. As a public defender I might win a case, or get a dismissal, or persuade the judge to give my client a good disposition like probation. But the victories were short-lived. The kids kept coming back with new charges.

I often felt like I was just setting them up for failure—running around trying to find programs for them that didn't exist, or wouldn't truly meet their needs. After a while I began to ask my clients and their families some simple questions: What do you want? What would work for you? What would keep you from coming back to court? And the answer was always the same: help with school, and a job.

I shared my frustration with a friend named David Domenici (about whom you will hear more shortly), and eventually we decided to start a school for kids in the juvenile justice system. Our idea was simple, if radical: the kids who needed the most should get the best. The smallest classes, best teachers, most robust counseling and mental health services, and a chance to work. We called it the Maya Angelou Public Charter School, after the poet who still visits our campus once a year. We started with 20 kids, in 1997. In the 15 years since we have grown to serve over 300 students in our high school now located in the far eastern section of Washington, DC.[2]

We had been doing this alternative school work for about a decade when we got a call from Vinnie Schiraldi. Trained as a social worker, Schiraldi spent most of his career trying to reform juvenile justice from outside the system. Then, in a twist of fate, DC Mayor Anthony Williams asked him to run the District's system. Mayor Williams more or less told Schiraldi, "You've been complaining for so long, you fix it."

Schiraldi took up the challenge, and as head of the DC's Department of Youth Rehabilitation Services, he called David and me with a startling proposal: he wanted to reform the city's long-term secure facility, and he didn't want to overlook the school. So he issued a request for proposal (RFP) seeking providers who wanted to start from scratch and remake the school inside the juvenile prison. He was calling people in DC and around the country whose work he admired and encouraging them to apply.

We had our doubts. Despite our background working with kids from the juvenile justice system, we had never operated a school *inside* a prison. We eventually overcome our hesitation, put in a proposal, and were selected.

I'm glad we took that risk. The Maya Angelou Academy now educates all sixty of the young men inside New Beginnings, the District's long-term, secure facility for adjudicated youth.[3] Most of our students (or scholars, as we call them) are 15 or 16 years old and will spend 9 to 12 months at our school and in the facility. We spend approximately $35,000 a year per student, which is more than is spent in schools in the city generally.[4] The higher cost reflects how many of our students require additional services—typically more than half of the students in the school have individual education plans or IEPs (meaning they are in the special education system), and many of those who do not have IEPs nonetheless require individual attention and services.

In the four years since we took over, our school has made an important difference in the lives of hundreds of young men. Our students improve their reading and math scores at a rate of nearly 1.5 grade levels for each year they are with us. Student retention rates (students remaining in school or at work after release to the community) have doubled during the Academy's tenure.[5]

DC's juvenile justice has long operated under a consent decree, and in July 2010 the monitor overseeing the agency called the school an "extraordinary educational program."[6] The monitor's educational expert reached a similar conclusion:

> The Maya Angelou Academy at the New Beginnings Youth Development Center is one of the best education programs in a confinement facility I have had the opportunity to observe. Scholars in the model units are

> receiving an excellent education. The strength of the leadership and the staff, the people and material resources available to them, and the processes and program design all contribute to the overall effectiveness of the program.[7]

Even the *Washington Post*, long critical of the District's juvenile justice system, was complimentary—citing the monitor's report, the *Post* noted that the school had been transformed "from one of the nation's worst programs to one of its finest."[8]

I emphasize our school's history and success for two reasons. First, I want to emphasize that if you are moved to try education programs in secure settings, you can do this too. This is hard work, but it is not impossible. We didn't begin with degrees in the field of educating incarcerated teens. We had a lot to learn, and we still are learning. But we did have the right beliefs: we believed that the young people we had met behind bars had extraordinary potential, and we had a firm conviction that although they had failed, the system had failed them too.

The Maya Angelou Academy is important for another reason as well. It disproves the myth that kids behind bars can't learn. The success at the Academy is like the black swan. Just as the existence of one black swan proves that not all swans are white, the existence of one successful school inside a juvenile facility proves that failure is not inevitable. Success is possible.

* * *

But how do we move beyond the one black swan? How do we create success across the field? How do we foster success in other states? This is the central question, and it is one where I come today with great optimism. The organization whose work gives me that hope is the Center for Educational Excellence in Alternative Settings (CEEAS).

Why am I so enthused about this organization and its work? In part it is due to leadership; CEEAS is run by David Domenici, who was a pioneer in the DC adventure. He was the principal of the Maya Angelou Academy who produced the academic results I just described. But my optimism stems from more than David's personal abilities.

His organization is beginning to do what nobody has been able to do before. CEEAS is beginning to help states dramatically enhance the educational programs inside their juvenile facilities.

David and his team have traveled around the country to find states with leaders who want to improve, and they have chosen eleven states to be initial members of an educational consortium. These states were not chosen because they are providing a good education already—few are. In fact, David and his team have compiled a depressing litany of statistics documenting the low quality of education being provided in juvenile facilities around the country.

For example, when David's team visited classrooms in over seventeen states, one of the things they looked for was whether teachers were, in fact, teaching. Now, this is a terribly low bar for measuring educational effectiveness. They only wanted to see if there was instruction in the classroom. Not quality instruction—just whether there was *any* instruction at all.

Overall, in 17 states, in 35 schools, and in hundreds of classrooms, they found instruction of any sort occurring in only 55 percent of the classrooms. Incredibly, that means in almost half the classrooms there is nothing that you could even call teaching, using the most charitable definition of the term.

The 11 states were chosen because of the sincerity of their commitment to improve. In each of them, David and his team found some caring individuals who would like to do better and know that they need help. CEEAS provides that help, through a series of policy and practice initiatives.

Why do I think any of this might work? Because I've seen it. I've seen it work in DC. I've seen how education can transform lives, including those of young people deep in the juvenile justice system, kids who many say are just too far gone.

Let me close with one example of such a transformation: Samantha, a successful product of our early efforts, who now works with us to help others. David and I met Samantha when she was 15, and was trying to get out of juvenile detention and into our school. This was in the late 1990s.

In 2008, Samantha was interviewed about her experiences in the juvenile justice system, and here is what she said then:

I was locked up for a year and a half when I was about 15. I was originally there on a first-degree murder charge, but I didn't do it and eventually was able to prove it and ended up with an accessory assault charge.

There was some schooling there, but what I remember of it was watching movies the whole time. There were no pencils or school supplies at all that I remember.

It was maybe two hours a day that was considered school and then we went back into lockup.

The way I found my way to Maya Angelou Charter School was that David Domenici knew my public defender, so he knew a little bit about my situation and wanted to help me get my life back on track once I got out.

He was starting a new school, and he was saying it was going to be for students like me who had gotten off track.

At first the whole idea was denied by the judge. He said I was a menace to society and that I didn't belong in such a school, and it wasn't until David followed through that I was allowed to attend.

Due to the fact that I came from unstable living conditions, my household just was not ever going to be stable for me. One of the first and most important things the school did was to recognize that. They opened up a residential home that I was able to live in, and they also looked at my concerns and my issues that I had going on in my life.

They had high expectations for me, because they believed in me and they believed in what they were trying to accomplish. They helped me mentally, physically, emotionally, everything.

They helped me see where different paths might lead, and helped me think through the consequences of different actions. No one had ever really provided a blueprint like that for me to be able to see where I might be headed.

The thing about Maya Angelou is that the support was there. For someone like myself who never really had any support of any kind . . . let's just say a little inch goes a long way.

No one in my household had ever graduated from anything, so all this talk about getting through high school and maybe going to college would have just been some crazy talk if it weren't for the support.

Once I learned to trust in it, knowing I had that support was what got me through.

Another important thing I got from Maya Angelou was my work ethic. They were straight up about it. They'd say things like, "You're really far behind and your dreams are really big, and you're going to have work to get there, but it's not impossible." They even sent me to a precollege exploration course at Wellesley College, to give me a taste of what was possible.

But they weren't just talking about schoolwork either. I worked at internships and my last internship at Maya Angelou was in the human resources department at Marriott, and when I graduated from high school Marriott offered me a job. That was my first real job.

Not everybody who graduates from high school and goes to college is going to graduate in four years and become a huge success story.

Some of us have to really work our butts off for it, and that's something I learned from Maya Angelou too.

I've been at Montgomery College on and off for some years now, and I'm considering transferring to Trinity College to finish it up.

I'm working towards a degree in special education and a teacher's license, because I've seen the good teachers can do in the world through my own life.

Samantha said those words five years ago. Samantha is an educator now, working at the Maya Angelou Academy. She was featured in a recent national profile of the Maya Angelou Academy on NBC's Rock Center with Brian Williams.[9]

Samantha is providing young people locked up today what she never got when she was incarcerated some 15 years ago. She's providing them a skilled, compassionate adult who knows where they are coming from.

She's providing them an adult who knows the value of education—because, as she put it, she's seen the good teachers can do. Samantha is putting education at the center of juvenile justice reform.

So should we.

NOTES

1. National Conference of State Legislatures, Trends in Juvenile Justice Legislation, 2001–2011 (2012).
2. For a more detailed discussion of the history of the school, see James Forman Jr. & David Domenici, "A Circle of Trust: The Story of the See Forever School,"

in *Starting Up: New Schools in New Times* (Marv Hoffman & Lisa Arrastia, eds., 2012, New York: Teacher's College Press, pp. 46–60).

3. The District currently sends very few girls to secure juvenile facilities; when it does, they are housed elsewhere.
4. I have not been able to obtain reliable data on the per-pupil education costs in other states, and from what I can tell, such data have never been collected in most jurisdictions. Some data exist regarding the overall cost of juvenile incarceration. The American Correctional Association estimates that states spend, on average, just over $88,000 a year for each juvenile behind bars. For a discussion of various cost estimates, see Justice Policy Institute, *The Costs of Confinement: Why Good Juvenile Justice Policies Make Good Fiscal Sense* (2009), Washington, DC, p. 4.
5. For more on the Maya Angelou Academy, see David Domenici & James Forman, Jr., "What It Takes to Transform a School Inside a Juvenile Facility: The Story of the Maya Angelou Academy," in *Justice for Kids: Keeping Kids Out of the Juvenile Justice System* (Nancy E. Dowd, ed., 2011, New York: New York University Press, pp. 283–305).
6. The Special Arbiter's Report to the Court (2010). Filed in *Jerry M. et al. v. District of Columbia*, Civil Action No. 1519-85.
7. Exhibit 6A to Special Arbiter's Report to the Court. (2010). Filed in *Jerry M. et al. v. District of Columbia*, Civil Action No. 1519-85.
8. Editorial, "Rehabilitating Juveniles: Commendable Progress, But Work To Be Done," *Washington Post*, July 12, 2010, p. A14.
9. "On Assignment: Setting High Expectations for Troubled Teens," *Rock Center with Brian Williams*, NBC News, July 5, 2012; http://rockcenter.nbcnews.com/_news/2012/07/05/12579909-on-assignment-setting-high-expectations-for-troubled-teens?lite.

6

A Tale of Two Systems

Juvenile Justice System Choices and Their Impact on Young Immigrants

DAVID B. THRONSON

Introduction

Decisions and actions in juvenile justice systems across the United States serve as de facto immigration decisions every day. But juvenile justice and immigration are not the two systems referenced in the title of this chapter. When immigrant youth are involved with law enforcement and juvenile justice, subsequent interactions with immigration authorities are common. The immigration repercussions that flow from immigrant youth involvement with juvenile systems, however, are largely determined by choices that juvenile justice systems make about the treatment of immigrant youth. Rigid immigration laws and enforcement practices react to the outcomes of juvenile justice system involvement by noncitizen youth in ways that often are harsh, but also are relatively predictable.

This means that the decisions made by a variety of players in juvenile justice systems about the treatment of immigrant youth will largely determine whether immigration authorities are involved at all, and how any such involvement will impact a young person's ability to remain in the United States. This chapter first explores the size and growth of the child immigrant population in the United States, a youth population over a million strong that is at risk of deportation under current immigration law. It then examines immigration law's peculiar treatment of children and its rejection of the widely held notion that youth, by virtue of their youth, should be treated differently.

Second, this chapter analyzes how the pervasive failure of immigration law to differentiate youth from adults results in harsh immigration consequences for immigrant youth that are not tailored to their culpability or capacity. This means that a variety of decisions made by juvenile justice systems will be determinative of the immigration fate of youth. These can range from decisions made by detention or law enforcement personnel to inform and involve immigration authorities, to more complex decisions by prosecutors or judges such as trying youth as adults or imposing blending sentencing schemes. Choices, even those that share identical rehabilitative goals within the juvenile justice system, can result in wildly different immigration impacts. Juvenile justice systems should not function in ignorance of the immigration consequences that flow from their actions.

Finally, this chapter argues that juvenile justice systems have defining choices in how they work with immigrant youth. Juvenile justice systems that place their core mission of working positively with youth ahead of collateral efforts to enforce federal immigration law can leverage the equitable flexibility of juvenile systems to improve the lives and well-being of immigrant youth. Punitive juvenile justice systems that choose affirmative efforts to involve immigration enforcement authorities in the lives of youth, or carelessly take actions without regard to the foreseeable immigration consequences, subvert their mission of providing an alternative to adult courts and punishments for youth. The starkly different choices that systems make about immigrant youth create two systems of juvenile justice. For immigrant youth involved with a juvenile justice system, the type of system that they encounter will result in fundamentally different life options.

I. Immigrant Youth and the Nature of Immigration Law

A. By the Numbers

The reality that large numbers of immigrant youth interact with juvenile justice systems is not an indication that immigrant youth are less law abiding than native-born youth. Indeed, evidence indicates the opposite and consistently demonstrates that immigrant populations, at any age, are more law-abiding than later generations (Rumbaut et al. 2006; Rumbaut & Ewing 2007; see also American Immigration Council 2008). But the population of noncitizen youth is large, and from this large group inevitably there are many immigrant youth who become involved with law enforcement. To get a sense of the range and scale of the immigrant youth population, a closer look is warranted.

Immigrant youth form a significant part of the population of the United States, both through and outside legal channels of migration. For starters, hundreds of thousands of immigrant youth arrive annually. They comprise approximately one quarter of all lawful immigration. For example, in fiscal year 2009 children constituted about 26.6 percent of all family-sponsored immigration (Department of Homeland Security 2009).[1] Similarly, 24.7 percent of employment-based visas and 26.2 percent of diversity visas were issued to children, as derivatives of their parents who qualified for immigration visas (Department of Homeland Security 2009).[2] These immigrants arriving as children and youth are not yet US citizens, so despite their current lawful status, they are still at risk of deportation based on encounters with law enforcement. As discussed more fully below, critical to all these immigrant youth who arrive lawfully is a relationship to a parent who has or is obtaining lawful status. But not every young person has such a parent in his or her life, and many youth arrive outside the legal framework of immigration law with or without parents.

Unaccompanied children arrive in the United States by the tens of thousands each year. Bucking the trend of generally declining unauthorized migration, the number of unaccompanied children arriving in the United States has risen sharply (Preston 2012, noting that from October 2011 through July 2012 "the authorities detained 21,842 unaccompanied minors, most at the Southwest border, a 48 percent increase over a year earlier"). According to the Congressional Research Service,

> more than 80,000 children have been apprehended annually since 2001, the vast majority having migrated from Mexico. Of those who are apprehended, most are turned away or placed in removal proceedings. Children from Mexico and Canada are nearly always repatriated immediately, since most lack asylum claims and because the United States has expedited repatriation agreements with these countries (Levinson 2011, 1; see also Haddal, noting that in fiscal year 2007, the Department of Homeland Security detained 8,227 unaccompanied children, 2007, 1).

Many of those not immediately turned back across a land border are detained. In the majority of instances, these youth do not have an avenue to obtain immigration relief and ultimately are removed. In the United States, deportations of children are not a rare anomaly, but rather a routine part of immigration enforcement.

Of course, not all youth attempting to enter or remain in the United States without authorization are unaccompanied, and not all are apprehended. The US Department of State estimates that between 14,500 and 17,500 persons are trafficked into the country each year, and that approximately half of global trafficking victims are minors (2008). Other children arrive with family members or other adults, and approximately 1.8 million children live in the United States without authorization, including some children without lawful status whose parents have legal immigration status or US citizenship. In total, youth constitute around 16 percent of the unauthorized migrant population in the United States (Passel 2006, 8).

Still, youth who themselves lack authorized immigration status are but a small part of the larger group of young people whose families are directly affected by immigration laws. Children in immigrant families now account for approximately one fourth of all children in the United States (Hernandez & Cervantes 2011, 6). Of these, more than five million children have at least one parent who lacks authorization to remain in the United States (Terrazas & Batalova 2009), while 3.8 million parents of US citizen children lack authorized immigration status (Passel & Cohn 2009, 7; see also Thronson 2010, 243, "having a child in the United States does nothing to alter the parents' immigration status and in all but the most extreme situations has no impact on parents' immigration options"). Combining the numbers of adults and children living in the United States with authorization, almost 9 million people live in families with at least one unauthorized immigrant (Passel & Cohn 2009).

Even without transgressions of criminal laws, many immigrant youth and youth in immigrant families find themselves living outside the law, and immigration status can significantly impact their lives. As immigrant youth without lawful status mature and gain an expanding appreciation of their tenuous relationship with broader US society, they come see mounting obstacles to their futures. Schools, at least since *Plyler* v. *Doe* (1982), can serve to welcome and integrate children regardless of their immigration status. But as immigrant youth branch out into the world they encounter status-based barriers to everyday rites of passage such as obtaining drivers licenses, jobs, and financial assistance to attend college. And those who find themselves involved with juvenile justice systems soon learn that the risks and potentially life-altering outcomes of their brush with the law, however minor, are far different from those faced by US citizen youth.

B. Children and Youth in Immigration Law

The numbers of youth who lack lawful immigration status or who are unable to naturalize provide strong evidence that immigration law is not guided by the notion that children should be treated more generously than adults in matters of immigration law. In its primary task of separating those permitted to remain in the United States from those who are not, immigration law generally fails to afford differential treatment to children and in many instances affirmatively prejudices those it identifies as children. While the very existence of juvenile justice systems arises from the notion that children and youth must be treated differently from adults, immigration law roundly rejects this premise (Tanenhaus 2012, 419–441). Before examining the intersection of immigration law with juvenile justice systems, a baseline explanation of the treatment of children in immigration law is needed.

1. CHILDREN, JUVENILES, MINORS, AND ADULTS

Before it even reaches the question of how a person should be treated prior to reaching adulthood, US immigration law demonstrates wildly inconsistent views on when the threshold is crossed. The term "child" is a defined by statutory provisions which look not to characteristics of children, but rather to the relationships or lack thereof between children and adults. In immigration law, a "child" is defined with circularity as a child who also meets other qualifying conditions set out in seven distinct categories. Among the criteria that make a child a child are qualifications such as being born in wedlock, being adopted before age 16, or having a father who has taken specified steps to "legitimate" the child (Immigration and Nationality Act [INA], 8 U.S.C.A. § 1101(b)(1); West 2005).

In contrast to this notion of a child who is defined only in relation to a parent, the Trafficking Victims Protection and Reauthorization Act of 2008 introduced the term "unaccompanied alien child," which now encompasses:

> a child who . . . has no lawful immigration status in the United States; . . . has not attained 18 years of age; and . . . with respect to whom . . . there is no parent or legal guardian in the United States; or . . . no parent or legal guardian in the United States is available to provide care and physical custody (6 U.S.C.A. § 279(g)(2)).

Being a child for immigration purposes thus turns on either having the right relationship to a parent, or having no parent available at all.

Federal regulations expand upon the restrictive yet "particularly exhaustive" (*INS v. Hector* 1986, per curiam) statutory definition of child and introduce the term "juvenile" as "an alien under the age of 18 years" (8 C.F.R. § 236.3 (2012)).[3] Other regulations utilize, but do not define, the term "minor," and the regulations treat these terms in some instances as distinct yet in other situations as interchangeable, as in the regulation noting, "*Juveniles* may be released to a relative . . . not in Service detention who is willing to sponsor a *minor* and the *minor* may be released to that relative notwithstanding that the *juvenile* has a relative who is in detention" (emphasis added, 8 C.F.R. § 212.5(b)(3)(i) (2012)).

Knowing who immigration law considers a child is important, not because they are afforded extra protections, but rather because children typically fare worse under immigration law than adults.

2. HOW DOES IMMIGRATION LAW TREAT CHILDREN?

With one exception, in meeting the substantive criteria that immigration law establishes for eligibility for a lawful immigration status or relief from removal, children are afforded no benefits based on their "childness"—that is, because of any of the various characteristics that frequently are attributed to children such as immaturity, lack of capacity or competence, innocence, or particular vulnerability. While children are not precluded from seeking immigration relief, they are held to the same criteria as adults. For example, while children are theoretically eligible for employment-based immigration, they are unlikely to meet the immigration law requirements related to education and experience, let alone overcome restrictions on the employment of child labor (INA 8 U.S.C.A. § 1151(b); West 2005 & Supp. 2013). Immigration provisions simply are not tailored to the experiences and abilities of children.

Like adults, children can independently seek humanitarian forms of immigration relief, such as asylum and protection from removal under the Convention Against Torture (e.g., *Gonzalez* v. *Reno* 2000, 1347 n.8, affirming that any person, regardless of age, may apply for asylum; Nugent 2006, 219–236), but the "normative and legal substantive framework for unaccompanied children in removal proceedings is based upon an adult framework and does not incorporate a child-oriented framework" (Somers, Herrera, Rodrigues 2010, 372). Moreover, the dominant conception in immigration law of children as dependents inhibits the recognition of individual rights and perspectives of children (Thronson 2002, 992–994, for the negative impact that the dominant paradigm of immigration law has on the plight of unaccompanied minors; see also Carr 2009, 122–123, for the significant differences between accompanied and unaccompanied or separated children in the immigration system). One place this is manifest is in the bar to naturalization for youth under age eighteen. Youth may be deported despite their minority, but they are not considered sufficiently mature that they may be permitted to naturalize as US citizens and lock in their right to remain in this country.

The one form of immigration relief solely available to youth, special immigrant juvenile status, is available to youth not because of their youth, their experiences, or their characteristics, but rather because they have been declared dependent on a juvenile court. This provision emphasizes youth's dependency, not agency (INA 8 U.S.C.A. § 1101(a)(27)(J); West 2005 & Supp, 2013).

Just as the substantive eligibility criteria for immigration relief apply to children as they do adults, no distinction is made between children and adults in grounds of inadmissibility that apply generally to all immigrants (INA 8 U.S.C.A. § 1182(a)(6)(A); West 2005, establishing documents-related inadmissibility grounds regardless of age). Furthermore, penalties and barriers that immigration laws impose on persons who enter the United States without inspection and fail to maintain lawful status apply to children as well as adults (INA 8 U.S.C.A. § 1255(a); West Supp. 2013), limiting adjustment of status to persons "inspected and admitted or paroled into the United States" (8 U.S.C.A. § 1255 (c)(7); West Supp. 2013, barring adjustment of status of persons "not in a lawful immigration status"). For example, even children too young to be capable of exercising independent judgment and volition in entering the United States, such as infants carried across the border, are forever barred from an important immigration law procedure known as adjustment of status and thus foreclosed from establishing eligibility for lawful immigration later in life through other avenues, such as marriage or employment (INA 8 U.S.C.A. § 1255 (c)(7); West Supp. 2013; see also Bhabha 2006, 198–199). This is but one example demonstrating that there is no proportionality between immigration law's imposed consequences and youth's perceived culpability for violations of immigration law (Bhabha 2004, 95). Rather than special treatment based on the nature of childhood, youth are punished for the choices of adults in their lives or for choices that they made at very early ages.

Perhaps the most stark example of the failure of immigration law to respond to children as individuals is the imposition of higher eligibility standards in family-sponsored immigration and derivative naturalization cases to children born out of wedlock. Outside immigration law, it is clear that attaching punishment to children for circumstances of birth outside their control

> is contrary to the basic concept of our system that legal burdens should bear some relationship to individual responsibility or wrongdoing. Obviously, no child is responsible for his birth and penalizing the illegitimate child is an ineffectual—as well as an unjust—way of deterring the parent (*Weber* v. *Aetna Cas. & Sur. Co.* 1972; see also Kraus 1966, 829–859; and *Levy* v. *Louisiana* 1968, finding invidious discrimination in state law denying child born of wedlock the right to recover for the wrongful death of his mother).

Indeed, the notion of deterring adult behavior by penalizing children runs counter to the mainstream recognition of children as autonomous individuals (Brown 2005, 150, arguing that deterring adult activity by punishing children rather than the adults who engaged in that activity is "grossly unfair"). Yet immigration law persists in attaching consequences to actions that are outside the control of youth.

Recent legislative reforms have improved some procedures for unaccompanied minors in removal proceedings and detention policies for children (Homeland Security Act, 6 U.S.C.A. § 279 (f)-(g)(2)(A)-(C); West 2007), transferring custody, care, and placement of "unaccompanied alien children" from the disbanded Immigration and Naturalization Service to the Office of Refugee Settlement (William Wilberforce Trafficking Victims Protection Reauthorization Act of 2008, Pub. L. No. 110-457, 122 Stat. 5044 (2008), codified at 8 U.S.C.A. §§ 1232, 1375 b-c, 18 U.S.C.A. §§ 1351, 1593A, 1596, 22 U.S.C.A. §§ 212a, 2370c-2379c-1, 7205a-b; for a thorough discussion of procedural and detention policy evolution, see Somers et al. 2010). Despite these procedural reforms, for unaccompanied minors "the removal system has structurally remained largely intact and . . . with the advent of new actors and roles in the system, the dependency and developmental constructions of childhood have found greater expression in the structure of the removal system" (Somers et al. 2010, 372). Moreover, even with procedural reforms, youth in removal proceedings have a right to an attorney, but only if they are able to find one. No legal representation is afforded by the government.

The Supreme Court recognizes that "children are constitutionally different from adults for purposes of sentencing" (*Miller v. Alabama* 2012, 2464). First, "children have a 'lack of maturity and an underdeveloped sense of responsibility,' leading to recklessness, impulsivity, and heedless risk-taking" (*Miller* v. *Alabama* 2012, quoting *Roper v. Simmons* 2005, 569). Second, "children 'are more vulnerable . . . to negative influences and outside pressures,' including from their family and peers; they have limited 'contro[l] over their own environment' and lack the ability to extricate themselves from horrific, crime-producing settings" (*Miller*, quoting *Roper*, 569). And third, "a child's character is not as 'well formed' as an adult's; his traits are 'less fixed' and his actions less likely to be 'evidence of irretrievabl[e] deprav[ity]'" (*Miller* quoting *Roper*, 570). Given children's diminished culpability and heightened capacity for change, age matters in assigning blame and consequences to the actions of youth.

Immigration law, however, thoroughly and consistently rejects the idea that youth, by virtue of their youth, should be treated differently. The enforcement of immigration law against youth frequently results in deportation, the harshest consequence that immigration law can impose. No notions of lowered capacity, responsibility, competence, culpability, agency, susceptibility to deterrence, or heightened need for protection can explain the arbitrary patchwork of immigration law's treatment of children. Once a juvenile justice system decides to involve immigration authorities in a young person's life, it loses the ability to tailor consequences in proportion to the culpability or capacity of the child as rigid immigration laws are applied.

II. Immigration Consequences Flowing from Juvenile Justice Involvement

Immigration law's failure to make reasoned distinctions between its treatment of children and adults does not mean that immigration law fails to recognize distinctions between adult criminal behavior and juvenile delinquency made in other systems. Importantly, however, to the extent that different consequences attach to youth in the operation of immigration law, these are distinctions that are imported from the outside criminal or juvenile justice systems with which the young person has been involved.

Involvement in criminal activity can have far reaching effects on immigrants, both those without lawful status who face grounds of inadmissibility (INA, 8 U.S.C.A. § 1182; West 2005 & Supp. 2013) and those who have or had lawful status who face grounds of deportation (8 U.S.C.A. § 1227; West 2005 & Supp. 2013). Regardless of how long someone has been present in the United States or what their status, any noncitizen is potentially subject to removal from the United States based on criminal activity (e.g., *Padilla* v. *Kentucky* 2010). Transgressions of law can serve as the direct cause of deportation in some instances. But even when a criminal matter is not enough itself to trigger deportation, it can limit access to certain forms of relief from removal for which person lacking lawful status might otherwise qualify. Criminal involvement also works an indicator of moral character, which must be shown for some benefits such as naturalization.

In determining the immigration consequences that will attach to transgressions of the law, the labeling that the criminal or juvenile justice system attaches to conduct is critical. Many, but not all, references in immigration law to criminal activity attach specific consequences to "convictions" as specifically defined by immigration statute (INA 8 U.S.C.A. § 1101(a)(48); West 2005). For immigration purposes, many adjudications that criminal or juvenile courts would not consider convictions are swept under the broad definition of the term. In general, a finding or admission of guilt coupled with imposition of any punishment or consequence is sufficient to meet the definition of conviction, even if the matter is subsequently dismissed, sealed, or even expunged (Kesselbrenner & Rosenberg 2013, 29–32).

Critically, immigration case law has long acknowledged that "juvenile delinquency proceedings are not criminal proceedings, that acts of juvenile delinquency are not crimes, and that findings of juvenile delinquency are not convictions for immigration purposes" (*In re Devison-Charles*, B.I.A. 2000, 1365). Looking to the Federal Juvenile Delinquency Act as a guide, the Board of Immigration Appeals agreed that "a juvenile delinquency proceeding results in the adjudication of status rather than a conviction for a crime" (1365).

It is important to recognize that in making this distinction immigration law is not making a decision regarding how a young person should be treated based on an independent judgment about what immigration consequences should flow from the particular acts and circumstances. Immigration law simply reacts to the label as either adult criminal behavior or juvenile delinquency that is imported from outside. A court action that fits under the label "conviction" triggers all the various consequences attached to that particular conviction under immigration law. A court action that is labeled a juvenile adjudication is just not a conviction, and thus does not automatically trigger such consequences. Yet this does not mean that a juvenile adjudication is without immigration impact.

Sometimes juvenile proceedings can establish facts that can trigger harsh immigration consequences even in the absence of a conviction. For example, being a drug trafficker, addict, or abuser can result in inadmissibility or deportability even in the absence of a conviction: (INA 8 U.S.C.A. § 1182(a)(2)(C); West 2005), inadmissibility based on drug trafficking; (8 U.S.C.A. § 1182(a)(2)(H); West 2005 & Supp. 2013), inadmissibility based on human trafficking; (8 U.S.C.A. § 1227 (a)(2)(F); West Supp. 2013), deportability based on human trafficking; (8 U.S.C.A. § 1182(a)(1)(A)(iv); West 2005), inadmissibility of drug addicts and abusers; (8 U.S.C.A. § 1227 (a)(2)(B)(ii); West 2005), deportability of drug addicts and abusers. Likewise, prostitution and false claims to US citizenship can lead to removal in the absence of convictions. In some instances, such as trafficking in controlled substances, the government needs only reason to believe that a person has engaged in the proscribed conduct to find that person inadmissible. Conduct established in juvenile proceedings, standing alone without a conviction, is often sufficient to result in a removal order.

Moreover, even juvenile adjudications that do not make a youth inadmissible or deportable can be used to influence immigration decisions to withhold forms of relief for which a youth otherwise qualifies. This can mean, for example, that a youth who qualifies for asylum or adjustment of status based on facts unrelated to any delinquency may be denied immigration relief in consideration of juvenile adjudications (INA 8 U.S.C.A. § 1229a (c)(4); West 2005).

When juveniles are charged as adults, immigration law will not look to the nuanced considerations that may accompany the decision to certify a youth to adult court. Immigration law simply will respond the label ultimately attached to the action, as a conviction or a juvenile adjudication.

> If a youth is charged and convicted of a crime as an adult, that youth may face mandatory deportation—even if the deportation means that the child is returning to a country with no one to care for him or her. Judges do not consider the type of evidence normally put forward at a hearing where an adult or child faces a loss of liberty, such as ties to the community, family, and rehabilitation (Frankel 2011, 94).

In the stark world of immigration court, where the outcome choice is deportation or not, there is no room for mitigation of the type that a sentencing judge might apply for a youth even if the youth's case proceeds in adult court.

Blended proceedings or dual sentencing schemes that mix adult and juvenile procedures and sentences are perhaps the biggest point of disconnect between the intent of juvenile systems and the outcomes in immigration law. Some of the schemes are structured in a way that, consciously or not, avoid immigration law's broad notion of a conviction. Others schemes that share identical rehabilitative goals but employ only slightly different mechanisms can result in adjudications that will be characterized as adult convictions despite clear intent on the part of the juvenile system to ameliorate the consequences that would flow from such a characterization.

For example, a New York scheme that permits a court to immediately vacate a conviction to substitute a youthful offender finding was determined to not be a conviction for immigration purposes, even where the youth was subsequently sentenced to jail time following a probation violation (*In re Devison-Charles*, B.I.A. 2000, 1365). In contrast, a deferred adjudication under a Michigan scheme where "no judgment of conviction is entered . . . [and] defendant is assigned to youthful trainee status" was found to ripen into a conviction where the judge later revoked the youthful trainee status based on a probation violation (*Uritsky* v. *Gonzalez* 2005, 728). As the Sixth Circuit noted, the "two statutes evince a similar underlying purpose and the distinction drawn by the Board may seem to some to be less than compelling, particularly in light of the serious consequences that potentially flow from the distinction: in this case, the removal of [the youth] from the United States" (734).

A detailed analysis of the distinctions between the multitude of such programs across jurisdictions is well beyond the scope of this chapter. For our purposes here, it is vital to recognize that immigration law will respond technically in characterizing the outcomes of various juvenile justice proceedings, and will not always do so in line with the intent and spirit of the juvenile system. Rehabilitative goals that are central to the mission of juvenile courts can be of no consequence to immigration law. Immigration law applies a strict formalistic analysis rather than a flexible exercise of equitable power, and often reaches results that are at odds with the underlying goals of juvenile justice systems.

While some convictions are cause to trigger immigration enforcement actions, for youth without lawful immigration status deportation often follows from nothing more than being brought to the attention of Immigration Customs and Enforcement (ICE). In some jurisdictions, when "a noncitizen child is arrested for a juvenile offense, it has become common practice for state authorities to contact ICE or allow ICE officers to question the youth about his or her immigration status" (Frankel 2011, 65). In such instances, youth "are targeted by ICE *not* because of the underlying delinquency or criminal offense, but because of their unlawful status" (65). Whether a juvenile case is ultimately pursued or dismissed, youth lacking lawful immigration status may find themselves in immigration detention, in immigration court, and ultimately deported simply because a juvenile justice system directed or facilitated ICE attention to their situation (INA 8 U.S.C.A. § 1182(a)(6); West 2005 & Supp. 2013, inadmissibility of persons present without permission or parole; 8 U.S.C.A. § 1227(a)(1)(B); West 2005, for deportation of persons present in violation of the law).

At the same time, other jurisdictions have chosen to adopt policies and practices of not reporting youth to ICE and limiting access to youthful detainees by ICE. For example, in Illinois, Cook County adopted an ordinance declining to respond to ICE detainers (Ordinance 11-O-73 (2011)). Santa Clara County in California adopted a policy prohibiting County personnel from expending time and resources responding to ICE inquiries and communicating regarding incarceration status and release dates (Board of Supervisors Policy 3.54 (2011)).

The different choices regarding their approach to immigrant youth demonstrate a wide variation in practice that will result in completely different outcomes for immigrant youth. There truly are two different systems.

III. The Choices of Juvenile Justice Systems Have Consquences

Involvement with juvenile justice systems can lead to entirely different outcomes for immigrant youth based on choices that systems make. These decisions are of enormous impact, and should be made thoughtfully and systemically (see table 6.1). Baseline choices about reporting youth to ICE will determine if youth lacking authorized immigration status in the United States will face the same consequences for their actions as US citizen youth, or if the additional penalty of deportation looms in their future. This is true whether a system makes a conscious choice to make such reports or turns a blind eye to the actions of rogue individuals in any part of the system. Given the enormity of the consequences, this justice by geography should not be left to chance or uninformed replication of past practice (Feld 1991, 206–210).

Similarly, choices to charge a youth as an adult will lead to different outcomes than choices to keep matters in juvenile court. Systems that seek to emphasize rehabilitative possibilities cannot ignore the actual consequences that flow from the procedural and structural choices built into their frameworks. Decisions—sometimes about proceeding in juvenile or adult court, most often by prosecutors but sometimes by juvenile courts—have clear impacts on youth. If disproportionate immigration consequences will attach to certification decisions for immigrant youth, juvenile justice decision makers must examine their true goals and expected outcomes before pushing a youth into an adult system.

Even choices in the design of statutes and sentencing procedures have immigration implications. As the New York and Michigan examples demonstrate, two systems with purportedly similar juvenile justice goals can cause wildly different immigration consequences to attach to their actions. Responsible juvenile justice officials must understand the immigration impact of their various procedures and consider alternatives where the actual outcomes are disproportionate with the underlying juvenile justice goals and values.

In all these instances, the enforcement of immigration law will not include a decision in the immigration realm regarding how a young person should be treated based on an independent judgment about what immigration consequences should flow from the particular acts and circumstances. Immigration law simply reacts to the label as either adult criminal behavior or juvenile delinquency that is imported from outside. The choice of label lies with the juvenile justice system.

Juvenile justice systems must not shy from the choices that face them, or pretend that their hands are tied. Under our federal system, state and local systems are empowered to make choices that reflect their true values and priorities in working with youth. In working with immigrants, state and local governments cannot make grants of immigration status (*Arizona* v. *United States* 2012). Only the federal government can make "a determination of who should or should not be admitted into the country and the conditions under which a legal entrant may remain" (*DeCanas* v. *Bica* 1976, 355, superseded by statute, see *Chamber of Commerce of U.S.* v. *Whiting* 2010). At the same time, the choices that juvenile justice systems make in many instances determine the immigration rights and options that youth will have. In making these choices, systems must look to their own missions and values and not feel compelled to assist in the blind enforcement of federal immigration law. Just as states cannot pass their own immigration laws, the federal government cannot force state and local law enforcement officials to enforce federal immigration laws (see, e.g., *New York* v. *United States* 1992, 166; *Printz* v. *United States* 1997, 927).

Juvenile justice systems must commit to advancing the welfare of all youth subject to their jurisdiction, including those without lawful immigration status. This requires a thorough understanding of the immigration consequences that flow from the decisions they make. In reviewing processes and procedures, they must stay true to their core values and central principles. Practices that burden immigrant youth with immigration risks and penalties that are unrelated to the youth's involvement with the juvenile justice system must be avoided and eliminated.

Table 6.1. Juvenile Justice System Features That Protect Immigrant Youth

Youth-Centered Practices	Efforts and Emphasis
• Adopt policies preventing personnel from expending time and resources responding to and communicating with ICE.	• Educate juvenile justice personnel on goals and mission and ways in which immigration enforcement can undermine these.
• Understand immigration status of youth and how this can impact behavior and family dynamics.	• Seek training and input from experts on working with immigrant communities.
• Develop knowledge and consciousness of the immigration consequences that will result from local juvenile justice processes and procedures, and train personnel accordingly.	• Attorneys working with immigrant youth must learn clients' immigration status, research possible immigration consequences, and discuss these with client as an integral part of legal representation.
• Consider disproportionate immigration consequences in making charging and sentencing decisions, including decisions to charge youth as adults or under dual sentencing schemes.	• All stakeholders in juvenile justice systems must research and understand immigration impact that adjudication and sentence will have, and conform decisions to advance, not frustrate, system goals.
• Proactively review state statutes that permit youth to be charged as adults or subjected to dual sentencing schemes, and advocate for reforms that will minimize disproportionate immigration consequences while preserving the rehabilitative intent of the systems.	• Work with juvenile justice stakeholders, policy makers and legislators to advance reforms that keep immigration consequences from undermining the broader goals and mission of juvenile justice programs.
• Ensure that youth have legal representation from attorneys who understand the immigration consequences of sentences and pleas. When necessary, seek outside immigration expertise for system and youth.	• Attorneys representing immigration youth need to seek training and resources related to immigration consequences of involvement law enforcement as part of providing competent representation.
• Limit Immigration and Customs Enforcement access to youth, their families, and information and records about them.	• Establish or advocate for formal policies that prevent ICE interviews and the sharing of records of and information about youth with ICE.
• Explore and facilitate options for youth to obtain lawful immigration status, such as special immigrant juvenile status or provisions available to victims of trafficking, domestic violence, and other crimes.	• Develop in-house knowledge of immigration options or seek outside counsel to fully explore youth's immigration options.
• Seek alternatives if immigration status presents barriers to participation in programs or access to services for youth or families.	• Challenge any denial of services that is purportedly on immigration grounds. Make sure the court is aware of denials and seek orders to obtain needed services via alternative means.
• Notify consulates in conformity with the Vienna Convention on Consular Relations when foreign national youth are detained.	•Establish protocols for communicating with consulate and develop relationships with consulate personnel.

Table 6.1 provides a list of ways in which juvenile systems can protect immigrant youth.

Deportation is a destructive punishment, uprooting a youth from home and family (Zimring 2005, 142). If juvenile justice systems purport to place value on the future life opportunities of youth, they must make choices that reflect that value. Decisions that disproportionately and permanently destroy future opportunities for immigrant youth cannot be reconciled with the mission of juvenile justice.

NOTES

1. Of 747,413 persons admitted under immediate relative and family preference categories, 198,751 were children.
2. Of 144,034 employment visas, 35,570 were issued to derivative children. Child derivatives were 11,479 of 47,879 admissions under the diversity lottery.
3. In addition to seemingly excluding the possibility that US citizens might be juveniles, the definition is inconsistent with provisions that a person may be eligible for classification as a "special immigrant juvenile" if under 21 years of age (8 C.F.R. § 204.11(c)(1) (2012)).

REFERENCES

American Immigration Council, Immigration Policy Center. 2008. "Immigrants and Crime: Are They Connected?" October 25. www.immigrationpolicy.org/just-facts/immigrants-and-crime-are-they-connected-century-research-finds-crime-rates-immigrants-are.

Bhabha, Jacqueline. 2004. "The 'Mere Fortuity' of Birth? Are Children Citizens?" *Differences: A Journal of Feminist Cultural Studies* 15, no. 2:91–117.

Bhabha, Jacqueline. 2006. "'Not a Sack of Potatoes': Moving and Removing Children Across Borders." *Boston University Public International Law Journal* 15:197–218.

Brown, Richard L. 2005. "Disinheriting the 'Legal Orphan': Inheritance Rights of Children After Termination of Parental Rights." *Missouri Law Review* 70:125–176.

Carr, Bridgette A. 2009. "Incorporating a 'Best Interests of the Child' Approach into Immigration Law and Procedure." *Yale Human Rights and Development Law Journal* 12:120–159.

Department of Homeland Security. 2009. "Table 7 Persons Obtaining Legal Permanent Resident Status by Type and Detailed Class of Admission: Fiscal Year 2009." *Yearbook of Immigration Statistics: 2009*. www.dhs.gov/files/statistics/publications/LPR09.shtm.

Feld, Barry C. 1991. "Justice by Geography: Urban, Suburban, and Rural Variations in Juvenile Justice Administration." *Journal of Criminal Law and Criminology* 82:156–210.

Frankel, Elizabeth M. 2011. "Detention and Deportation with Inadequate Due Process: The Devastating Consequences of Juvenile Involvement with Law Enforcement for Immigrant Youth." *Duke Forum for Law and Social Change* 3:63–108.

Haddal, Chad C. 2007. *Unaccompanied Alien Children: Policies and Issues*. Congressional Research Service (March 1), RL 33896.

Hernandez, Donald J. and Wendy D. Cervantes. 2011. *Children in Immigrant Families: Ensuring Opportunity for Every Child in America*. First Focus. www.firstfocus.net/sites/default/files/FCDImmigration.pdf.

Kesselbrenner, Dan and Lory D. Rosenberg. 2013. *Immigration Law and Crimes*. Eagan, MN: West.

Krause, Harry D. 1966. "Bringing the Bastard into The Great Society—A Proposed Uniform Act on Legitimacy." *Texas Law Review* 44:829–859.

Levinson, Amanda. 2011. "Unaccompanied Immigrant Children: A Growing Phenomenon with Few Easy Solutions." *Migration Information Source*. January. www.migrationinformation.org/Feature/display.cfm?ID=823.

Nugent, Christopher. 2006. "Whose Children Are These? Towards Ensuring the Best Interests and Empowerment of Unaccompanied Alien Children." *Boston University Public Interest Law Journal* 15:219–236.

Passel, Jeffrey S. 2006. *The Size and Characteristics of the Unauthorized Migrant Population in the U.S.: Estimates Based on the March 2005 Current Population Survey*. Pew Hispanic Center. March 7. www.pewhispanic.org/2006/03/07/size-and-characteristics-of-the-unauthorized-migrant-population-in-the-us/.

Passel, Jeffrey S., and D'Vera Cohn. 2009. *A Portrait of Unauthorized Immigrants in the United States*. Pew Hispanic Center. April 14. http://pewhispanic.org/files/reports/107.pdf.

Preston, Julia. 2012. "Young and Alone, Facing Court and Deportation." *New York Times*, August 26, p. A1..

Rumbaut, Ruben G., Roberto G. Gonzales, Golnaz Komaie, and Charlie V. Morgan. 2006. "Debunking the Myth of Immigrant Criminality: Imprisonment Among First- and Second-Generation Young Men." *Migration Information Source*. June. http://migrationinformation.org/Feature/display.cfm?ID=403.

Rumbaut, Rubén G., and Walter A. Ewing. 2007. "*The Myth of Immigrant Criminality and the Paradox of Assimilation: Incarceration Rates Among Native and Foreign-Born Men*," *Immigration Policy Center* (Spring). www.immigrationpolicy.org/special-reports/myth-immigrant-criminality-and-paradox-assimilation.

Somers, M. Aryah, Pedro Herrera, and Lucia Rodrigues. 2010. "Constructions of Childhood and Unaccompanied Children in the Immigration System in the United States." *U.C. Davis Journal of Juvenile Law and Policy* 14:311–382.

Tanenhaus, David S. 2012. "The Elusive Juvenile Court: Its Origins, Practices, and Re-Inventions," in *The Oxford Handbook of Juvenile Crime and Juvenile Justice*. Edited by Barry C. Feld and Donna M. Bishop, 419–441. New York: Oxford University Press.

Terrazas, Aaron, and Jeanne Batalova. 2009. "Frequently Requested Statistics on Immigrants and Immigration in the United States." *Migration Policy Institute*. October. www.migrationinformation.org/USfocus/display.cfm?ID=747#7.

Thronson, David B. 2002. "Kids Will Be Kids? Reconsidering Conceptions of Children's Rights Underlying Immigration Law." *Ohio State Law Journal* 63:979–1016.
Thronson, David B. 2010."Thinking Small: The Need for Big Changes in Immigration Law's Treatment of Children." *U.C. Davis Journal of Juvenile Law and Policy* 14: 239–262.
U. S. Department of State. 2008. *Trafficking in Persons Report.*
Zimring, Franklin E. *American Juvenile Justice.* New York: Oxford University Press, 2005.

CASES CITED

Arizona v. *United States,* 132 S. Ct. 2494 (2012).
Chamber of Commerce of U.S. v. *Whiting,* 131 S. Ct. 1968 (2010).
De Canas v. *Bica,* 424 U.S. 351 (1976).
Gonzalez v. *Reno,* 212 F.3d 1338, 1347 n.8 (11th Cir. 2000).
INS v. *Hector,* 479 U.S. 85 (1986) (per curiam).
In re Devison-Charles, 22 I. & N. Dec. 1362 (B.I.A. 2000).
Levy v. *Louisiana,* 391 U.S. 68 (1968).
Miller v. *Alabama,* 132 S. Ct. 2455 (2012).
New York v. *United States,* 505 U.S. 144 (1992)
Padilla v. *Kentucky,* 559 U.S. 356 (2010).
Plyler v. Doe, 457 U.S. 202 (1982).
Printz v. United States, 521 U.S. 898 (1997).
Roper v. Simmons, 543 U.S. 551 (2005).
Uritsky v. Gonzalez, 399 F.3d 728 (6th Cir. 2005).
Weber v. Aetna Cas. & Sur. Co., 406 U.S. 164 (1972).

STATUTES CITED

Homeland Security Act, 6 U.S.C.A. § 279; West 2007.
Immigration and Nationality Act, 8 U.S.C.A. § 1101; West 2005 & Supp. 2013.
Immigration and Nationality Act, 8 U.S.C.A. § 1151; West 2005 & Supp. 2013.
Immigration and Nationality Act, 8 U.S.C.A. § 1182; West 2005.
Immigration and Nationality Act, U.S.C.A. § 1227; West 2005 & Supp. 2013.
Immigration and Nationality Act, U.S.C.A. § 1229a; West 2005.
Immigration and Nationality Act, U.S.C.A. § 1255; West Supp. 2013.

7

Juvenile Criminal Record Confidentiality

JAMES B. JACOBS

> While opening access to the juvenile record is a policy based on legitimate public safety concerns, it threatens to reverse nearly 100 years of juvenile justice policy that stresses rehabilitation, treatment and individual privacy. How to balance the use of juvenile justice records in today's climate presents unique challenges to juvenile justice administrators, public policy makers, and others in the criminal justice arena involved in aspects of collecting, maintaining, using or disseminating juvenile justice record information.
> —Jan Chaiken, Director, US Bureau of Justice Statistics (1997)

This chapter examines juvenile criminal records, an important but understudied topic in the history of American juvenile justice. Beginning with an analysis of the theory and uneven practice of keeping juvenile police and court records confidential from the early 1900s to the 1960s, the chapter then examines recent trends that have further eroded confidentiality and increased the collateral consequences for juveniles. The chapter next traces the role of the police and juvenile arrest records in this history before analyzing how the information technology revolution complicates matters. The conclusion focuses on the fundamental principles that should guide sensible policy making in this area.

Franklin Zimring (2002) has pointed out that the founders of the juvenile court had two main goals: 1) to avoid burdening and harming youth with a criminal stigma, and 2) to rehabilitate wayward youth. To achieve the first goal, they proposed that juvenile court proceedings and records be kept confidential (Belair 1982). Anticipating what sociologists would later call "labeling theory" (Lemert 1951; Becker 1963), they believed that to label a child "criminal" is itself "criminogenic"; that is, that when prosecutors, judges, corrections personnel and peers treat a child as a criminal, the child begins to form attachments with others similarly situated, becomes estranged from prosocial peers, and self-defines as and acts like a criminal. They insisted that stigmatizing a child with a "criminal" label was not in the best interest of the individual child or society (Platt 1969; Tanenhaus 2004).

The juvenile court movement began at the turn of the twentieth century. One of its founders, Judge Julian Mack (1909), urged getting "away from the notion that the child is to be dealt with as a criminal; to save it from the brand of criminality, the brand that sticks to it for life; to take it in hand and instead of first stigmatizing and then reforming it, to protect it from the stigma—this is the work which is now being accomplished [by the juvenile court]." The first challenge in keeping confidential the juvenile's contacts with the police and the court was to cabin all information about the youth's criminal activity in the hands of a small group of juvenile court personnel. This would be accomplished by closing the courtroom to all but court insiders—in other words, the public would not be admitted to juvenile court proceedings. There would be no jurors who might later talk about what they had seen and heard.

The juvenile court sought to avoid creating records that would impose a stigma that a youth would necessarily carry forward into adulthood. It attempted to accomplish this by defining its procedures as civil rather than criminal, and by decriminalizing the language used by the court. The child would be called a "respondent," not defendant. The respondent would be held in "detention," not jail. The proceeding would be referred to as an "adjudication," not a trial. The respondent would not be convicted, but "adjudicated as delinquent." The respondent would receive a "disposition," not a sentence. If the disposition included confinement, the delinquent would be sent to "training school," not prison. No transcript of the proceeding would be prepared. In the event that an appeal or postconviction petition reached an appellate court, the appellate court's published opinion would anonymize the juvenile respondent's name (i.e., "In re J.B.").

Although the founders of the juvenile court wanted to protect children from the negative consequences of labels and records, they also urged the juvenile court judge to obtain as much information as possible about the respondents over whom it exercised authority. This meant creating a copious file on each respondent. Court personnel prepared a "social file" that included information about the respondent's contacts with social service agencies, behavior at school, parents' description of the respondent's behavior at home, use of alcohol and drugs, sexual activity, and the probation officer's perception of the respondent's remorse. (Judges sometimes ordered a psychological report.) These reports typically included much rumor and hearsay. The more information that flowed to and through the court, the more serious the consequences (embarrassment and stigma) to the respondent if the information was inadvertently or purposefully disclosed to unauthorized parties.

Juvenile court historian David S. Tanenhaus (2004) points out that in the first three decades of the twentieth century, efforts to keep juvenile court proceedings and records confidential met significant resistance in some jurisdictions. In Illinois, for example, opponents declared that "secret courts might operate to enslave poor children." However, by the late 1920s, proponents of confidentiality had achieved substantial success. The majority of states passed laws limiting disclosure of information about adjudications and arrests, albeit permitting disclosure to law enforcement agencies, adult courts, and other government agencies. Some states required that the case file automatically be sealed when the respondent turned 21 years old so that the delinquent youth could embark upon adulthood without a criminal stigma.

Some state statutes provided that an individual with a sealed or expunged juvenile adjudication could, when asked, deny ever having been found guilty of a crime or adjudicated delinquent. (This could be very confusing when, for example, law schools or bar committees ask applicants if they have ever been arrested or adjudicated, even as a juvenile and even if purged.) In 1950, Congress passed the Federal Youth Corrections Act in order to spare "rehabilitated youth offenders the common and pervasive social stigma and loss of economic opportunity that in this society accompany the 'ex-con' label." The Act made federal offenders between 18 and 26 years old eligible to have their convictions "set aside" if the court released them early from probation.

Despite the philosophical and statutory commitment to confidentiality, it is unclear how effectively juvenile courts maintained the confidentiality of respondents' identities. It should not be assumed that the identities of and charges against juvenile arrestees and respondents remained secret. No doubt there was considerable variation from court to court. In small towns, it was nearly impossible to keep a young person's contact with the juvenile court completely confidential; the community would know that a youngster had gotten into trouble. Because sealing statutes always gave judges discretion to unseal a case file upon a showing of good cause, judges in all jurisdictions could disclose information to those agencies, organizations, and individuals deemed to have a legitimate need to know. This might include military recruiters, social service caseworkers, school authorities, and some private employers. It is unlikely that much attention was given to information security, and in any case, a court insider might be willing to oblige a nosy acquaintance, curious friend, or potential employer.

In its watershed 1967 decision in *In re Gault*, the US Supreme Court cast doubt on the extent to which Arizona's and other states' juvenile courts kept information confidential:

> It is frequently said that [the juvenile court protects] juveniles from disclosure of their deviational behavior. As the Supreme Court of Arizona phrased it, in the present case, the summary procedures of the juvenile courts are sometimes defended by a statement that it is the law's policy to "hide youthful errors from the full gaze of the public and bury them in the graveyard of the forgotten past." This claim of secrecy is, however, more rhetoric than reality. Disclosure of court records is discretionary with the judge in most jurisdictions. Statutory restrictions almost invariably apply only to the court records, and even as to those the evidence is that many courts routinely furnish information to the FBI and the military, and on request to government agencies and even to employers.

The *Gault* Court held that the constitution guarantees to juvenile court respondents most of the criminal procedure rights enjoyed by adult criminal defendants: the constitutional right to counsel, the opportunity to confront witnesses, the right against self-incrimination, and the right to a transcript of the hearing and the right to appeal the court's decision (Tanenhaus 2011). However, the Supreme Court did not require the juvenile court to open its proceedings or records to the public, and emphasized the importance of protecting youth from being labeled criminal.

Some juvenile court critics charged that secrecy of proceedings and records invited abuse of authority, arbitrariness, and discrimination. For example, Massachusetts Justice Gordon A. Martin Jr. wrote: "Elimination of juvenile delinquency's historic cloak of confidentiality is essential to rebuilding trust and dissipating the fear that the closed juvenile system fosters" (Martin Jr. 1995). In the years that followed, several states responded to these criticisms by opening up juvenile court proceedings to the public (Bazelon 1999; Martin 2002–2003).

Further Erosion of Confidentiality

In the 1970s, the Supreme Court heard three cases that challenged the confidentiality of delinquency records. The proponents of confidentiality lost all three. In *Davis v. Alaska* (1974), the Supreme Court considered whether a criminal defendant has a constitutional (confrontation clause) right to cross-examine a prosecution witness about that witness's juvenile criminal record. Alaska, like many states, did not allow lawyers to impeach a witness by exposing prior delinquency adjudications. The state claimed to have a compelling interest in protecting a person from having his juvenile criminality disclosed. In *Davis*, the Court held that a criminal court defendant's Sixth Amendment right to impeach a juvenile prosecution witness outweighed the state's interest in protecting that witness from having his juvenile criminality disclosed. Chief Justice Burger's majority opinion stated: "Whatever temporary embarrassment might result to Green [the prosecution's witness] or his family by disclosure of his juvenile record—if the prosecution insisted on using him to make its case—is outweighed by petitioner's right to probe into the influence of possible bias in the testimony of a crucial identification witness." It concluded "that the State's desire that Green fulfill his public duty to testify free from embarrassment and with his reputation unblemished must fall before the right of petitioner to seek out the truth in the process of defending himself." (In accord with the *Davis* decision, Rule 609 of the Federal Rules of Evidence, like state evidentiary rules, now provides that a juvenile adjudication is admissible to impeach a witness *other than the defendant* if an adult's conviction for that offense would be admissible to attack the adult's credibility, and admitting the evidence is necessary to fairly determining guilt or innocence.)

Oklahoma Publishing v. District Court (1977) and *Smith v. Daily Mail Publishing* (1979) dealt with whether, in order to preserve confidentiality of juvenile offenders, states can prohibit media from naming juvenile arrestees and respondents. The Supreme Court ruled that a state cannot, either by court order (*Oklahoma Publishing*) or statute (*Smith*), prevent the media from revealing a juvenile arrestee's identity as long as the information was legally acquired. In *Smith,* Justice Rehnquist concurred in striking down West Virginia's law because it prohibited newspapers, but not electronic media, from disclosing the name of an accused juvenile offender: "It is difficult to take very seriously West Virginia's asserted need to preserve the anonymity of its youthful offenders when it permits other, equally, if not more, effective means of mass communication to distribute this information without fear of punishment." However, in a passage that now reads like a swan song for the ideal of confidential juvenile court records, Rehnquist observed:

> The prohibition of publication of a juvenile's name is designed to protect the young person from the stigma of his misconduct and is rooted in the principle that a court concerned with juvenile affairs serves as a rehabilitative and protective agency of the State. . . . Publication of the names of juvenile offenders may seriously impair the rehabilitative goals of the juvenile justice system and handicap the youths' prospects for adjustment in society and acceptance by the public. . . . Such publicity also renders nugatory States' expungement laws, for a potential employer or any other person can retrieve the information the States seek to "bury" simply by visiting the morgue of the local newspaper. The resultant widespread dissemination of a juvenile offender's name, therefore, may defeat the beneficent and rehabilitative purposes of a State's juvenile court system.

In the 1980s, there was bipartisan support for greater transparency in juvenile justice proceedings. Conservatives and many liberals had soured on rehabilitation and now embraced retributive ("just deserts") and incapacitative rationales for criminal sentencing. Liberals charged that juveniles were being accorded second-class justice and urged that juvenile charged with crime be accorded the same procedural rights as adult criminal defendants (Feld 1998). They recommended opening up the juvenile court to public scrutiny. (Some advocates of abused and neglected children, also adjudicated by the juvenile or family court, sought to open up those proceedings and records in order to expose and remedy abuses.)

Law-and-order conservatives argued that prosecutors and judges in adult court should have access to a defendant's delinquency adjudications in order to make sensible charging, plea-bargaining, and sentencing decisions. They insisted that because adult offenders whose criminal careers started when they were juveniles had a higher risk of future offending than adult offenders without delinquency adjudications, it was foolish and dangerous to treat an adult with previous delinquency adjudications as a first time offender.

Public support for confidentiality protections significantly eroded during the 1980s and 1990s in response to a sharp spike in both the prevalence and violence of juvenile crime. State legislatures enacted laws emphasizing accountability rather than confidentiality. In 1984, Congress repealed the Youth Corrections Act. Every state made it easier to prosecute in adult court juveniles who were charged with serious crimes.

Many states passed laws requiring juvenile criminal records to remain accessible well into adulthood. Florida, for example, required records about juveniles considered habitual offenders to be preserved until the offender reaches age twenty-six. Other states repealed laws protecting juvenile offenders' confidentiality, especially in cases involving violent or serious offenses. By 1997, half the states had enacted laws cutting back on sealing or expunging juvenile records (Butts 2009).

At a 1997 conference on juvenile records, Robert R. Belair, a leading privacy law expert, reported that the confidentiality of both police and court records pertaining to juvenile offenders had significantly diminished. The juvenile court's original commitment to rehabilitation and protection of minors had been eclipsed by commitment to community protection and the "public's right to know." Support for forgiving and forgetting juvenile misconduct had significantly diminished, while support for governmental and judicial transparency had significantly increased.

Currently, at least 21 states require or permit the court to open juvenile proceedings if the respondent is charged with a serious offense or is a repeat offender. In California, the public can be admitted to hearings when a juvenile is alleged to have committed felony criminal street gang activity, such as carjacking or drive-by shooting. In Illinois, the public has the right to find the name and address of a juvenile who is at least 13 years old and has been criminally convicted of a serious crime or been connected to criminal street gang activity. A Pennsylvania law provides for public access to juvenile court proceedings when the respondent in felony cases is over 14 and charged with conduct that would be a felony if she or he was in adult court; in cases involving the most serious felonies, the public has a right of access when the respondent is older than twelve. In 1997, New York State created a presumption that family court proceedings would be open to the public. Wisconsin opened up juvenile court proceedings to the media on condition that those attending do not disclose the respondent's name (Reporters Committee For Freedom of the Press 1999). Of course, when a juvenile is tried in adult court, the proceedings are fully open to the public.

Collateral Consequences

The disclosure of delinquency adjudications is important, because significant consequences flow from disclosure. Increasingly, delinquency adjudications are being taken into account by criminal justice system and other decision makers. For example, the Federal Sentencing Guidelines (1987) instruct federal judges to assign the same weight to a delinquency adjudication (for conduct that would be criminal if committed by an adult) as to an adult conviction. Every state provides that adult criminal court judges have access to at least some delinquency adjudications for purposes of pretrial release, detention, and sentencing. Some states, including 14 with sentencing guidelines, *require* criminal court judges to consider juvenile adjudications (Redding 2002).

Delinquency adjudications increasingly trigger collateral consequences outside of the criminal justice context (see Shepherd 2000; Pinard 2006; Love et al. 2013). For example, the 1993 (Brady) Handgun Violence Control Act imposes a lifetime disqualification from firearms ownership on individuals who had been adjudicated delinquent for conduct that would have been a felony if committed by an adult. A delinquency adjudication has serious and wide-ranging immigration consequences, such as barring adjustment of legal status and requiring or permitting secure detention pending deportation. It also can disqualify a juvenile from living in public housing (Gowan et al. 2011).

In many states, a juvenile sex offense adjudication bars the record-subject from working with children and other vulnerable populations. Every state has a Megan's Law (see Garcia 2010) that requires convicted sex offenders, *including juvenile sex offenders*, to register with a designated state agency (Zimring 2004). Individuals who have committed more serious sex crimes must provide a designated agency information on residence, place of employment, school, automobile license plate number, and so on. This information, plus the individual's photo, is posted to a publicly accessible website. The federal Adam Walsh Child Protection and Safety Act requires that state sex offender registries include juveniles convicted in adult court of sex offenses. The "Amie Zyla Law" amended the federal Sex Offender Registration and Notification Act (SORNA) to require that certain juvenile sex offenders be included in state sex offender registries (42 U.S.C. sex.16911).

The collateral consequences discussed in the previous paragraph are policies imposed by law or regulation. In addition, an individual with a recorded delinquency adjudication faces being discriminated against by colleges and universities, private employers, landlords, volunteer organizations, and other entities and individuals. For example, since 2007 the common entrance application used by 500 colleges and universities asks applicants if they have ever been adjudicated delinquent and, if so, to explain the circumstances. Many employers ask job applicants to disclose delinquency adjudications and, in any event, become aware of them via reports from commercial background checking companies.

Police Records

The history of juvenile justice has always been court-centric, paying much less attention to police and corrections. This is especially short-sighted when it comes to juvenile records policy, because police juvenile record policies and practices significantly affect the effectiveness of judicial policies. If the police freely disclose information about juveniles' criminal history, the court's confidentiality policy is substantially undermined, even rendered irrelevant.

Historian David Wolcott points out that "one of the [juvenile court's] reformers' basic goals has been to remove children from the punitive control of the police" (2005, 106). The founders were not oblivious to the fact that police officers created and disseminated information about juvenile delinquents (Flexner and Baldwin 1914). They and their intellectual and ideological descendants sought, with some degree of success, to prevent juvenile criminality from being recorded on permanent rap sheets. They supported laws restricting police photographing and fingerprinting of juveniles. Practically every state limits fingerprinting of juveniles, except for juveniles accused of serious crimes. Even today, some states require a court order to fingerprint a juvenile; others authorize fingerprinting only for serious offenses. If the juvenile is not fingerprinted, no rap sheet (record of arrest and conviction) is created. In the event that the juvenile is fingerprinted, some states have laws requiring police authorities to keep juvenile fingerprints separate from adult fingerprints and to keep juvenile and adult rap sheets in different data bases. Other states maintain a single rap sheet system for all arrests.

While criminal record confidentiality was fundamental to the juvenile court, it was not central to police departments' mission or ideology. Other than in very large cities with specialized units (e.g., youth bureaus), police departments did not have officers assigned to policing juveniles. Of course, specialized juvenile policing units did not have a monopoly on police contacts with juvenile offenders. Moreover, officers in specialized units were not necessarily committed to keeping juvenile offender information confidential (Handler 1965).

The police could (and can) also be a source of *informal information disclosure*. It is much easier to maintain control of juvenile court information than to control the dissemination of police information. Even a fairly large jurisdiction might have only one or two juvenile court judges and a handful of juvenile court officers, as compared to hundreds or thousands of police officers who come into contact with juveniles. Furthermore, juvenile court judges are often volunteers committed to the ideals of the juvenile court, including its goal of keeping information confidential. This is not necessarily true of police who come into contact with juvenile offenders.

Police who monitor and arrest juveniles are not selected on the basis of their commitment to preventing juveniles from being labeled as criminals. Patrol officers might arrest a juvenile in response to a reported crime in progress or a call complaining about an unruly and noisy clique that is disturbing or frightening some neighborhood adults. Unlike a juvenile court judge, who may define her mission as "child saving," a police officer's primary goals are maintaining public order, preventing crime, and apprehending criminal perpetrators (Wolcott 2005). Unlike the judge, who sees a nervous and contrite child in court, the police officer confronts surly teenagers on the street or at a crime scene. Police officers regularly interact with members of the community who feel threatened by and complain about "delinquents" and "gang members." The officers also see and interview victims (sometimes juveniles themselves) of juvenile crime perpetrators. Many police officers are cynical about juvenile offenders' contrition and rehabilitative prospects.

In the *In re Gault* case, the state (Arizona) argued that opening up juvenile courts' practices to outside eyes would stigmatize and thereby harm juvenile respondents. The Supreme Court rejected this argument, in part because the police routinely disseminated information about the juvenile offender's criminal justice system contacts to the armed forces, various federal, state, and local government agencies, and even to private businesses.

Police officers create quasi-criminal files and databases on juveniles who are suspected of past or future crimes. They routinely compile intelligence about young people (perhaps gang members) who might have committed unsolved crimes or who might commit future crimes. Some police departments, at some points in time, have required their officers to keep records on all juvenile contacts (Spalty 1972). For example, in the 1970s, the New York City Police Department's (NYPD's) Youth Division (YD) created "contact cards" on youths whom they suspected of delinquency (New York State Division of Criminal Justice Services 1990; Coffee 1972). These reports, routinely shared with the juvenile court, probation services, schools, and social welfare agencies, frequently had negative repercussions for the contact-card subject; at a minimum, the police would monitor the juvenile more closely. In addition, they might leak their suspicions to government and private agencies and employers. Consequently, a class action challenged the constitutionality of these records, arguing that creating, maintaining, and disseminating intelligence information about suspicious juveniles violated their rights to procedural due process and privacy (*Cuevas v. Leary* 1970). In effect, according to the plaintiffs, the contact cards labeled them as delinquents or quasi-delinquents without providing any opportunity to challenge the label. Ultimately, the parties settled the case. The NYPD agreed to inform juveniles and their parents when officers created a YD report, providing them an opportunity to challenge the report, and agreed to destroy the record when the report-subject turns seventeen years old.

In most states the police keep a complete file of juvenile police contacts, and have complete discretion to disclose this information. Police departments often comply with requests for information about juveniles from the FBI and other law enforcement agencies, the Armed Forces, and social service agencies. Some departments and individual officers comply with private employers' requests for juvenile record information.

The same 1980s political pressures that eroded confidentiality of juvenile court records also eroded restrictions on police information gathering, record keeping, and dissemination (Office of Juvenile Justice and Delinquency Prevention 1997). In 1992, the FBI changed its long-standing policy against accepting juvenile arrest information from state and local police. Henceforth, it would accept fingerprints and arrest information for "serious and significant juvenile offences" (Bishop 1997). Federal law requires that when a juvenile is found guilty of an act that would be a violent felony if committed by an adult, the juvenile must be photographed and fingerprinted. Moreover, a federal court must transmit to the FBI the court record and fingerprints of a juvenile who has twice been adjudicated for an offense that would be a felony if committed by an adult and those of a juvenile over the age of 13 who committed a felony with a firearm.

Practically every state passed laws allowing more juvenile arrestees to be fingerprinted and making juvenile records more accessible to police, prosecutors, and courts. A 1995 Institute for Law & Justice (ILJ) survey found that 40 states explicitly authorized, while only two states prohibited, fingerprinting arrested juveniles, almost a complete reversal from 20 years earlier. In 1995, Pennsylvania broadened its existing fingerprinting law to allow the fingerprinting of youth arrested for committing misdemeanors. Connecticut authorizes law enforcement agencies to photograph and fingerprint a child charged with a felony. Idaho requires fingerprinting and photographing juvenile offenders in detention. Missouri requires law enforcement officials to fingerprint juveniles arrested for felonies. North Dakota expanded the criteria for fingerprinting and photographing juvenile arrestees (Bureau of Justice Statistics 1997). At the end of the twentieth century, 27 states maintained juvenile records in a centralized state-level database; only five prohibited juvenile record centralization (Miller 1997). Many states included juvenile arrests and adjudications on adult rap sheets ("one record, one system").

The clear trend is passage of state laws authorizing or requiring police and juvenile court personnel to share criminal record information with schools and other agencies and organizations that provide services to children. The goal is to protect students from criminally inclined classmates by informing school authorities when students have been adjudicated delinquent or are even suspected of criminal activity. Even when it is not legally required, a police department may voluntarily notify the school when a student is arrested (Henning 2004).

Some states have laws requiring school officials to bring certain disciplinary problems to the attention of the police (Henning 2004). Many localities have established interagency partnerships (collaboratives) among police, parole, probation, school, and prosecutor's offices. Police resource officers, stationed in schools, facilitate information sharing between schools and police. More contact between police and schools inevitably means greater information sharing.

In at least 30 states, the names and photos of violent and repeat juvenile offenders can be released to the public (Snyder and Sickmund 2006). Maine, for example, allows anyone to obtain any person's delinquency adjudications for a $31 fee (Maine State Police, Maine Criminal History Record & Juvenile Crime Information Request 2013). The Florida Department of Law Enforcement sells juvenile arrest records along with all other rap sheet information. Several states (e.g., Utah; Maryland) have opened juvenile court proceedings to the public and the media. Strangely, some of those states still seal juvenile court records, a policy significantly undermined when information about the adjudicated juvenile has already been widely disseminated by court observers, media, or commercial information vendors (Markman 2007).

While the trend toward wider access to and dissemination of juvenile records is clear, it should not be exaggerated. There are still many laws and regulations, even some new ones, that treat juvenile criminal records as confidential. For example, in March 2013, the House of Representatives in Washington State unanimously passed a bill that would seal juvenile records from public view, thereby reversing a four-decade-old policy of open juvenile records. Moreover, a majority of states have procedures that allow a person who has been adjudicated delinquent to request that his juvenile record be sealed. Unfortunately, we do not know how often such requests are made and how often they are granted.

New Types of Juvenile Records and Databases

The information technology revolution makes possible the collection, classification, and retrieval of vastly more information than the juvenile court founders could have imagined. Local, state, and federal "gang databases" are a good example (Jacobs 2009). Their purpose is to aid law enforcement and other government agencies identify and monitor suspected gang members whom, it is assumed, pose a high risk of current and future criminality. The police populate these databases with suspected gang members' names, gang affiliation, residence, school, and other identifying information. Michelle Alexander points out that:

> In Los Angeles, mass stops of young African-American men and boys resulted in the creation of a database containing the names, addresses and other biographical information of the overwhelming majority of young black men in the entire city . . . In Denver, displaying any two of a list of attributes—including slang, "clothing of a particular color," pagers, hairstyles or jewelry—earns a youth a spot on the Denver Police gang database (2010, 36).

The police use gang databases to obtain leads on unsolved crimes and to prevent future crimes by taking preemptive action against gang members. When there is a crime with an unknown perpetrator, known gang members will be among the first to be investigated. If a known gang member is arrested, police and prosecutors will press the case harder than they otherwise would. Where the option exists, prosecutors are more like to charge gang members in criminal court rather than juvenile court. Whether adjudicated in juvenile court or convicted in adult court, the gang member will be sentenced more severely. Gang databases are not public—but police, probation, and parole officers, as well as school and social services personnel, have direct or indirect access to them. A database that is accessible to hundreds or even thousands of police officers cannot be considered confidential. Undoubtedly, information from the gang database is sometimes leaked to employers and others who have a strong interest in (and may be willing to pay for) such information.

Conclusions

For sixty years there was a consensus that American juvenile court records and, to a lesser extent, police contacts should be treated as confidential or at least as quasi-confidential. Indeed, the US juvenile court influenced international standards and many other countries' laws. For example, the United Nations Standard Minimum Rules for the Administration of Juvenile Justice state:

> RULE 8.1: The juvenile's right to privacy shall be respected at all stages in order to avoid harm being caused to her or him by undue publicity or by the process of labeling.
>
> RULE 8.2: In principle, no information that may lead to the identification of a juvenile offender shall be published.

The International Covenant on Civil and Political Rights (ICCPR), to which the United States became a party in 1992, specifically emphasizes special treatment and rehabilitation of children in the criminal justice system. While most of the world embraces the principle that rehabilitation requires confidential treatment of information about juvenile delinquents, the United States, which invented a juvenile court committed to recording confidentiality, now is exceptional for the amount of juvenile offender information that is disclosed to diverse government agencies and the public.

Our examination of juvenile criminal records policy needs to distinguish between confidentiality afforded juvenile criminal record information while the record-subject is still a juvenile and confidentiality afforded that information after the record-subject crosses the threshold of legal adulthood. Before adulthood, juvenile criminal record information is important to the police (e.g., gang intelligence databases), juvenile court, schools, social service, and immigration agencies. However, juvenile criminal record is increasingly treated as relevant to assessing an adult's character and recidivism risk. When an adult—especially a young adult—is arrested, the police, prosecutors, and adult court judges want access to his or her juvenile offending history in order to inform their decision making. Confidentiality was meant to protect the youth (first for the remainder of adolescence and then as an adult) from the indiscretions and poor decisions of his adolescence so that he could embark upon adult life with a clean record. The rationale for concealing youthful delinquency no longer applies when the former delinquent is charged as an adult. Because a juvenile record is a significant predictor of an adult offender's future criminality (Miller 1997), that record will be important for the prosecutor's charging and plea-bargaining decisions and for the judge's bail and sentencing decisions. Some employers, landlords, volunteer organizations, and colleges also seek delinquency information when handling applications from young adults.

The majority of individuals with delinquency adjudication are not later charged with adult crimes. For them, sealing and expunging juvenile adjudications will have facilitated their successful transition to adulthood. Many youth, especially males, go through a troublemaking phase, but "only a relatively small proportion of adolescents who experiment in risky or illegal activities develop entrenched patterns of problem behavior that persist into adulthood" (Scott and Steinberg 2003). As the Supreme Court recognized in *Roper v. Simmons* (2005), *Graham v. Florida* (2010), and *Miller v. Alabama* (2012), judgment and self-discipline are far from fully developed at age 13, 14, or fifteen. In holding that the Constitution does not permit the death penalty to be imposed on juvenile offenders, the *Roper* majority highlighted three important characteristics that distinguish juvenile from adult offenders: (i) recklessness and impulsiveness; (ii) susceptibility to outside influences and peer pressure; and (iii) still-forming (and thus, more redeemable) moral character. Five years later, in *Graham,* the Court reiterated these observations in holding that the constitution does not permit a juvenile who has not committed homicide to be sentenced to life without possibility of parole. The majority opinion stated that "developments in psychology and brain science continue to show fundamental differences between juvenile and adult minds," particularly those parts of the brain involved in behavior control. In *Miller,* Justice Kagan wrote for the Supreme Court's 5 to 4 majority that a mandatory life without parole sentence for an offender who committed murder when younger than 18 constitutes cruel and unusual punishment because "it precludes consideration of his chronological age and its hallmark features—among them, immaturity, impetuosity, and failure to appreciate risks and consequences," and that life without parole "prevents taking into account the family and home environment that surrounds him—and from which he cannot usually extricate himself—no matter how brutal or dysfunctional."

For the reasons articulated by the Supreme Court, adolescent criminal conduct should not be treated as an indelible mark of bad character or as a strong predictor of future offending. Character evolves throughout adolescence and early adulthood. Because there is a strong societal interest in encouraging and facilitating juvenile offenders' rehabilitation makes, it is highly desirable that a delinquency adjudication not become a scarlet letter. Unless and until the adjudicated delinquent is later charged as an adult, it is desirable to keep his or her juvenile record as confidential as possible. That means that juvenile court files and dockets should not be available for inspection by journalists, commercial information vendors, or for use by employers and curious members of the public. Unfortunately, maintaining juvenile criminal record confidentiality is increasingly difficult given the revolution in information technology and the routinization of criminal background checking. One government report is aptly titled "The Criminal Backgrounding of America" (SEARCH 2005). If juvenile criminal records become as publicly accessible as adult criminal records, the first raison d'etre of the juvenile court, preventing the juvenile from being publicly marked as a criminal, will have been negated. Unable to assure respondents of confidentiality, the juvenile court would survive as a kind of problem-solving court, like the drug court and mental health court. It would still have value on account of its expertise in deploying juvenile-specific rehabilitative services, but a great deal of its potential will have been lost.

REFERENCES

Alexander, Michelle. 2010. *The New Jim Crow: Mass Incarceration in the Age of Colorblindness*. New York: The New Press.

American Bar Association Criminal Justice Section, Committee On Legal Aid & Indigent Defendants. 2012. *Commission on Homelessness and Poverty Standing, Recommendation: Report to the House of Delegates*. No. 102A, February 8–9.

Bazelon, Emily. 1999. Public Access to Juvenile and Family Court: Should the Courtroom Doors Be Open or Closed? *Yale Law and Policy Review.* 18(1): 155–194.

Becker, Howard S. [1963] 1973. *The Outsiders: Studies in the Sociology of Deviance.* Revised, New York: Free Press.

Belair, Robert. 1982. *Criminal Justice Information Policy: Privacy and Juvenile Records.* Bureau of Justice Statistics, US Department of Justice.

———. 1997. The Need to Know Versus Privacy. Paper presented at the National Conference on Juvenile Justice Records: Appropriate Criminal and Noncriminal Justice Uses, Washington, DC, May 22–23, 1996. www.bjs.gov/content/pub/pdf/NCJJR.PDF.

Bishop, Demery R. 1997. Juvenile Recordhandling Policies and Practices of the Federal Bureau of Investigation. Paper presented at the National Conference on Juvenile Justice Records: Appropriate and Noncriminal Justice Uses, Washington, DC, May 22–23, 1996. www.bjs.gov/content/pub/pdf/NCJJR.PDF.

Bureau of Justice Statistics. 1997. *Privacy and Juvenile Records: A Mid Decade Status Report.* http://ia410331.us.archive.org/peth04/20041026012503/; www.ojp.usdoj.gov/bjs/pub/pdf/pjjr.pdf.

Butts, Jeffrey A. 2009. Can We do Without Juvenile Justice? In *You Decide! Current Debates in Criminal Justice*, edited by Bruce N. Waller. 321–331. Upper Saddle River, NJ: Prentice Hall.

Coffee, John C. 1972. Privacy Versus Parens Patriae: The Role of Police Records in the Sentencing and Surveillance of Juveniles. *Cornell Law Review.* 57(4): 571–620.

Gowen, Christopher, Lisa Thurau, and Meghan Wood. 2011. The ABA's Approach To Juvenile Justice Reform: Education, Eviction, And Employment: The Collateral Consequences Of Juvenile Adjudications. *Duke Forum for Law and Social Change* 3(1): 187–203.

Henning, Kristin. 2004. Eroding Confidentiality in Delinquency Proceedings: Should Schools and Public Housing Authorities Be Notified? *New York University Law Review.* 79 (2): 520–611.

Feld, Barry. 1998. Abolish the Juvenile Court: Youthfulness, Criminal Responsibility and Sentencing Policy. *Journal of Criminal Law and Criminology.* 88(1) 68–136.

Flexner, Bernard and Roger Baldwin. 1914. *Juvenile Courts and Probation.* New York: Century Co.

Garcia, David A. 2010. Juveniles Crowd Michigan Sex Offender Registry. *Michigan Messenger*, February 10. http://michiganmessenger.com/34538/juveniles-well-represented-on-mich-sex-offender-Registry.

Handler, Joel. 1965. The Juvenile Court and the Adversary System: Problems of Function and Form. Wisconsin Law Review 1965:7–51.

Jacobs, James B. 2009. Gang Databases: Context and Questions. *Criminology and Public Policy.* 8(4): 705–709.

Jacobs, James B. and Elena Larrauri. 2012. Are Criminal Records Private? A Comparison of Law & Policy in Spain and the U.S. *Punishment and Society.* 14(1): 3–28.

Lemert, Edwin. 1951. *Social Pathology*. New York: McGraw-Hill.
Love, Margaret et al. 2013. *Encyclopedia of Collateral Consequences.*
Mack, Julian. 1909. The Juvenile Court. *Harvard Law Review.* 23(2): 104–122.
Markman, Joanna S. 2007. In re Gault: A Retrospective in 2007: Is it Working? Can it Work? *Barry Law Review.* 9: 123–411.
Martin, Stefani. (2003). Confidentiality of Juvenile Proceedings vs. The First Amendment Guarantee of Public Access: Does The Federal Delinquency Act Require Closed Proceedings? *Juvenile Law Review*. 23: 79–80.
Martin Jr., Gordon A. 1995. Open the Doors: A Judicial Call to End Confidentiality in Delinquency Proceedings. *New England Journal on Criminal and Civil Confinement*. 21:393, 394–395.
Maine State Police. 2013. Maine Criminal History Record and Juvenile Crime Information Request. www5.informe.org/online/per/.
Miller, Neal. 1997. Prosecutor and Criminal Court Use of Juvenile Records: A National Study, Paper presented at the National Conference on Juvenile Justice Records: Appropriate Criminal and Noncriminal Justice Uses, Washington, DC, May 22–23, 1996.. www.bjs.gov/content/pub/pdf/NCJJR/PDF.
Nelson, Kara. 1998. Release of Juvenile Records under Wisconsin's Juvenile Justice Code: A New System of False Promises. *Marquette Law Review*. 81(4): 1101–1159.
New York State Division of Criminal Justice Services. 1990. *Juvenile Justice Processing Study, Volume II: Juvenile Justice Information Policy*. Albany, NY. www.ncjrs.gov/App/Publications/abstract.aspx?ID=130478.
Office of Juvenile Justice and Delinquency Prevention. 1997. Juvenile Justice Reform Initiatives in the States 1994–1996. www.ncjrs.gov/pdffiles/reform.pdf.
Pinard, Michael. 2006. The Logistical and Ethical Difficulties of Informing Juveniles About the Collateral Consequences of Adjudications. *Nevada Law Journal.* 6: 1111–1126.
Platt, Anthony M. 1969. *The Child Savers: The Invention of Delinquency*. Chicago: The University of Chicago Press.
Redding, Richard. 2002. Using Juvenile Adjudications for Sentencing Enhancement Under the Federal Sentencing Guidelines: Is it Sound Policy? *Virginia Journal of Social Policy and Law.* 10: 231, 231–232.
Reporters Committee For Freedom of the Press. 1999. Access to Juvenile Courts: A Reporters' Guide to Proceedings and Documents in the 50 States & D.C. www.rcfp.org/rcfp/orders/docs/ACCJUVCTS.pdf.
Scott, ES and L. Steinberg. 2003. Less Guilty by Reason of Adolescence: Developmental Immaturity, Diminished Responsibility, and the Juvenile Death Penalty. *American Psychologist*. 58 (12): 1009–1014.
SEARCH. 1988. *SEARCH, State Law and the Confidentiality of Juvenile Records*, Bureau of Justice Statistics, *US Department of Justice, 1982*. Washington, DC: Bureau of Justice Statistics, Juvenile Records and Recordkeeping Systems.

SEARCH. 2005. Report of the National Task Force on the Criminal Backgrounding of America. San Francisco. www.search.org/files/pdf/ReportofNTFCBA.pdf.
Shepherd, Robert E. Jr. 2000. Collateral Consequences of Juvenile Proceedings: Part II. *Criminal Justice*. 15(3): 4–6.
Snyder, Howard N. and Melissa Sickmund. 2006. Juvenile Offenders and Victims: 2006 National Report. Office of Juvenile Justice and Delinquency Prevention. 108–109. http://ojjdp.ncjrs.org/ojstatbb/nr2006/downloads/NR2006.pdf.
Spalty, Edward R. 1972. Juvenile Police Record-Keeping. *Columbia Human Rights Law Review*. 4: 461– 478.
Tanenhaus, David S. 2002. The Evolution of Juvenile Courts in the Early Twentieth Century: Beyond the Myth of Immaculate Construction. In *A Century of Juvenile Justice*, ed. Margaret Rosenheim, et al. 42–61. Chicago: University of Chicago Press.
———. 2004. *Juvenile Justice in the Making*. Oxford: Oxford University Press.
———. 2011. *The Constitutional Rights of Children: In re Gault and Juvenile Justice*. Lawrence: University Press of Kansas.
Wolcott, David. 2005. *Cops and Kids: Policing Juvenile Delinquency in Urban America, 1890–1940*. Columbus: Ohio State University Press.
Zimring, Franklin. 2002. The Common Thread: Diversion in the Jurisprudence of Juvenile Courts, in *A Century of Juvenile Justice*, ed. Margaret Rosenheim et al., 142, 144–147. Chicago: University of Chicago Press.
———. 2004. *An American Travesty: Juvenile Sex Offending*. Chicago: University of Chicago Press.

CASES CITED

Cuevas v. Leary, 70 Civ. 2017 (S.D.N.Y., filed May 13, 1970).
Davis v. Alaska, 415 U.S. 308 (1974).
Graham v. Florida, 130 S.Ct. 2011 (2010).
In re Gault, 387 U.S. 1 (1967).
Miller v. Alabama, 567 U.S. ------ (2012).
Oklahoma Publishing v. District Court (1977).
Roper v. Simmons, 543 U.S. 551 (2005)
Smith v. Daily Mail Publishing, 443 U.S. 97 (1979).

8

Minority Overrepresentation

On Causes and Partial Cures

FRANKLIN E. ZIMRING

The overrepresentation of disadvantaged racial and ethnic minorities in the courtrooms and detention cells of American juvenile justice is both an undeniable fact and a serious problem. Throughout the world, the poor and disadvantaged get caught up in the machinery of social control in numbers far greater than their share of the population. In the United States, the long shadow of racism adds another important dimension to concern about young persons already at serious disadvantage. Punishment and stigma make a bad situation worse. What to do?

The issues we confront in trying to fix the damages of disproportion in juvenile justice are a mix of the obvious and the obscure. There can be no doubt that the handicaps imposed on youth by arrest, detention, adjudication, and incarceration fall disproportionately on males from disadvantaged minority groups in the United States. It is equally obvious that the hardships imposed on formally sanctioned youth are substantial by themselves and even worse when they aggravate the other byproducts of social disadvantage. But this chapter is about the not-so-obvious choices that we confront when attempting to reduce the harms that disproportionate minority concentration produces. There are a variety of different approaches that can be taken to reforming juvenile justice to protect minority youth, and not all of them are of equal effectiveness.

My ambition in these pages is to identify some of the key policy choices that must be made in reducing injustices found in American juvenile courts. A clear definition of goals and priorities is absolutely essential to intelligent policy planning. My argument is that reducing the hazards of juvenile court processing may be a better approach to protecting minority youth than just trying to reduce the proportion of juvenile court cases with minority defendants.

The chapter is divided into two large segments and then subdivided into smaller units. Part I concerns the conceptual equipment necessary to assess the impact of legal policies on minority populations. A first section of Part I discusses whether it is best to consider the minority concentrations in juvenile justice as a special problem in the juvenile justice system or as part of the generally higher-risk exposures found in criminal justice and other state control systems. A second section proposes harm reduction as the principal criterion by which policies designed to respond to minority disproportion should be judged. A third section contrasts two competing measures of disadvantage on minorities, relative and aggregate disadvantage as the appropriate goal of reforms. A fourth section compares two overall approaches to minimize harm—cutting back on the harms that juvenile justice processing produces versus cutting back on the number and proportion of minority youth who are pushed through the system.

Part II attempts to apply the apparatus developed in Part I to discuss recent chapters in juvenile justice law reform—changes in transfer policy, the deinstitutionalization of status offenders, and the embrace of diversion programs. A final subsection of Part II contrasts the harm to minority youth from exposure to juvenile courts with the harm from criminal courts. If the proper standard for judging the impact of institutions on minority kids is reducing the harms these kids suffer, the current juvenile justice system—warts and all—is vastly less dangerous to minorities than the machinery of criminal justice.

I. Conceptual Issues

A. Juvenile Justice in Context: A Special or General Case?

The first issue on my agenda is whether the kind and amount of minority overrepresentation is importantly different in the juvenile justice system. How does the African American and Hispanic overrepresentation we observe for delinquency cases in the juvenile system compare to the pattern of concentration of disadvantaged minorities found in the criminal justice system in the United States?

But why should a question about the generality of the pattern that produces minority disadvantage be a starting point for seeking remedial measures? The reason is that the data reveal whether the special organizational and substantive provisions of juvenile justice should be regarded as the proximate causes of the problem, so that shifting the special provisions or procedures of juvenile courts could be expected to provide a remedy. If so, the specific approaches of the juvenile court should be a high priority for reform. If, however, the extent of minority overrepresentation in juvenile justice is about the same as that found in criminal justice, it is less plausible that this pattern is the product of any special characteristics of the juvenile system.

One example of the usefulness of this type of analysis concerns the relative concentration of young girls in incarcerated populations in juvenile justice. Figure 8.1 turns back the clock to compare juvenile and adult incarcerations by gender for 1974, as a familiar example of looking for special patterns in juvenile justice. The 1974 vintage for this data is to summarize patterns at the time when federal legislation first mandated deinstitutionalizing status offenders.

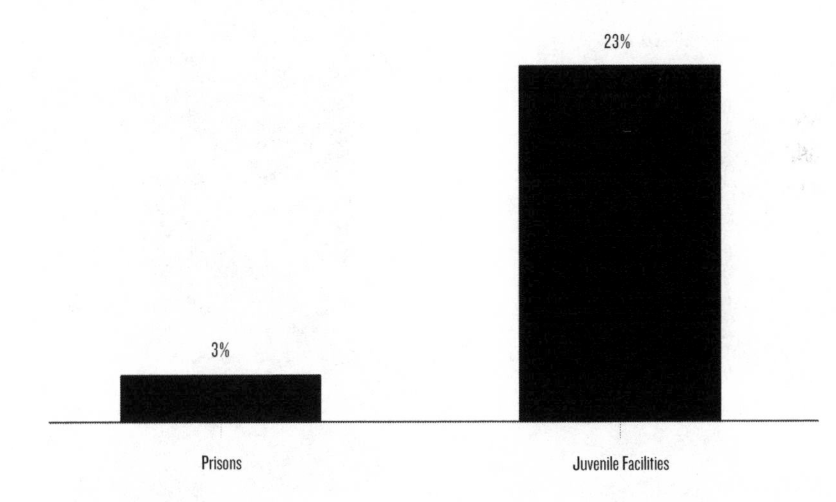

Figure 8.1. Percentage of Female Incarcerated Persons in 1974
Source: Bureau of Justice Statistics (Prisoners); US Department of Justice, *Children in Custody* (Juveniles).

The 23 percent of incarcerated juveniles who were female in 1974 is over seven times the proportion of females then found in prisons. The larger concentration of females in the juvenile distribution is an indication that different motives (including paternalism) and different substantive legal provisions (so-called status offenses) are producing different outcomes in juvenile justice. In such circumstances, reforming these special provisions should be an early priority of those concerned with the high traditional exposure of girls to juvenile incarceration. The juvenile system's rules and procedures have been clearly implicated in female incarceration.

Figure 8.2 contrasts the percentage of African American males in juvenile and adult incarceration facilities in 2010. I dichotomize populations in prisons, jails, and juvenile facilities into African American and other groups to simplify the analysis. The other major minority group in criminal justice institutions—Hispanic populations—are more difficult to define and more uncertain in current measurements.

The 41 percent of incarcerated juveniles who are African American are grossly out of proportion to the African American percentage

Figure 8.2. Percentage of Incarcerated Persons that are African American in 2010
Sources: Sickmund, M., Sladky, T.J., Kang, W., and Puzzanchera, C. (2011). "Easy Access to the Census of Juveniles in Residential Placement," www.ojjdp.gov/ojstatbb/ezacjrp/; Paul Guerino, Paige M. Harrison, and William J. Sabol, *Appendix Table 13. Estimated Number of Sentenced Prisoners under State and Federal Jurisdiction, by Sex, Race, Hispanic Origin, and Age, December 31, 2010*, National Prisoner Statistics Program, http://bjs.ojp.usdoj.gov/index.cfm?ty=pbdetail&iid=2230.

of the youth population (about 15%). Thus, overrepresentation is both obvious and substantial. But the concentration of African Americans incarcerated in adult criminal justice populations is about the same at 38 percent. If we could add in other minority populations the size of the total minority shares would increase, but the contrast between systems would remain close to that portrayed in Figure 8.2.

The importance of finding this general pattern is not to minimize the problem of juvenile minority overrepresentation, but to alert policy analysts that the pattern extends beyond juvenile justice and is therefore less likely to have been generated by the peculiar rules and procedures that the juvenile system uses. So it appears that minority boys are at a disadvantage in the juvenile system, but no more so than minority persons are in the rest of the criminal process. What disadvantages minority kids in delinquency cases is part of a broader pattern that probably should be addressed by multiple system approaches.

B. Equalize Disadvantage or Minimize Harm?

My friend and teacher Hans Zeisel once published a note showing that a peculiar kind of disproportion was evident in the death sentences accumulating in the state of Florida. Zeisel found that 95 percent of the death sentences in that state were imposed on defendants who were charged with killing white victims (Zeisel 1981). Zeisel showed that some Florida prosecutors believed that the solution to this problem was to add more murder cases with black victims to Florida's burgeoning death row populations (Zeisel 1981 at 464–466). The reason for Zeisel's anger at this tactic was that expanding a cruel and inhuman punishment was the last thing he wished to do, and moving closer to proportional representation by adding black victim cases to death row was a cynical manipulation of the system that again established its arbitrary cruelty. For Hans Zeisel, much more than proportional overrepresentation was wrong with the death penalty system in Florida.

I wonder whether this story has exemplary value for many of us who worry about the overrepresentation of minorities in dead-end detention centers and training schools in 2014. The test question is this: imagine a prosecutor who responds to a finding of imbalance not by releasing minority youth, but by trying to lock up many more Anglo-Saxon whites. Would this brand of affirmative action please or trouble the social critic? Why?

Many persons who justly worry about the burden of disproportionate impact on minority youth believe that the deep end of the juvenile justice system harms kids, and they wish to minimize that harm. Expanding the number of kids harmed through an "affirmative action" plan that only adds nonminority targets is perverse from this perspective for two reasons. First, such an expansion of negative controls does not improve the life chances of any of the minority kids. They continue to suffer the same harms at the same rate. Second, the expansion of harms over a wider population hurts many new kids, placing them in positions of disadvantage close to those that troubled the critics about minority kids. Most of those active in addressing issues of minority overrepresentation care deeply about youth of all colors and backgrounds. This grisly form of affirmative action would be, in their view, a step backward.

My point here is that there are two problems that are rather different when addressing the impact of the system on minority kids, the disproportionate use of sanctions on minorities and the negative effects that these sanctions have on the largely minority kids who are captured by the system. A critic of the system will have two goals—reducing the harm to kids and reducing the proportion of minority kids in the system. But which goal should have the larger priority?

In my view, the more pragmatic a system reformer becomes, the more she will choose measures that reduce the harms that minority kids suffer over programs of better proportional representation. If this is true, then harm reduction creates the opportunity to use concerns about the impact of the system on minority kids as a wedge to reduce the harmful impact of the system on all processed through it. The shift in emphasis from proportional concerns to harm reduction also means that there is no competition between minority and nonminority delinquents, but rather a natural community of interest across group boundaries to make the deep end of the juvenile system less hazardous.

There is also a dark side to the case for emphasizing harm reduction. The sharp edge of the blade in criminal justice almost always falls on disadvantaged minorities, and it is not clear that procedural reform can undo the damage. Some areas of criminal law (traffic and drugs) may respond to administrative controls that reduce the impact on minorities.

Spreading traffic stops into nonminority areas can reduce the proportion of traffic arrests and fines that involve minorities. Drug arrests are often a function of where police concentrate drug enforcement efforts, and this can be altered by administrative measures. But other arenas, including violence, will remain problematic. Street crimes involve minority suspects more often than white kids for different reasons, and changes in law enforcement procedures will not end the overrepresentation of minority youth arrested for robbery and burglary. As long as minority crime victims are well-served by city police, minority suspects will be a disproportionate segment of violence arrests in the United States.

C. Absolute versus Proportionate Standards of Harm in Choosing Reforms

The choice between harm reduction and proportional approaches to overrepresentation will lead to different judgments about which reforms work best. Assume that one reform will leave the proportion of incarcerated delinquents who are minorities the same but reduce the number of kids locked up by 10 percent. Another approach will lower the proportion of incarcerated minority kids by 10 percent but leave the number of minorities locked up the same. Which is better? The "least worst" outcome for minority kids in some settings will depend on what standard is selected as the most important measure of the problem. If a proportionate approach is most important, an observer will pick the outcome that results in the smallest percentage of total harm falling on the minority youth population. If a harm-reduction standard is used, the observer will try to minimize the amount of harm the minority population suffers regardless of what share of total bad outcomes are absorbed by minority youth.

If highly selective styles of law enforcement also concentrate bad outcomes on minorities, then the law enforcement approach that punishes minority kids in the highest percentage of total arrests might still punish fewer minority kids than a system that spreads a much larger number of harmful outcomes somewhat more evenly across the youth population. The highly discretionary system may be more proportionally unjust than the system that spreads a larger level of punishment more evenly over the youth population, but the amount of harm the broader system does to vulnerable minorities is greater. A principled argument for preferring either outcome can be made. But more important than pointing to a particular preference is recognizing the potential conflict in reform priorities.

My suspicion is that persons with backgrounds in child welfare will be more apt to choose the aggregate harm reduction standard and discount its distributive implications, while persons with stronger legal orientations may be more likely to select higher aggregate harm if it is more evenly distributed.

Whatever might separate those who prefer harm reduction to reducing disproportion when hard choices have to be made, I do not think that different choices can be explained as a liberal versus conservative distinction. Instead, I think the conflict highlights the difference between two competing strains of opinion on the left side of the political spectrum that point to different priorities in some circumstances. I will briefly revisit this problem when discussing rules versus discretion competitions in reforming the law of transfer of juveniles to criminal court.

D. Evening Out versus Softening Consequences in Delinquency Cases

If minimizing the harm that falls on minority youth becomes the dominant standard for choosing policy in this area, there are many different policy levers available to seek this end. One contrast is between trying to reduce the number of minority kids subjected to harmful results without attempting to alter the consequences of a delinquency finding, as opposed to trying to lower the amount of aggregate harm suffered by minority kids by reducing the harm produced by juvenile justice sanctions. The first approach tries to alter the distribution of sanctions but not the sanctions themselves. The second tries to take some of the sting out of the sanctions.

Ultimately, which approach to take when choosing how to attempt reform is an empirical question that general statements cannot illuminate very well. But there are some generalizations about such a choice that teach important lessons. The first point is that softening the bite of sanctions only becomes a path to a priority reform because harm reduction is selected as a priority. It is only when harm reduction has been isolated as a goal that shifts in the content of sanctions rather than their distribution can compete with redistribution strategies on an equal footing in protecting minority kids.

A second point about taking some of the harm out of sanctions relates to its distributional advantage over reducing the number of minorities punished. The benefits of sanction reform reach all of those unlucky enough to be punished after the reform. All the members of minority groups who are sanctioned benefit, rather than just those who are spared the punishment as the result of a distributional reform. And all delinquents benefit, not merely the minority population. Further, since most youth held for serious acts of delinquency are at social disadvantage, the nonminority beneficiaries of the process are not all that different than the minority kids who are its core concern.

There is one potential problem with sanction-softening approaches that carries no practical weight in current conditions. A strategy that pushes for reducing the harm in sanctions would generate conflict where the youth advocate feels there are strong social and justice benefits in severe sanctions. However, most youth advocates dislike severe juvenile sanctions, so that it seems safe to discount the prospect that youth advocates would be reluctant to reduce the negative impact of recent levels of sanction in American juvenile justice.

A third contrast between proportional reduction strategies and harm-reduction strategies concerns the inferences about overrepresentation that justify the approach. A focus on reducing the share of sanctions absorbed by minorities may not require the assumption that some form of discrimination has produced the overrepresentation, but it is certainly much easier to justify proportional remedies when discrimination is suspected. But what if the large percentage of delinquents incarcerated for robbery and homicide from minority backgrounds is matched by arrest rates of minorities for robbery and homicide? By contrast, the question of establishing discrimination is not implicated by attempts to reduce the negative impacts on sanctions for all delinquents.

I will not speculate here on the political circumstances that favor emphasis on reducing the concentration of minorities as opposed to reducing the harmful content of sanctions for all youth. These two strategies can complement each other in a coordinated program to reduce harm. Here, I suspect, is the reason that one rarely encounters hardline policies toward criminal offenders in those interest groups that serve disadvantaged minorities. Minority interest groups become penal reform advocates by structural necessity (Ward 2012).

A further implication of the close connection between concern about proportional disadvantage and concern about the harms of juvenile sanctions is that often our worry about disproportion reflects concern about the justice of the harshness of a penal measure. One reason for special concern about the overrepresentation of minorities on American death rows is the feeling that capital punishment is too degrading a sanction for a civilized nation. Our prison populations are just as skewed racially as our death rows, but ambivalence toward the death penalty makes the concentration in death cases a larger concern.

This pattern of larger distrust of more extreme sanctions would predict that the expansion of sanctions in blended-jurisdiction juvenile systems and the legislative trends toward more frequent transfer to criminal court should exacerbate fears about minority overrepresentation in juvenile justice. Just as lowering the punitive stakes may take some of the bite out of disproportionate minority representation, raising the punitive stakes for juveniles can be expected to increase concerns about the extent to which this heavier burden falls on members of disadvantaged minorities.

II. Minority Disproportion and Modern Juvenile Justice Reforms

The first section of this chapter attempted to provide tools for policy analysis. The aim of this section is to apply the perspectives just outlined to consider the impact of three changes in juvenile justice policy over the past generation: (1) the proliferation of legislative transfer standards to supplement discretionary waiver by juvenile court judges; (2) the attempt to protect status offenders from secure confinement by creating separate legal categories with restricted dispositional options for status cases, and (3) diversion programs to resolve minor delinquency charges without formal juvenile court charges or adjudications. None of these three reform programs was centrally concerned with minority overrepresentation in delinquency cases, but each set of changes has an impact on minority presence in juvenile and criminal justice. Further, evaluating the impact of such changes on minority prospects is a critical task in contemporary policy analysis. A final part of this section views the substitution of juvenile court for the criminal process as a law reform that has had a positive long-range impact on minority youth in the United States.

A. Automatic Transfer Rules and Minority Harm

Almost all juvenile justice systems provide some method for transferring some accused delinquents close to aging out of the juvenile system who are charged with serious crimes into criminal court to face much harsher sanctions that are available in the juvenile system (see Fagan and Zimring 2000). The traditional method of determining whether an older juvenile would be transferred was for a hearing to be held in the juvenile court, and for the judge to decide whether he should waive the juvenile court's jurisdiction and therefore allow criminal prosecution (Dawson 2000). The issue before a juvenile judge in such a hearing is whether the youth is a fit subject for the juvenile court. This was always a discretionary decision, difficult to review and quite rarely reversed on appeal (Frost-Clauson and Bonnie 2000).

This type of discretion would seem an ideal breeding ground for attitudes that prejudice the prospects of African American and Hispanic juveniles. No precise studies have been done, but the track record of waiver for transferring high proportions of minority youth is not encouraging (Bortner, Zatz, and Hawkins 2000). At the same time, however, the signal virtue of traditional discretionary waiver was the low rate at which juveniles were transferred.

An almost universal addition to discretionary waiver provisions in recent years has been legislation that provides for automatic transfer of juveniles to criminal court if one from among a list of serious charges is brought against the juvenile. The charges frequently listed include murder, armed robbery, rape, and many other serious offenses (Feld 2000). The advantage of this legislative system is that it substitutes a clear rule for personal discretion. The disadvantage is that many more kids of all kinds, including many more minority kids, will be shipped to criminal court under mandatory transfer rules than under systems that only transfer juveniles after juvenile court waiver hearings. Even if the *proportion* of all kids transferred who are African American or Hispanic goes down with automatic transfer rules, the *number* of minority kids disadvantaged will increase. The rule versus discretion choice looks at this first impression like a competition between proportional representation and harm reduction. When automatic transfer replaces discretionary waiver, the number of minority kids harmed will increase even if the share of transferred kids from minority backgrounds declines.

A second look, however, suggests that automatic transfer standards may have nothing to offer minority kids, not even the certainty of the application of a uniform set of rules. The only discretion less reviewable than a juvenile court judge's is that of a prosecutor, and the adoption of automatic transfer standards really substitutes a prosecutor's discretion for that of a judge. A prosecutor can select the charge to bring against a juvenile, and that charging decision will determine whether the case goes to juvenile or criminal court. No review can force a prosecutor to file more serious charges than he wants to file, or indeed to file any charges at all.

My guess is that the proportion of minorities transferred might go down somewhat in regimes of prosecutorial rather than judicial discretion, but not because prosecutors are more sensitive to minorities. Instead, as the number of juveniles transferred increases substantially, the population transferred will tend to become somewhat more like the general population of accused delinquents. By disadvantaging a much larger fraction of the youth population, the proportional share of minorities hurt by prosecutorial discretion systems may decline, but this is nobody's definition of youth welfare. The number of minority youth at risk of criminal sanctions will expand, and it is small comfort that they have been joined in this vulnerability by larger numbers of nonminority youth. Legislative transfer's effects are close to Florida's adding black victim cases to its death row to create the appearance of even treatment.

Further, there is no enforceable legal principle behind this change, only the substitution of prosecutorial for judicial discretion—a shift that moves the locus of authority from a legal actor with a formal commitment to consider the welfare of the accused to a legal actor under no such obligation.

B. Deinstitutionalization of Status Offenders

Since the original juvenile court was presumed to be taking power only for the welfare of its youthful clients, that court was given power to order institutional placements including detention and training schools for young people who were truant or disobedient but had not behaved in ways that harmed others. Since juvenile court sanctions were not regarded as punishment, it was said that there was no need for proportionality limits on power assumed over delinquents, and thus no need to differentiate between burglars and runaways when distributing the juvenile court's helpful interventions.

From the start, this theory suffered from two linked problems. First, the detentions and commitments of juvenile courts were punitive in effect and often in intent, so that imposing them on kids who did not deserve punishment or imposing much more punishment than disobedience would merit was manifestly unjust. Second, there was no evidence that the punitive treatment of delinquents in twentieth-century juvenile justice was effective either as therapy or social control (Titlebaum 2002). The same legal realism about juvenile justice that produced decisions like *In re Gault* also demanded that proportional limits be placed on the power exercised by the state over runaways, truants, and adolescents in conflict with parents. The particular target of the Federal Juvenile Justice and Delinquency Prevention Act of 1974 was to discourage the states from the practice of putting status offenders in secure confinement. While the effort to break status offenders out of juvenile jails was neither an instant nor an unqualified success, its core judgment that unlimited detention is unjust and ineffective for noncriminal misbehavior has stood the test of time, even with shifting sentiments about many other aspects of juvenile justice.

The shift in status-offender policy is rarely considered as an important aspect of policies relating to minority group overrepresentation. The paternalistic excesses of juvenile justice were concentrated on girls, but the status offenders pushed into state processes were no more concentrated among minorities than were delinquents.

But did the emphasis on this policy goal help minority kids? Considering this question again raises the contrast between aggregate and proportional measures of minority disadvantage. The number of African American and Hispanic kids locked up in detention centers and training schools decreased as a direct result of successful deinstitutionalization. But the proportion of detained kids who were minorities may have increased as a result of the program. Although fewer African American kids were locked up, a greater proportion of the kids locked up might have been African American. Was this progress? I would suggest the answer is yes.

But didn't the deinstitutionalization of status offenders strip the veneer of child welfare from the court and thus make harsher policy toward other classes of delinquency more acceptable (Empey 1979 at 408–409)? After all, the intense pressure to crackdown on "juvenile super-predators" happened after the welfare facade of the court had been removed. So why not conclude that the latent function of status-offender reforms was additional hardship for the largely minority residual of delinquents that stayed in juvenile court systems?

The first problem with such a spin on status-offender reforms is that those who supported such reforms were skeptical about secure confinement for delinquents generally. There was no push to fill empty cells with burglars and joyriders from the policy analysts who had pushed the 1974 reforms onto the public agenda. Nor did a juvenile court crime crackdown stem in any clear way from the status-offender reforms. The get-tough rhetoric and punitive pressure that arrived in juvenile court policy debates in the 1980s was a spillover from crime policy changes in criminal justice that began in the late 1960s (Zimring, Hawkins, and Kamin 2001 at Chapter 9). The premises and the example of the status-offender reforms probably worked against the push for punitive policy in juvenile justice, and thus were consistent with the youth–welfare interests of minority advocates. I will revisit this issue in the last section of this analysis.

C. Diversion and Minority Justice

What is the impact of reforms aiming to divert first-time and minor offenders from formal processing on the interests of minority offenders in juvenile justice? The policy thrust of diversion seems in harmony with lower levels of coercive controls and concern for youth welfare, but what are the results? Here again, the method of scorekeeping may determine the result. The aggregate impact of diversion on the number of minority youth in formal processing will be a benefit, unless the diversion program is a complete sham. If substantial numbers of kids escape detention and adjudication, many of them will be African American and Hispanic. But even if the number of minority youth benefited is high, the proportion of those not diverted who are members of disadvantaged minorities will not go down, and it might increase. So a proportionate standard would not produce evidence that diversion had a positive impact on the problem of overrepresentation. Because I believe that harm reduction is the appropriate standard, my conclusion is that diversion programs benefit minority populations.

D. Juvenile versus Criminal Court

The last comparison that teaches us about harm reduction is between the rate of minority incarceration from juvenile versus criminal courts. The comparison is instructive for two reasons. First, comparing the exposure to harm associated with these two systems is one way of forming a judgment about the aggregate impact of the juvenile court—itself a special reform in American law—on the welfare of minority populations. The second reason to compare aggregate juvenile versus criminal court outcomes is to provide an indirect test of the effects that reforms like diversion and deinstitutionalization of status offenders have had on the welfare of minority youth. Comparing a system performing with these features against an alternative system for processing accused criminals might help us decide whether these major thrusts in juvenile justice over recent decades have made the system more or less sympathetic to interests of minorities.

Table 8.1 repeats one measure of minority overrepresentation used in Figure 8.2, the percentage of incarceration populations who are African American, but adds for the age groups 13 to 17 and 18 to 24 the rate per 100,000 African American males of incarceration in the mostly

Table 8.1. Comparing Percentage African American and Rate of African American Confinement in Juvenile Facilities and Prisons, 2010

	Juvenile Facilities	Prison (ages 18–24)	Ratio
Percentage African American of Total	41%	38%	
Rate per 100,000 of African American Confinement	606	1,899	3.31/1

Sources: Sickmund, M., Sladky, T.J., Kang, W., and Puzzanchera, C. (2011). "Easy Access to the Census of Juveniles in Residential Placement," www.ojjdp.gov/ojstatbb/ezacjrp/; Paul Guerino, Paige M. Harrison, and William J. Sabol, *Appendix Table 13. Estimated Number of Sentenced Prisoners under State and Federal Jurisdiction, by Sex, Race, Hispanic Origin, and Age, December 31, 2010*, National Prisoner Statistics Program, http://bjs.ojp.usdoj.gov/index.cfm?ty=pbdetail&iid=2230.

juvenile justice age brackets of 13 to 17 and the early criminal court age brackets of 18 to twenty-four.

The juvenile versus adult data based on proportionate overrepresentation of African Americans shows that about 40 percent of both juvenile incarcerations and young adults in prison are African American, a much higher proportion of the total incarcerated population than African American youth are of the total youth population. A slightly higher percentage of the younger group is African American.

But the important statistic for my argument is the rate of minority incarceration in juvenile and adult facilities. The incarceration rates for African American kids in the age 13 to 17 rate is 606 per 100,000. The rate for African American males ages 18 to 24 is over three times higher than for 13- to 17-year-olds. A proportional approach suggests that the two systems are equally problematic, but the criminal system is confining three times as many kids of color. I suspect that the same juvenile versus criminal court pattern would hold for other discrete and overrepresented minority male populations. The big difference in incarceration rates suggests that the aggregate protective impact of juvenile justice policy on minority youth appears to be substantial when compared with criminal justice impact. To borrow a phrase from legal Latin, *res ipsa loquitur*.

Conclusions

The overrepresentation of disadvantaged minorities in the juvenile justice system is part of a broader pattern observed throughout law enforcement in the United States and in most other places. The particular doctrines and processes of juvenile courts do not appear to exacerbate overrepresentation when compared to criminal courts.

This analysis has contrasted two approaches to the problem of overrepresentation, a legalist view that emphasizes reducing disproportionate impact and a youth–welfare view that attempts to reduce the harms suffered by minority youth.

The major positive reforms in juvenile justice over the past generation—deinstitutionalization of status offenders and diversion—have not had dramatic impact on the disproportionate involvement of minority youth in the deep end of the juvenile system. But the lower levels of incarceration embraced by juvenile courts mean that the harms suffered within juvenile courts by all sorts of youth are much smaller than the harms imposed on young offenders in America's criminal courts. It turns out that the entire apparatus of juvenile justice is functioning as a substantial harm-reduction program for minority delinquents.

What I have called a harm-reduction perspective shows clearly that those concerned about the healthy development of minority youth must also be invested in the continued operation of the juvenile court as by far the lesser evil in modern crime control. That the institutions of juvenile justice need reform should not obscure the fact of their lesser harm or its policy implications.

REFERENCES

Bortner, M. A., Marjorie S. Zatz, and Darnell F. Hawkins. 2000. "Race and Transfer: Empirical Research and Social Context." In *The Changing Borders of Juvenile Justice.* Jeffery Fagan and Franklin E. Zimring, eds. , pp. 277–320. Chicago: University of Chicago Press,

Dawson, Robert O. 2000. "Judicial Waiver in Theory and Practice." In *The Changing Borders of Juvenile Justice.* Jeffery Fagan and Franklin E. Zimring, eds., pp. 45–81. Chicago: University of Chicago Press.

Empey, LaMar T. 1979. *The Future of Childhood and Juvenile Justice.* Charlottesville: University Press of Virginia.

Fagan, Jeffrey, and Franklin E. Zimring, eds. 2000. *The Changing Borders of Juvenile Justice.* Chicago: University of Chicago Press.

Feld, Barry C. 2000. "Legislative Exclusion of Offenses from Juvenile Court Jurisdiction: A History and Critique." In *The Changing Borders of Juvenile Justice.* Jeffery Fagan and Franklin E. Zimring, eds., pp. 83–144. Chicago: University of Chicago Press.

Frost-Clauson, Lynda E. and Richard J. Bonnie. 2000. *Juvenile Justice on Appeal.* In *The Changing Borders of Juvenile Justice.* Jeffery Fagan and Franklin E. Zimring, eds., pp. 181–206. Chicago: University of Chicago Press.

Guerino, Paul, Paige M. Harrison, and William J. Sabol, *Appendix Table 13. Estimated Number of Sentenced Prisoners under State and Federal Jurisdiction, by Sex, Race, Hispanic Origin, and Age, December 31, 2010.* National Prisoner Statistics Program. http://bjs.ojp.usdoj.gov/index.cfm?ty=pbdetail&iid=2230.

Moone, Joseph. 1993. *Children in Custody 1991: Private Facilities. Prevention Fact Sheet 2, 5.* Washington, DC: Office of Juvenile Justice and Delinquency Prevention.

Sickmund, M., Sladky, T.J., Kang, W., and Puzzanchera, C. 2011. "Easy Access to the Census of Juveniles in Residential Placement." www.ojjdp.gov/ojstatbb/ezacjrp/.

National Criminal Justice Information and Statistics Service. 1974. *Children in Custody.* Washington, DC: National Criminal Justice Information and Statistics Service.

Titlebaum, Lee. 2002. "Status Offenders." In *A Century of Juvenile Justice*. Margaret Rosenheim, Franklin E. Zimring, David S. Tanenhaus, and Bernardine Dohrn, eds., pp. 158–175. Chicago: University of Chicago Press.

US Department of Justice, Bureau of the Census. 1997. *Current Population Reports: Estimates of the Population of the United States by Age, Sex, and Race*. Washington, DC: US Government Printing Office.

US Department of Justice, Bureau of Justice Statistics. 1974, 1997. *Correctional Populations in the United States*. Washington, DC: US Government Printing Office.

US Department of Justice, Bureau of Justice Statistics. 1997. *Children in Custody*. Washington, DC: US Government Printing Office.

Ward, Geoff. 2012. *The Black Child Savers: Racial Democracy and Juvenile Justice*. Chicago: University of Chicago Press.

Zeisel, Hans. 1981. "Race Bias in the Administration of the Death Penalty: The Florida Experience." *Harvard Law Review* 95:456.

Zimring, Franklin E., Gordon Hawkins and Sam Kamin. 2001. *Punishment and Democracy: Three Strikes and You're Out in California*. New York: Oxford University Press.

PART III

Making Change Happen

The last section of this book shifts the focus from the types of legal and institutional change that should take place in the next decade to the strategies and appeals that might facilitate reforms. In Chapter 9, Terry Maroney surveys the changes in both neuroscience and legal rhetoric about brain development that have been a prominent feature of policy debate in the recent past. Maroney's reading of the case law suggests that the primary focus of reform arguments should not be brain-based. Reformers should instead place their primary emphasis on the traditional understandings of youth and the process of maturity.

Chapter 10 provides a detailed analysis of the normative and behavioral arguments for progressive policies toward young offenders. We then survey both the impediments to law reform and the important leading indicators of whether and to what extent the next decade will be an era of positive reform of legal policy toward young offenders in the United States.

9

The Once and Future Juvenile Brain

TERRY A. MARONEY

Introduction

From the comfortable perch of a decade out, it seems clear that twentieth-century juvenile justice passed through three distinct eras.[1] The founding era, often referred to by reference to the rehabilitative ideal by which it was motivated and shaped, began at the century's turn (Tanenhaus, 2004). Its quickly proliferating systems of separate adjudication and sanction for minors were left relatively to their own devices until the 1960s, when the court-driven revolution that was transforming adult criminal procedure took children under its wing. This due process era was highlighted not only by blockbuster cases like *In re Gault* (1967), but also by blockbuster legislative enactments like the Juvenile Justice Delinquency Prevention Act of 1974. After only two decades this shift was supplanted by the so-called superpredator era—a highly concentrated undertaking to move far more children out of the juvenile courts and to gut protections for those left in it, driven by fears of a "new breed of juvenile superpredator" that would soon overrun existing systems (DiIulio, 1995). That the last century can be thus divided is a story well told (Zimring, 2005; Rosenheim et al., 2002).

We surely now have moved into a new era of juvenile justice. In the space of the last decade we have seen the courts—most notably the US Supreme Court—abolish the juvenile death penalty, severely cut back juvenile life without parole sentences, and demand greater attention to youths' vulnerability in police interactions; we also have seen a steady drip of state legislative measures to return older youth to the juvenile courts. The story of this era has yet to be told, unfolding as it is around us, but its advent has been enthusiastically noted (Levick, 2012).

What to call this new era? Not long ago, and only a little tongue-in-cheek, I suggested that we were in "the decade of the adolescent brain" (Maroney, 2009, at 90). Perhaps, then, we might peg our emerging reality with a moniker relating to the brain. It's tempting. The popular media evidence our continued cultural fascination with teen brains: widely circulated magazine articles promise that science explains teens' exasperating behavior, including criminal acts (Wallis, 2004; Begley, 2000; Sabbagh, 2006). A major national ad advocating teen driving restrictions claimed that young people are literally missing a part of their brains—with an accompanying cartoon showing a car-shaped hole in the grey matter (Allstate Insurance, 2010). Parents can buy books offering brain-based explanations for why their adolescents are "primal" and even "crazy" (Strauch, 2003; Bradley, 2002; Walsh, 2004). As explained in the pages to follow, the developmental immaturity of the teen brain was elevated by juvenile-rights champions into a central meme of the legal advocacy that has begun so rapidly to bear fruit. All right, then: the juvenile brain science era it is.

Or not. There's a reason why history often waits to be written, and eras may be known best in their decline. With just a little hindsight it will be clear that this new era is not really about the juvenile brain. In fact, we can see that right now, if we are willing to push back at the meme. Adolescent brain science has contributed to our new reality—less than many think it has, but a contribution all the same. But the point is not, and never has been, the juvenile brain itself. The point is the stable truths about children and their environments that we currently enjoy thinking and talking about through that frame.

It's a highly imperfect frame, for reasons I shall explain. But then all our prior frames have been imperfect in their own way. Just as it would have been preferable had the founders foreseen the procedural disasters their informal model would engender, had the due process reformers anticipated the possibility of substantive backlash and had the panicked denizens of the 1990s seen the extent of their overreach, we should try today to see our chosen memes as those who come after us will.

In this chapter I will trace how adolescent brain science came so quickly to appear so promising, locating both the prior narratives into which it fit and the new narratives it made seem possible. The science was rapidly integrated into advocacy strategies, reflecting a pronounced empirical move within criminal law—indeed, law—more generally. A look at how those strategies fared on the ground reveals that they generally were effective only as a rhetorical device: an efficient, modern-sounding way to signal endorsement of a host of ideas about children's differences.

Again, temptation arises, this time to conjure visions of old wine and new bottles. The metaphor is apt, so far as it goes. It could be read with a disparaging tone, implying that stale arguments are being disingenuously repackaged. But of course old wine can be quite good, and new bottles can be quite handy, particularly if they attract a new audience to that lovely, overlooked vintage. This latter view comes closer to our present experience. Talk of the juvenile brain has become a twenty-first-century way to inject certain core values back into the juvenile justice system. But using the science for that purpose has significant downsides and limits. Now that we are firmly ensconced in this new era, we stand to make the most of it by highlighting child-protective values directly and letting the brain frame gently recede.

The Juvenile Brain, Ascendant

The Scientific Moment

Adolescent brain science came to occupy its current prominence within juvenile justice because of the confluence of three distinct phenomena. First, developmental psychology—a science with which juvenile justice long has enjoyed a close historical relationship—began a significant expansion. Second, neuroscience, including developmental neuroscience, experienced an even more radical and time-compressed period of growth. Third, legal scholars and scientists began a spirited dialogue over the legal implications of those scientific advances. This confluence created a cultural moment in which we could entertain the notion that juvenile brain development had something important to do with juvenile justice.

The move in developmental psychology came first. Theories of adolescence as a distinct developmental stage always have been central to juvenile justice. Such theories underlie not only the core idea—that of having a separate system for those who are no longer children but not yet adults—but also the attributes of that system, such as preservation of future life chances through limited sanctions. However, for most of the twentieth century developmental psychology was in a fairly primitive state. Further, it focused primarily on young children, the population whose misbehavior is least likely to be addressed in any coercive legal environment. In the 1980s, however, a sustained program of relevant empiricism about adolescents took hold.

Scientists found, for example, that normal teens show a marked, temporary increase in risky behaviors, despite displaying an adult-level cognitive understanding of risk. Researchers were able to document typical adolescent differences in a wide range of other domains as well, including sensation-seeking (temporarily increased); ability to adopt a future-time perspective (greater than a child's, less than an adult's); perceptions of personal vulnerability (low); self-concept (evolving); and peer orientation (higher than in either children or adults) (Scott & Steinberg, 2008). Soon psychologists and legal scholars began a collaborative effort to define and measure teens' law-relevant psychological attributes, such as competence to waive Miranda rights (Grisso & Schwartz, 2000).

The takeaway from all of this research would likely be entirely unsurprising to any parent, but was surprisingly underdocumented as a scientific matter: in terms of typical behaviors and patterns of thought, teenagers are indeed distinct from both children and adults. By the 1990s, psychologists had validated that general proposition and rapidly were filling in its substance, including the substantive juncture between developmental psychology and law (Buss, 2009).

At just that time, a revolution was taking place in neuroscience. Historically, most brain science had relied on postmortem examination or opportunistic study of those with dramatic injuries—approaches with rather obvious limitations. Technological breakthroughs suddenly allowed for sophisticated observation of live, normal human brains, including those of young people. Structural studies were the first to evolve. Such studies are helpfully analogized to a very advanced x-ray, generating detailed, static pictures of the brain. A number of reputable structural studies of adolescent brains appeared in prominent journals, together demonstrating that the typical brain undergoes a distinct developmental stage during the teen years (Giedd et al., 1999; Paus et al., 1999; Sowell et al., 1999; Gogtay et al., 2004). Adolescent structural maturation appeared to revolve around two distinct processes. Myelination, the insulation of neural axons with a fatty substance referred to as "white matter," facilitates fast, efficient communication among brain systems. Healthy brains show linear increases in white matter from childhood until adulthood. The second process is nonlinear. Early adolescence typically coincides with an increase in the volume and density of "gray matter," or neuron cell bodies and synapses—something that previously had been observed only very early in the life course.

Following this second wave of neural exuberance, over the course of adolescence gray matter is sharply pruned back, a process shaped by factors such as use and life experiences. Finally, neuroscientists observed that the processes of myelination and pruning start at the back of the brain and spread toward the front, meaning that the evolutionarily new frontal cortices—responsible for higher-order reasoning and a host of other aspects of mature thought and behavior—are reached last.

The takeaway: normal development results in a relatively mature adult brain that is better equipped quickly and efficiently to respond appropriately to life's challenges and to perform the types of tasks for which a person has trained. While the average normal adolescent's physical capacity for such brain maturity far exceeds that of a child, it falls short of that of the average normal adult.

Functional studies—those seeking to track activity within the brain in real time—followed. This is the area of neuroscience currently undergoing the most rapid expansion, as functional MRI (fMRI) machines proliferate in university and commercial laboratories. Relying as they do on a newer technology, and implicating as they do more complex questions, functional studies of the teen brain are less firmly established than structural ones and their takeaway points are far less clear (Blakemore, 2012). In the early 2000s, when juvenile advocates began most enthusiastically to take note of neuroscience, relatively few such studies were available; but those consistently suggested that adolescents might tend to employ different brain processes than adults when carrying out identical tasks, with potential implications for their relative competence to carry out such tasks under varying conditions (Baird et al., 1999). The less dramatic but still notable takeaway: structural differences in how the brain is built and wired appeared likely to correlate with differences in how the brain operates to facilitate mind and action.

By the early 2000s, then, neuroscience supported the notion that typical teen brains are structurally and functionally different from those of both children and adults. Importantly, the developmental findings from neuroscience and psychology appeared to fit neatly together. Well before the advent of fMRI, neuroscientists had built up an impressive level of understanding of the highly specialized nature of the brain, providing relatively reliable guides to which substructures did what—think, for example, of speech centers, or areas responsible for smell or taste or motor control (Gazzaniga, 2004). These functional maps would prove to be critical.

Psychology could show that teens' real-life proclivities and aptitudes matured in a way that seemed to correspond with physical maturation in the brain areas thought to regulate such proclivities and aptitudes. Research demonstrating that some level of delinquent behavior is normal, particularly for boys, provides a nice example. According to these studies, the vast majority of teens age out of offending (Zimring, 2005). This finding lends itself to an easy pairing with brain studies that show a leveling-off of maturational processes through aging. The science offers a plausible physiological mechanism underlying a known developmental trajectory. And thus the coin acquired two sides: to "the extent that transformations occurring in adolescent brains contribute to the characteristic behavioral predispositions of adolescence," one scholar wrote, "adolescent behavior is in part biologically determined" (Spear, 2000, at 447).

The third and final thread was the one beginning to be drawn between neuroscience and law. The early to mid-2000s saw a growing fascination with that link. Scholars predicted that emerging brain science would be particularly relevant to criminal law, given the centrality of mental states to criminal responsibility (Zeki & Goodenough, 2004). The most aggressive claim, one that tended to be made early in this academic moment, was that neuroscience would upend entrenched concepts of free will and responsibility. A more modest prediction, one that has gradually taken over intellectual market space, was that neuroscience might improve identification and understanding of issues already relevant to criminal law such as incompetence, insanity, impulse control, addiction, and lying. Either of these iterations was potentially relevant to juvenile justice (Baird & Fugelsang, 2004).

These threads wove together in the following way. Progress in developmental psychology put detailed empirical substance on a core tenet of parental experience since time immemorial: teens think and act differently. Advances in neuroscience showed that teen brains are physically changing and acting in ways that appear to dovetail nicely with those processes of behavioral maturation. Increasingly, these insights seemed obviously relevant to law.

*The Pre-*Roper *Advocacy Moment*

Enter the juvenile advocacy community. Recall that the late 1990s were the tail end of the superpredator era, in which virtually every state committed to treat far more juveniles as adults and to shrink the benefits—such as confidentiality—youth previously had enjoyed, even if they remained in the juvenile courts. Scholars and advocates with a commitment to traditional juvenile justice values began to see brain research as a tool to close an apparent disjuncture between science, which increasingly showed that juveniles and adults are different, and law, which increasingly treated juveniles and adults as if they were the same.

The highest-profile test case for this new strategy was, of course, *Roper v. Simmons,* over which the U.S Supreme Court took certiorari in 2004. Important though *Roper* was, it was not the original test balloon: by that time the advocacy community was already swinging hard with the brain-science findings. Since 2000, a small group had been coordinating a state-by-state effort to legislatively abolish the juvenile death penalty, and made a strategic decision to rely heavily on those findings nearly the second they hit the ground (Boyle, 2005). Researchers incorporated testimony about the teen brain into legislative testimony, even bringing along plastic brain models to illustrate their points (Boyle, 2005; Aronson, 2007). Then in 2002, in a dissent from denial of certiorari in a different juvenile case, Justice Stevens sent an important signal that he wanted to hear more, writing:

> Neuroscientific evidence of the last few years has revealed that adolescent brains are not fully developed, which often leads to erratic behaviors and thought processes in that age group. Scientific advances such as the use of functional magnetic resonance imaging—MRI scans—have provided valuable data that serve to make the case even stronger that adolescents "'are more vulnerable, more impulsive, and less self-disciplined than adults'" (*In re Stanford*, 537 U.S. 968, 971 (2002) (Stevens, J., dissenting).

Within the space of a year, scholars had gone to press on an impressive number of articles tying psychology and neuroscience to arguments for lesser juvenile sanctions (Fagan, 2003; Feld, 2003; Scott & Steinberg, 2003; Steinberg & Scott, 2003). An entire PBS *Frontline* episode was devoted to the teen brain (Spinks, 2002). At a closely watched sentencing hearing, the attorney for convicted "DC sniper" Lee Malvo called jurors' attention to a recent *Newsweek* article on the teen brain, pleading with them to spare Malvo's life because a teen's "frontal lobe is not developed," impairing judgment, and explaining why we don't give teens full responsibility for their lives and actions (Shepherd, 2004, at 73–74). It appears to have worked: some jurors reported voting for a life sentence in part because they found that plea persuasive.

So when in late 2003 the Missouri Supreme Court ruled the juvenile death penalty unconstitutional, in direct defiance of the higher court's 1989 decision upholding the death penalty for 16- and 17-year-olds, the advocacy community was ready. It went all in.

The condemned teen's lawyers chose prominently to highlight adolescent brain science in their briefs, arguing that "the parts of the brain that enable impulse control and reasoned judgment," as well as "competent decision-making, control of emotions, and moral judgment," are "not yet fully developed in 16- and 17-year-olds" (Brief for Respondent at 10, *Roper v. Simmons*). His counsel, the prominent former Solicitor General Seth Waxman, similarly emphasized neuroscience in oral argument, repeatedly using the terms "science" and "scientific" (Oral Argument at 18, 22, *Roper v. Simmons*). Indeed, Waxman devoted more argument time to brain science than to any other issue. His focus was complemented by a number of amicus parties. The American Psychological Association, for example, made a number of explicitly neuroscientific arguments, and brain science was the exclusive focus of the American Medical Association's brief, a text that has acquired a devoted following and cultural salience of its own. Very much a coordinated effort, the advocacy message was united and clear: neuroscience gave irrefutable gravitas to the long-held (if at that time embattled) notions that juveniles are by virtue of their developmental status less culpable than adults who commit similar crimes; less deterred by the specter of punishment; and less than the "'fully rational, choosing agent[s]' presupposed by the death penalty" (Brief for Respondent at 23, *Roper v. Simmons*).

In terms of outcome, *Roper* was a home run. In striking down the juvenile death penalty, the Court fully endorsed those conclusions. In language that is likely to shape all major juvenile cases for the foreseeable future, it noted three relevant, general differences about teens: their propensity to "immaturity and irresponsibility," resulting in overrepresentation in "virtually every category of reckless behavior"; increased vulnerability and susceptibility to negative influences, including "peer pressure"; and "more transitory, less fixed" personalities, reflective of a less "well formed" character (*Roper v. Simmons*, 543 U.S. at 569–70, 2005). These attributes, the Court held, make it extremely unlikely that the juvenile death penalty serves a meaningful deterrent function, and prevent any teen from being truly among the worst of the worst.

Whether brain science was particularly persuasive in getting to that outcome was, however, difficult at that time to determine. In a grand total of one phrase, the Court noted that its conclusions tended to find support in the "scientific and sociological studies" cited by Simmons and "his *amici*."

It was an ambiguous signal, but was received by many as a full-throated endorsement. Developmental neuroscience quickly came to be regarded as a major influence on the highest-profile juvenile case in decades. The resulting flurry of activity was astonishing. A highlight reel: policy advocates in multiple states issued brain-heavy position papers; in the words of Action for Children North Carolina, the science offered a way to put "the juvenile back in juvenile justice" (Action for Children North Carolina, 2007; Wisconsin Council on Children & Families, 2006). Juvenile defenders started rolling out studies and experts in the courtroom (Paget Henderson, 2009), and prosecutors started training themselves to respond (American Prosecutors Research Institute, 2006; National District Attorneys Association, 2007; National Juvenile Justice Prosecution Center, 2004). Edward Kennedy convened a Senate hearing (Hearing on Adolescent Brain Development and Juvenile Justice, 110th Congress, 2007). It became something like an article of faith that brain science had driven *Roper*, and could unlock a new future for juvenile justice in America.

*Taking Measure of the Post-*Roper *Moment*

Spoiler alert: there has been no juvenile brain-science revolution. What we have seen is something along the lines of a polite reform effort waving a radical banner. The courts have proven to be a moderately hospitable environment for the takeaway points, and a quite inhospitable one for the scientific nitty-gritty underlying them. The court of popular opinion has gone largely the same way. This is largely as it should be. The more we understand why it has gone down this way, I believe, the more clearly we can see that we're ending up in just about the right place.

Juvenile defenders and advocates in the immediate post-*Roper* moment advanced an impressive array of claims, both in the public square (through books, articles, trainings, and interviews) and before the juvenile and adult courts (the latter, of course, in cases in which chronological juveniles were being tried as adults, which tended to be the more serious cases). Again, a highlight reel. Neuroimmaturity, the community urged, might render juveniles less competent to consent to searches, waive Miranda rights, offer confessions, waive counsel, participate adequately in their own defense, or enter a guilty plea. Further, they might be less able to form specific intent, or to foresee consequences in such a way as to justify findings of recklessness or criminal negligence—or, in the case of felony murder determinations, presumptions of recklessness or negligence. These assertions all reflected an assessment of juveniles' present deficits. What juveniles had going for them, in contrast, was heightened capacity for change.

The promise of brain maturation over time counseled strongly in favor of eliminating or shaving back both transfer to adult court and the imposition of lengthy sentences. These arguments were nicely set out in Elizabeth Scott and Lawrence Steinberg's 2008 book *Rethinking Juvenile Justice*, regarded by many as a gold standard for "legal-developmental collaboration" (Buss, 2009). And all over the country, defenders began rolling them out in real cases.

Perhaps surprisingly, though, a lopsided majority of brain-science claims failed to hit their mark. Those that fell short tended to do so for one of three reasons.

First, many courts regarded brain-science claims as falling outside the narrow parameters dictated by legal doctrine. In many cases, the doctrinal constriction of juveniles' rights by which the neuroscientific reform effort was motivated was simply too tight to penetrate. One place where this was obvious was with challenges to transfer schemes. For years the courts had become progressively less willing to second-guess the legislatures' choices as to such schemes, even when they did highly unconventional things like give prosecutors unreviewable discretion to keep a child on the juvenile side or treat him like an adult. By the time the states expanded transfer in the 1990s, the doctrinal landscape had rendered courts largely impotent to respond. In a heavily litigated New Mexico case involving expert brain-science testimony, for example, defenders argued strenuously that automatic transfer for juveniles charged with murder represented a "rejection of biology"; the court simply found that the constitutionality of such transfer was well-established and moved on (*State v. Garcia*, 2007).

In many other cases, doctrinal constraints of a broader sort were the issue. This clearly was the case with the deluge of lower-court post-*Roper* challenges to juvenile life without parole sentences (now overtaken by subsequent events, as explained below). At that time, devotion to the mantra that "death is different" had erected an impenetrable wall between capital and term-of-years sentences, and the latter were evaluated by gross-disproportionality tests that had evolved in such a way as to apparently foreclose any consideration of the defendant's personal characteristics. These were not juvenile-specific sentencing principles; they were just sentencing principles. But they created virtually no room for juveniles to say anything about their brains—or any other part of them, for that matter. Overwhelmingly, courts disposed of these cases quickly—reciting the doctrine, noting that *Roper* itself appeared passively to endorse life without parole, ignoring the scientific arguments, and upholding the sentences. A similar fate befell most children who argued that by virtue of being juveniles, they were unable to form specific intent, foresee consequences, waive rights, and so on. Most courts (if they bothered even to respond to the arguments) took note of the extraordinarily low bars set by contemporary criminal doctrine for each of these determinations, and declared themselves unwilling to hold that juveniles were, as a class, unable to clear them. The Connecticut Supreme Court, for example, recognized that juveniles might be more vulnerable to duress, in part because of incomplete brain maturation, but believed itself unable to accommodate that reality without "rewrit[ing] the entire Penal Code, crimes, and defenses" (*State v. Heinemann*, 2007). Similarly, an Arizona court found neuroscientific arguments as to *mens rea* legally irrelevant because, even if true, they would amount to a diminished capacity defense, not permitted under state law (*State v. Torres*, 2010).

These cases made clear the impact of *Roper's* death-penalty frame. Being deemed death-eligible is a high bar. It is not hard to harmonize the ideas that no child can clear *that* one, but that all children deemed old enough to be handled in a juvenile court can clear the far lower ones—unless there is something special about that child.

Which leads to the second sort of case that tended to fare badly: ones in which brain science was alleged to have something to do with a juvenile not just as a member of a class, but also as an individual. In many of these cases, that specificity was itself the problem. Courts frequently rejected brain-science claims where they appeared to contradict record facts. Exemplifying this trend were cases contesting the *mens rea* element of specific intent. In perhaps the most extreme example, a Delaware youth charged with capital murder elicited extensive brain-science testimony from a nationally known expert. The expert told the judge and jury that the parts of juveniles' brains responsible for planning and foresight were not yet fully developed. So far, so good. Unfortunately for that juvenile, a neuropsychologist who had examined him individually promptly went on the stand to present clinical findings that his scores on measures for planning and foresight were "off the charts" (*State v. Jones*, 2005). This case is exceptional; most involve juveniles whose actions suggested relatively high levels of planning and forethought, taken to obviate the relevance of findings that juveniles generally lack adult levels of such capacity. In a high-profile South Carolina case in which a 12-year-old shot his grandparents, for example, the court relied heavily on the facts that the child had acquired the gun, waited for the victims to fall asleep, escaped the scene, and concocted a cover story (*State v. Pittman*, 2007). As such actions by an adult would be sufficient to infer either a conscious plan to cause death or an awareness that death would result, they were considered *a fortiorari* to allow the same inference for a child—again, a very low bar.

Finally, courts also sometimes deemed brain-science claims not contradictory of record facts, but rather duplicative. In these cases, courts believed brain science to add little to evidence of immaturity that already was before fact-finders, including those fact-finders' common sense. In upholding a life without parole sentence, for example, a Wisconsin appellate court took no issue with various neuroscientific claims but held that they "did not constitute a new factor," as the "trial court was well aware of the differences between juveniles and adults" and "a physiological explanation for the differences is not highly relevant" (*State v. Ninham*, 2009). Thus, if at some moments courts think the brain science claims too much, at others they think it offers too little.

Some brain-science claims, in contrast, have hit their mark. When they have done so, it has been in a very particular way.

The most obvious post-*Roper* success story for adolescent brain science has to be *Graham v. Florida* (2010). In *Graham*, the US Supreme Court invalidated juvenile life without parole sentences for nonhomicide crimes. In so doing, it gave brain science more than an oblique phrase: Justice Kennedy upgraded to two sentences and a shout-out, writing that "developments in psychology and brain science continue to show fundamental differences between juvenile and adult minds. For example, parts of the brain involved in behavior control continue to mature through late adolescence." No more mystery; the Court was in fact paying attention to the science. Since then it has repeated the shout-out, in *JDB v. North Carolina* (2011), clarifying that youth matters in the interrogation setting, and in *Miller v. Alabama* (2012), extending *Graham*'s holding to all mandatory life without parole sentences. It has not significantly expanded on its rhetoric, but it has solidified its commitment to it.

And this is where adolescent brain science has hit its stride. In each of these instances, the Court invoked the science as one source of data tending to confirm a general proposition about gross differences between adolescents and adults, about which the criminal law tends to care. The specific proposition in *Graham* about lesser physical capacity for behavioral control is a nice example: we care because if juveniles as a rule have less such capacity, they are by some margin less likely to be deterred by sanctions (sanctions serving as a source of external motivation for exerting self-control), and are more likely to become self-policing over time (and therefore are by some margin not as in need of permanent incapacitation). The Court has not suggested that these differences are absolute and invariable, but rather that they are relatively stable group characteristics, such that it is sensible to take account of them when shaping rules that apply to all members of that group. This is particularly sensible if, as the Court found, there is no reliable way to differentiate within the group as to these attributes at the moment of sentencing. To borrow a concept from the geneticist Steven Pinker, this approach reflects the view that "aggregate data" about youth should be considered when formulating "policy that will optimize the costs and benefits of treating a large similar group in a particular way" (Pinker, 2009). Nor has the Court treated the neuroscience as particularly significant on its own. Rather, it always has bundled it with complementary concepts from developmental psychology—the two sides of our coin.

Where lower courts have displayed similar openness to juvenile brain science, this is generally how they have done it. Most such cases (and there are not many of them) involve policy-level decisions, such as whether children should be able to claim that they are adjudicatively incompetent by virtue of age-typical immaturity, rather than being limited to arguing only mental illness or other disability (*Timothy J. v. Superior Court*, 2007). Importantly, these courts also have regarded neuroscience as only one source of relevant data. In several cases, the science is literally presented as an item on a list of reasons why the judge thinks as she does—reason three of eight for wanting to require an interested adult at juvenile interrogations (*In re Jerrell C.J.*, 2005), say, or reason four of five to invalidate extension of a sex-offender registry scheme to children (*In re Louis A.*, 2008). In all cases, the brain science is addressed in combination with complementary psychological findings.

So adolescent brain science has not revolutionized juvenile justice. But it does seem to have played a marginal role in helping some courts—including the Supreme Court—acknowledge developmental truths that matter at the 10,000-foot level. Moreover, some legislatures have responded in precisely the same way. Washington State partly justified its abolition of mandatory sentencing of juveniles convicted as adults by reference to that science (Wash. Rev. Code Ann. § 9.94A.540), and Texas legislators heard neuroscientific testimony before abolishing juvenile life without parole (Hearing on S.B. 839 Before the Comm. on Criminal Justice, 2009 Leg., 81st Sess., Tex. 2009). In neither the courts nor the legislatures does it seem clear that the science was a turning factor; it is far more plausible to conclude that it helped buttress conclusions to which certain judges and lawmakers already were inclined, and that were supported by ample other grounds. As Lawrence Steinberg has noted, perhaps a bit mournfully, "it is highly unlikely that lawmakers are going to rewrite statutes because of a new study of synaptic pruning, myelination, brain activity, or neurotransmission. If only scientists held such sway in our legislatures" (Steinberg, 2009).

We can quibble about the precise dimensions of causality: it's not fully knowable, and in any event is not terribly relevant going forward. What clearly is relevant going forward is that statements about the juvenile brain have rhetorical value. The future of the juvenile brain revolves around that value.

The Future of the Juvenile Brain

The brain is not what we are really talking about when we talk about the juvenile brain. We use the juvenile brain to talk about other things. Adolescent brain science has become a quick, culturally salient way to reference those qualities we think are special about juveniles, such as immaturity, impulsivity, and malleability. The future of the juvenile brain, then, is not really going to be about the juvenile brain either; it's going to be about those qualities. As it turns out, that's what the whole juvenile justice enterprise always has been about anyway. Hence the once and future juvenile brain.

Juvenile Brain Science as a Twenty-First-Century Rhetorical Device

Each of the dramatic US Supreme Court cases that have made clear the arrival of this new era—*Roper, Graham, JDB, Miller*—uses the brain science as a handy, timely bit of verbiage to undergird a bigger point. So too with the lower courts, when they have been open to the science at all.

Placed in a larger context, it is not at all surprising that talk of the juvenile brain has succeeded at this rhetorical level. Criminal law is experiencing a major empirical turn, one that has gained momentum in the last decade. Sentencing decisions, for example, increasingly are being influenced by actuarial risk assessment instruments (Slobogin, 2007). Instead of getting ever tougher on crime, we now talk about getting smart on crime, the smarts being supplied by data on what works—for example, to reduce recidivism. These moves are making significant inroads in juvenile justice. Indeed, they appear to have gotten even further, given the greater room for experimentation the juvenile system historically has made available. Actuarial risk and need assessments presently are used in many jurisdictions to shape juvenile dispositions (www.nysap.us/ provides many examples). As of 2009, Tennessee law has required that all its dispositional programming be evidence-based, grounded in scientific research using at least two separate client samples and demonstrating improvement in client outcomes (T.C.A. 37-5-121, 2007). Industries have sprung up around such moves: a company called Evidence-Based Associates, for example, contracts with state juvenile justice departments to improve youth outcomes while saving costs, by using models that have been validated by research meeting the highest standards of scientific scrutiny.[2]

If one widens the lens even further, it becomes apparent that the empirical turn pervades contemporary legal thought and debate far beyond juvenile and criminal law. Witness the impressive growth of organizations like the Society for Empirical Legal Studies, begun in the mid-2000s and now regularly offering trainings on topics such as advanced causal inference. Even the abortion debate—perhaps the high-water mark for a straight-up values conflict—has come to revolve around competing scientific claims. Women come to regret abortion or they don't; fetuses feel pain or they don't. We no longer simply argue about these things, digging into why we believe them and why we think those beliefs matter. We cite studies. And let's widen that lens even a bit more: we are increasingly a data society. We love Malcolm Gladwell, David Brooks, and anyone who distills and feeds us scientific tidbits that help us frame our experience, to understand our world. Empiricism is the new value. (Of course, we pretend that empiricism is devoid of value—*it's objective science, after all!*—even as we choose to credit only the empiricism that conforms to our values. On that, more in a minute.)

Further, there is a hierarchy of empiricism. We like the social sciences fine, especially if they are quantitative and not qualitative, and especially the rigorous-sounding ones like economics. (If you need proof of this, spend time at any major law school.) But we like the hard sciences best, and of those we might like brain science best of all. As a culture we are presently so enamored of brain science that ordinary people unduly credit neuroscientific explanations, even patently bad ones (McCabe & Castel, 2008; Weisberg et al., 2008). Scholars and advocates have openly embraced this hierarchy, privileging brain science in large part because it lends a hard-science edge to behavioral findings that might otherwise be dismissed as "soft" (Aronson, 2007, at 133).

All of this adds up to the juvenile brain as potent rhetorical device. It's current, fresh, even cool and fun. It fits nicely into contemporary schemes for thinking about justice policy. It has a concrete relationship to relevant policy considerations: immaturity and growth, vulnerability and potential. And it has achieved sufficient cultural penetration to reliably evoke that cluster of juvenile attributes with a minimum of words. (I have seen this play out many, many times at conferences, in meetings, and in the classroom; all a speaker has to do is say something along the lines of "We know the juvenile brain is still developing," and the satisfied nods of recognition and approval begin. No more need be said. In fact, for some of the reasons I discuss below, it's often most effective if no more is said: details reveal devils.) Indeed, a mention now seems positively de rigueur; it's hard to imagine saying something big about juveniles without at least uttering the word "brain."

Well, good for adolescent brain science. Evidence and data matter. Particularly in an area that can be marked by foolish folk wisdom and irrational policy choices, there are worse things with which to be aligned. Rhetoric matters, too: that's why, when it doesn't, we tag it with the descriptor "empty." Why else would Aristotle have thought so hard about it, and why do we still care what he had to say? So if periodic shout-outs to the juvenile brain remind us of first principles, it is a useful meme.

Juvenile Brain Science as Only a Rhetorical Device (and an Imperfect One at That)

The empirical and hard-science turns in our culture help explain why adolescent brain science has succeeded as rhetorical device. Other reasons show why that is the only level at which it *can* succeed, at least for now (and likely for some time to come)—and why even at that level it is far from perfect.

The meme works only at the 10,000-foot policy level, because the science yields conclusions that are valid only at that level. As the scientists themselves have taken pains to point out, the current generation of studies shows only group trends (Casey et al., 2008). While all humans will pass through the same basic stages of structural maturation at more or less the same stages of life, the timing and manner in which they do so will vary (Steinberg & Schwartz, 2000). Further, while functional capacity will in some way track structural maturation, we do not yet have a firm grip (or anything close to it) on that relationship (Casey et al., 2008;

Phelps & Thomas, 2003). Neither structural nor functional imaging can determine whether any given individual has a mature brain, and this is likely to be the case for quite some time. Thus, the bind in which the juvenile defendant sometimes finds herself. If she presents only general findings (which would be the most scientifically accurate approach), they can seem at best marginally relevant to a highly individualized determination, such as formation of *mens rea*. But if she tries to individualize those findings, there is no valid scientific mechanism for doing so. No MRI or fMRI report could validly be interpreted so as to reveal something meaningful about her position on a normal maturational trajectory; for that she must call on the old standbys, behavioral and psychiatric evaluation. Without some policy-level determination to which general juvenile traits are relevant, her age-typical brain claim falls between two chairs.

Further, in several discrete ways the juvenile-brain meme doesn't work so well at the 10,000-foot level either.

First, the studies reliably indicate that the described developmental trends extend into early adulthood, with full structural maturity likely in place by one's mid-twenties. Depressingly, other structural changes (of the "declining" variety) appear to kick in around one's mid-to-late forties. If neuroscience is the proper benchmark, perhaps the criminal justice system should systematically recognize the brain deficiencies of both young adults and the elderly. Despite some academic rumblings about extending juvenile-like solicitude to "emerging adults," this is not a battle the advocacy community appears to relish. It is left having to assert that all line-drawing is arbitrary, and that 18 is a reasonable guess as to when most people will have crossed an important developmental threshold even though they will continue to mature significantly. That's a good guess, and it may well be true. But it's interpreting the science to fit our social and legal reality, one in which we've decided to regard 18 as an important turning point. That collective decision, not the science, is what trumps.

A similar point can be made about gender and race implications. Boys and girls have different trajectories for structural maturation, likely linked to pubertal onset. Girls, on average, experience not only earlier puberty but also earlier second-wave neural exuberance. They show such exuberance at least a year before boys, particularly in the frontal lobes (Brizendine, 2006; Giedd et al., 1999). Add the idea of having boys and girls age in and out of juvenile-court jurisdiction at different times to the list of arguments juvenile advocates will *not* be making. Further, it is not hard to imagine race-level findings in the near future, given the well-documented fact that African American girls tend to begin puberty much earlier than white American girls (Dahl, 2004). To conform to legal and moral norms, any argument for law to track developmental neuroscience must demonstrate why unequal treatment that aligns with known gender and race differentials at the scientific level is not its logical outcome. And the only way to do so is to concede that the science must sometimes give way to other values.

Second, using brain development as the metric by which to dole out legal rights and protections could be—and has been—understood to threaten juvenile autonomy. Justice Scalia brought this issue front and center in his *Roper* dissent. He noticed, accurately, that the American Psychological Association had taken what appeared to be a rather different stance on adolescent capacity in an earlier amicus brief submitted on behalf of juveniles seeking to choose abortion without parental consent (*Hodgson v. Minnesota*, 1990). In that case the APA had asserted that teens had the moral reasoning skills and other internal resources to make that decision on their own. Much academic ink has now been spilled demonstrating how the APA's assertions can be harmonized: the state can, does, and should distinguish between the competence necessary to make certain critical choices about one's fate, and the relative moral blameworthiness and capacity for change that justifies differential treatment when accused of a crime (Steinberg et al., 2009; Mutcherson, 2006). But simple messages about brain immaturity make it harder to explain such complicated and contingent claims about autonomy. Scalia may have been too harsh on the APA, but his is not an idle concern. One prominent expert, frequently called to testify about these issues, has stated on the stand that he would be hesitant to let a 16-year-old decide to forego cancer treatment, specifically because of that child's brain immaturity. A California judge, in removing an infant from the custody of its 22-year-old father, opined that the father's brain would not be fully developed—and that he therefore would be an inadequate parent—until age 26 (*In re D.L.*, 2009). Imagine had the father been seventeen.

There are no simple answers to when teens deserve and can handle the right to direct the many aspects of their lives. Brain science appears (wrongly) to offer far too simple an answer, one that points away from autonomy. This is especially so when advocates and the media indulge (as they sometimes do) in blunt, materialist, even deterministic claims—for example, that "science tells us" that older children and teens can't control their emotions, make rational decisions, be deterred, or form a culpable *mens rea*. If that were true, we'd barely let them out of our houses, ever. I'm put in mind of a *New Yorker* cartoon in which a father tells his son, "Young man, go to your room and stay there until your cerebral cortex matures."

Brain science therefore does not answer a lot of the hardest questions in juvenile justice. It didn't create them—line-drawing, for example, has always been hard to justify theoretically—so perhaps that is not a fair criticism. But in some respects it has further muddied the waters. And the very simplicity of the meme, if one does not dive into the messy underlying studies and data and interpretations and open questions, does its own damage by suggesting that the science's implications are more straightforward than they are. Which, of course, seems like a very big problem indeed if one does not like the implied, straightforward conclusion—such as, "teenagers are incompetent at most important things."

A third and final flaw in the brain-as-meme story comes from confirmation bias; that is, the strong human tendency to filter factual assertions, including scientific ones, through our prior beliefs, values, and commitments (Kahan et al., 2009). We tend to accept evidence as relevant and plausible where it aligns with implicit views and judgments and to reject it when it does not. This simple reality means that the rhetorical value of juvenile-brain talk will vary considerably depending to whom it is directed. Put yourself back in the conferences, meetings, and classrooms I evoked earlier. Take out whomever you had imagined in those rooms (in my world that would be defenders, social workers, relatively liberal students, and the like) and repopulate them with groups of prosecutors. Better yet, let's make them prosecutors charged with trying juveniles transferred into adult court for very serious crimes, and police officers on a violent youth gang task force. When the speaker says "the juvenile brain is still developing," you may not see approving nods; you may instead see brows furrowing and arms crossing in front of chests. Legal actors evaluate brain science through implicit political, cultural, or role-based perspectives that predispose them to favor or disfavor juveniles' claims.

This bias confines even the rhetorical potential of adolescent brain science, as it is likely to be understood so as to support conclusions to which one already is inclined. The real task, then, is to influence beliefs, values, and inclinations directly rather than expect such influence to flow naturally from invoking the meme.

Which is what we have always been about in juvenile justice. Brain science may have given us a handy, quick way to communicate what we are about with people who either do (or are inclined to) agree with us. It probably has moved a few people, even a few very important people, further into that space. It has deepened our collective understanding of juvenile thought patterns and behaviors. It has not relieved us of the duty to keep talking—constantly—about the larger universe of reasons for giving juveniles special treatment. We can feed the desire for an empirically validated evidence base by, for example, continuing to trumpet data showing that transfer to adult court increases recidivism (Fagan, 1996; Redding, 2008); that many transferred youth are accused of property crimes (Deitch et al., 2009); that very few juvenile sex offenders become adult sex offenders, even if left untreated (Zimring, 2004); and that incarceration with adults frequently leads to physical and sexual abuse (Campaign for Youth Justice, 2007). We can continue to recognize that our juvenile policy choices are driven by a complex constellation of values and concerns that go far beyond diminished culpability and increased rehabilitative potential. These choices are also about availability and allocation of resources; political will; and the complementary capacities of other systems of child supervision and control, such as schools, medical and mental health facilities, child welfare agencies, neighborhoods, faith communities, and families. We care about addictions and gangs and poverty. We care about the availability and lethality of firearms. As the Court's decision to distinguish between homicide and nonhomicide crimes in *Graham* made clear, we also care about the harms that juveniles cause, and the victims they create. In short, juvenile justice cares about all the factors that make a kid's life what it is, and the impact that life has on others. The more parts of that life we add in, the less useful brain-talk feels.

Our talk about the juvenile brain therefore needs to settle into where those brains actually live: inside of juvenile skulls, on top of juvenile bodies—bodies that live in homes and have families; bodies that go to school, engage in activities, and have friends, needs, and desires; and bodies that live in societies and are surrounded by possibilities, limitations, and expectations.

Conclusion

Every generation must articulate what is special about juveniles in the language that speaks to that generation. Channeling our complex constellation of values through the prism of brain science makes a lot of sense for this new era: it takes what we long have known about juveniles and anchors it to a salient cultural narrative about the possibilities of empiricism, grounds it in the comfort and certainty we seek in science. It allows us to deploy early twentieth-century ideas in an early twenty-first-century package. But we need to know that one day—and likely soon—aspects of that package will seem as dated and misguided as did earlier ones. I've pointed out some such aspects that are in plain view right now. Together they counsel us to ease up on the rhetoric, to know what it's good for and what it's not, and to be prepared to articulate directly the core values it is meant to evoke.

In the future, perhaps we'll get more out of juvenile brain science. New studies continue to proliferate, and growth on the functional side is particularly robust. A lot of very smart people are continuing to elaborate the various ways in which law and neuroscience interact: witness the MacArthur Foundation's $10 million commitment to a research network, within which juvenile issues will continue to get some attention. The most realistic prediction is that developmental neuroscience will continue to offer more and better ways of detecting and understanding children's abnormalities, such as mental illness, addiction, and organic damage. This would be useful to a subset of juveniles, and such tools would nicely advance our present approaches to diagnosis and treatment.

But what about the science that is relevant to the typical juvenile? As a cultural observer of and participant in the juvenile advocacy world, I get the distinct sense that no one is paying much attention any more. I detect a feeling that we have gotten what we need. We might not even *want* to know more. After all, what if we did develop a sound method for placing an individual child's brain on a maturational trajectory—couldn't that be used to justify harsher treatment of kids who are unusually mature, just as surely as for the benefit of the unusually *im*mature? Might not the unusually immature be harmed as well, if that evidence were used to justify greater use of incapacitative controls rather than increased support? Perhaps advocates are better off if all juveniles get the benefit of presumed immaturity relative to adults, and we just leave it at that without poking around too much.

Similarly, what if functional studies eventually show few or no relevant behavioral correlates to the structural differences on which we've leaned so hard? Perhaps we would discover that juveniles get to mental and physical outcomes through different routes, but end up with similar levels of control over and competence at the things about which law cares.

As a general rule, I think, we should not enter the science game unless we really want to know the answers and are prepared to live with them. But we are in this game already. So we have to keep paying attention, and not lock ourselves into simplistic narratives from which we later will have to distance ourselves.

So now that I have stripped the juvenile brain science era of its title no sooner than I nominated it, the task remains to come up with a new contender. This contender would preferably have none of the be-careful-what-you-wish-for downsides I've identified, and would orient us toward a broader universe of juvenile concerns. I recently posed this challenge to my students on their final examination. I received a number of strong contenders, mostly along the "kids are different" theme. But one student, I think, captured the task of this new era and the spirit with which we must meet it.[3] She analogized the last part of the twentieth century to an earthquake. In her words, we "shook the very foundations of our juvenile system. Now, here we are in 2012, recovering from this earthquake, trying to rebuild some of the protections for children" that were the rock on which the system was built. She therefore proposed that we call our new era the rebuilding.

The rebuilding era. I like it. It's concrete, simultaneously realistic (damage has been done) and ambitious (we can always rebuild something better than what we tore down). I'm going with it. The juvenile brain has a role to play in this rebuilding process, most of which it's probably played already. The rest of the task calls for different tools. Let's use them all to keep building this new world, one in which all children have adequate opportunities to reach their potential, no matter what they have done.

NOTES

1. A number of the ideas explored in this chapter are discussed in far greater detail in Terry A. Maroney, *The False Promise of Adolescent Brain Science in Juvenile Justice*, 85 Notre Dame L. Rev. 89 (2009), and Terry A. Maroney, *Adolescent Brain Science after* Graham v. Florida, 86 Notre Dame L. Rev. 765 (2011).

2. See the website for Evidence-Based Associates at www.evidencebasedassociates.com/the_difference/evidence-based_programs.html.
3. My wonderful student's name is Alessandra (Alee) Pagnotti. If you like her nomination, please use it liberally; and if you ever run across her, please hire her.

REFERENCES

Action for Children. "Putting the Juvenile Back in Juvenile Justice." *Juvenile Justice Issue Brief* (Raleigh, NC: Action for Children NC, December 2007).

Allstate Insurance Company. Advertisement, *Why Do Most 16-Year-Olds Drive Like They're Missing A Part of Their Brain? Because They Are.* www.allstate.com/content/refresh-attachments/Brain-Ad.pdf (2010).

American Prosecutors Research Institute. *A Prosecutor's Guide To Psychological Evaluations And Competency Challenges In Juvenile Court* (Alexandria, VA: 2006).

Aronson, Jay D. "Brain Imaging, Culpability and the Juvenile Death Penalty." 13 *Psychology, Public Policy, and Law.* 13 (2007): 115–142.

Baird, Abigail, et al. "Functional Magnetic Resonance Imaging of Facial Affect Recognition in Children and Adolescents." *Journal of the American Academy of Child and Adolescent Psychiatry* 38 (1999): 195–199.

Baird, Abigail and Jonathan A. Fugelsang. *The Emergence of Consequential Thought: Evidence from Neuroscience,"* In Zeki, Semir and Oliver Goodenough, eds. *Law & the Brain.* (New York: Oxford University Press: 2004): 245-258.

Begley, Sharon. "Getting Inside a Teen Brain." *Newsweek* (February 28, 2000): 58–59.

Beschle, Donald L. "Cognitive Dissonance Revisited: *Roper v. Simmons* and the Issue of Adolescent Decision-Making Competence." *Wayne Law Review* 52 (2006): 1–42.

Blakemore, Sarah-Jayne. "Imaging Brain Development: The Adolescent Brain." *Neuroimage* 61 (2012): 397–406.

Boyle, Patrick. "Behind the Death Penalty Ban: Supreme Court Decision Caps State-by-State Combat by Unusual Coalition." *Youth Today* (April 2005), 1–39.

Bradley, Michael J. *Yes, Your Teen Is Crazy!* (Gig Harbor, WA: Harbor Press, 2002).

Brizendine, Louann. *The Female Brain* (New York: Broadway Books, 2006), 31–56.

Brooks, David. *The Social Animal: The Hidden Sources of Love, Character, and Achievement* (New York: Random House, 2012).

Buss, Emily. "Rethinking the Connection Between Developmental Science and Juvenile Justice." *University of Chicago Law Review* 76, no. 493 (2009), 499–506.

Campaign for Youth Justice, Jailing Juveniles 13 (2007). www.campaign4youthjustice.org/Downloads/NationalReportsArticles/CFYJ-Jailing_Juveniles_Report_2007-11-15.pdf.

Casey, B. J., et al. "The Adolescent Brain." *Annals of the New York Academy of Sciences* 1124 (2008), 111–122.

Dahl, Ronald E. "Adolescent Brain Development: A Period of Vulnerabilities and Opportunities." *Annals of the New York Academy of Sciences* 1021 (2004): 1–22.

Deitch, Michele, et.al. *From Time Out to Hard Time: Young Children in the Adult Criminal Justice System.* (Austin, TX: The University of Texas at Austin, LBJ School of Public Affairs, 2009).

DiIulio, Jr,. John. J. "The Coming of the Super-Predators." *Weekly Standard* (November, 23, 1995): 23–28.

Fagan, Jeffrey. "The Comparative Advantage of Juvenile Versus Criminal Court Sanctions on Recidivism among Adolescent Felony Offenders." *Law & Policy* 18 (1996): 77–114.

Fagan, Jeffrey. "*Atkins*, Adolescence and the Maturity Heuristic: Rationales for the Categorical Exemption For Juveniles from Capital Punishment." *New Mexico Law Review* 33 (2003): 207–254.

Feld, Barry C. "Competence, Culpability and Punishment: Implications of Atkins for Executing and Sentencing Adolescents." *Hofstra Law Revew* 32 (2003): 463–552a.

Gazzaniga, Michael S., ed. *The Cognitive Neurosciences III.* (Cambridge: MIT Press, 2004).

Giedd, J.N., et al. "Brain Development During Childhood and Adolescence: A Longitudinal MRI Study." *Nature Neuroscience* 2 (1999): 861–862.

Gladwell, Malcolm. *Blink: The Power of Thinking Without Thinking.* (New York: Back Bay Books, 2005).

Gogtay, N., et al. "Dynamic Mapping of Human Cortical Development during Childhood through Early Adulthood." *Proceedings of the National Academy of Sciences* 101 (2004): 8174–8179.

Graham v. Florida, 560 U.S. 48 (2010).

Grisso, Thomas and Robert G. Schwartz, eds. *Youth on Trial: Developmental Perspectives on Juvenile Justice.* (Chicago: University of Chicago Press, 2000).

Hearing on Adolescent Brain Development and Juvenile Justice Before the Subcom. on Healthy Families and Communities of the S. Comm. on Education and Labor and the Subcomm. on Crime, Terrorism, and Homeland Security of the S. Comm. on the Judiciary. 110th Congress (2007).

Henderson, Wendy Paget. "Life after *Roper*: Using Adolescent Brain Science in Court." *Children's Rights* 11 (Fall/Winter 2009): 1–7.

Hodgson v. Minnesota, 497 U.S. 417 (1990).

In re D.L., No. B205263, 2009 WL 43513, at *3–4 (Cal. Ct. App. Jan. 8, 2009).

In re Jerrell C.J., 699 N.W.2d 110, 139–40 (Wis. 2005).

In re Louis A., Nos. 51676–51696, slip op. at *2 (Nev. Sep 5, 2008).

J.D.B. v. North Carolina, 131 S.Ct. 2394 (2011).

Kahan, Dan M., et al. "Whose Eyes Are You Going to Believe? Scott v. Harris and the Perils of Cognitive Illiberalism." *Harvard Law Review* 122 (2009): 837–906.

Levick, Marsha. "From a Trilogy to a Quadrilogy: Miller v. Alabama Makes It Four in a Row For U.S. Supreme Court Cases That Support Differential Treatment of Youth." *BNA Criminal Law Reporter* 98 (September 12, 2012): 1–8.

Maroney, Terry A. "Adolescent Brain Science after *Graham v. Florida*." *Notre Dame Law Review* 86 (2011): 765–793.

Maroney, Terry A. "The False Promise of Adolescent Brain Science in Juvenile Justice." *Notre Dame Law Review* 85 (2009): 89–176.

McCabe, David and Alan Castel. "Seeing is Believing: The Effect of Brain Images on Judgments of Scientific Reasoning." *Cognition* 107 (2008): 343–352.

McGowan, Angela, et al. "Task Force on Community Preventive Services, Effects of Violence on Laws and Policies Facilitating the Transfer of Juveniles from the Juvenile Justice System to the Adult Justice System: A Systematic Review." *American Journal of Preventative Medicine* 32 (2007): S7–S28.

Miller v. Alabama, 132 S.Ct. 2455 (2012).

Mutcherson, Kimberly M. "Minor Discrepancies: Forging a Common Understanding of Adolescent Competence in Healthcare Decision-Making and Criminal Responsibility." 6 *Nevada Law Journal* 6 (2006): 927–965.

National District Attorneys Association. Course Schedule. (October 2007–March 2008). www.ndaa.org/pdf/nac_course_schedule_oct_07_mar_08.pdf.

National Juvenile Justice Prosecution Center. Two Training Opportunities. (May 2004). http://web.archive.org/web/20071112113393/www.ndaa.org/apri/programs/juvenile/inre_express_april_2004.html.

Paus, T., et al. "Structural Maturation of Neural Pathways in Children and Adolescents: In Vivo Study." *Science* 283 (1999): 1908–1911.

Phelps, Elizabeth A. and Laura A. Thomas. "Race, Behavior, and the Brain: The Role of Neuroimaging in Understanding Complex Social Behaviors." *Political Psychology* 24 (2003): 747–758.

Pinker, Steven. "My Genome, My Self." *New York Times Magazine* (January 11, 2009): 24–29.

Redding, Richard E. "Juvenile Transfer Laws: An Effective Deterrent to Delinquency?" *Juvenile Justice Bulletin.* (Washington, DC: Office of Juvenile Justice and Delinquency Prevention, US Dept. of Justice, August 2008). www.ncjrs.gov/pdffiles1/ojjdp/220595.pdf.

Roper v. Simmons, 543 U.S. 551 (2005).

Rosenheim, Margaret K., et al. eds. *A Century of Juvenile Justice.* (Chicago: University of Chicago Press, 2002).

Sabbagh, Leslie. "The Teen Brain, Hard at Work (No, Really)." *Scientific American Mind* (August/September 2006): 20–25.

Scott, Elizabeth S. and Laurence Steinberg, "Blaming Youth." *Texas Law Review* 81 (2003): 799–840.

Scott, Elizabeth S. and Laurence Steinberg, *Rethinking Juvenile Justice.* (Cambridge: Harvard University Press, 2008).

Shepherd, Jr., Robert E. "*Malvo* Closing Argument." *Criminal Justice* 19 (2004): 73, 76.

Slobogin, Christopher. *Proving the Unprovable: The Role of Law, Science, and Speculation in Adjudicating Culpability and Dangerousness.* (New York: Oxford University Press, 2007).

Sowell, E., et al. "In Vivo Evidence for Post-Adolescent Brain Maturation in Frontal and Striatal Regions." *Nature Neuroscience* 2 (1999): 859, 860–861.

Spear, Linda Patia. "Adolescent Brain Development and Animal Models." *Annals of the New York Academy of Sciences* 1021 (2004): 23–26.
Spear, Linda Patia. "The Adolescent Brain and Age-Related Behavioral Manifestations." *Neuroscience & Biobehavioral Revs.* 24 (2000): 417–463.
Spinks, Sarah. "Adolescent Brains Are Works in Progress." *PBS Frontline* (January 2002). www.pbs.org/wgbh/pages/frontline/shows/teenbrain/work/adolescent.html.
State v. Garcia, CR 2005-422 (N.M. Dist. Co. Dec. 14, 2007).
State v. Heinemann, 920 A.2d 278 (Conn. 2007).
State v. Jones, No. 9911016309, 2005 WL 950122 (Del. Super. Ct. Apr. 10, 2005).
State v. Ninham, 767 N.W.2d 326 (Wis. Ct. App. 2009).
State v. Pittman, 647 S.E.2d 144, 163 (S.C. 2007).
State v. Torres, No. 2 CA-CR 2009-0302-PR, 2010 WL 715994, at *1–2 (Ariz. Ct. App. Mar. 1, 2010).
Steinberg, Laurence, et al. "Are Adolescents Less Mature Than Adults? Minors' Access to Abortion, the Juvenile Death Penalty, and the Alleged APA 'Flip-Flop.'" *American Psychologist* 64 (2009): 583–594.
Steinberg, Laurence and Elizabeth S. Scott. "Less Guilty by Reason of Adolescence: Developmental Immaturity, Diminished Responsibility, and the Juvenile Death Penalty." *American Psychologist* 58 (2003): 1–10.
Strauch, Barbara. *The Primal Teen*. (New York: Anchor Books, 2003).
Tanenhaus, David S. *Juvenile Justice in the Making*. (New York: Oxford University Press, 2004).
Timothy J. v. Superior Court, 58 Cal. Rptr. 3d 746, 754 (Cal. Ct. App. 2007).
Wallis, Claudia. "What Makes Teens Tick?" *Time Magazine* (May 10, 2004): 56–65.
Walsh, David. "*Why* Do They Act That Way?" (New York: Free Press, 2004).
Weisberg, Deena Skolnick, et al. "The Seductive Allure of Neuroscience Explanations." *Journal of Cognitive Neuroscience* 20 (2008): 470–477.
Wisconsin Council on Children & Families, Rethinking the Juvenile in Juvenile Justice 4 (2006).
Zeki, Semir and Oliver R. Goodenough. "'*Introduction*' to Law and the Brain." (New York: Oxford University Press, 2006): xi, xiii–xiv.
Zimring, Franklin E. *American Juvenile Justice*. (New York: Oxford University Press, 2005).
Zimring, Franklin E. *An American Travesty: Legal Responses to Adolescent Sexual Offending*. (Chicago: University of Chicago Press, 2004).

10

On Strategy and Tactics for Contemporary Reforms

FRANKLIN E. ZIMRING AND DAVID S. TANENHAUS

The previous chapters have produced a persuasively argued agenda for changes in laws and institutions that will reduce many burdens of adolescent development and improve the life chances of the adults our children become. The shopping list for change is easy to construct:

- The 1990s shift toward prosecutorial dominance and administrative control of transfer to criminal court should be reversed.
- Secondary schools should be demilitarized, and educational reentry programs and opportunities should be as much an emphasis as dropout prevention.
- Juvenile courts can best serve educational goals for high-risk youth by using sanction policies that keep kids in communities and minimizing secure confinement. But providing quality education in secure youth settings must also be a priority.
- The extension of sex offender registration requirements to juvenile offenders is punitive, pointless, and provides no community protection or investigatory assistance to law enforcement. The federal mandate of the Amie Zyla law should be removed without qualification or any substitute strategy. Juvenile sex offense records only became useful when corroborated by adult sex violations.
- A critical area for reform is the criminal record information involving young persons. The trend toward the compromise of the privacy of traditional juvenile court delinquency proceedings should be rethought, and qualified by rules designed to remove public records once sustained periods of offense free behavior had separated a juvenile offense from the adult career it threatens to stigmatize. But controls on juvenile arrest records are also necessary.

- The juvenile court's commitment to the welfare of all the young persons subject to its jurisdiction extends as well to young persons without immigration documentation. The juvenile court cannot become a branch of the national government's immigration policing without violating its own distinctive mission. And court policy toward immigrant youth should be designed to minimize harmful immigration consequences.
- The trend in recent policy to increase the collateral consequences of juvenile adjudications is a critical battleground for regaining the protections that the juvenile court provides from stigma and permanent disadvantage. Increasing the breadth and duration of collateral consequences increases the negative effects of disseminating juvenile record information and of disproportionate overrepresentation of minorities. Reducing collateral consequences thus becomes a priority method of reducing the stigma and the disadvantage to minorities of juvenile justice exposure.

That shopping list of law reforms is one important product of this volume. There is, however, a world of difference between a shopping list and a pantry full of groceries. Even a detailed and well-articulated agenda of reform proposals stops well short of improving anyone's life chances. The central task of juvenile law reform and the central topic of this concluding chapter is identifying the proper places in government where changes need to take place and listing some of the political and institutional developments that can make changes possible.

Our survey of the means to reform the legal world of adolescent development is divided into a discussion of the governmental structures and institutions that determine policies toward young persons and an analysis of the institutional, political, and public attitudes that influence policy. The governmental structures we discuss in Part A are the hardware for governing juvenile justice and education. The attitudes and values discussed in Part B are the software that will motivate and sustain reforms. The final section of this chapter will address some of the leading indicators of future directions for juvenile justice.

A. Government Structures and Juvenile Justice

A precondition to creating change in juvenile justice policy is locating the places in the governmental structure where policies are determined.

First, there are issues about which *level of government* in the United States federal system determines policy—federal, state, or local. Within each distinct level of government there is commonly a division into separate *branches of government*—the common terms here are the legislative, executive, and judicial branches. And then within the branches of government, there are importantly different functional departments. Particularly within the executive branch of each level of American government, there will usually be very different functional departments that govern the young—the board of education, the police, the prosecutor, and the health department may all be situated in the executive branch of local government, but these departments will have quite different priorities and powers in juvenile justice policy.

Usually, the first question the would-be reformer needs to ask about a policy she wishes to change is what level, branch, and department of government has traditional power to control the policy that should be changed. The path of least resistance to policy change will often be found in the traditional place where policy has been made.

National Government

For law professors as a general rule and students of juvenile justice in particular, the tendencies when searching for the places to launch reform have been hierarchical and judicentric. We push reform campaigns to the national government first and see the US Supreme Court as a primary institutional actor. The national government is an attractive target because it is the center of more power than lower levels of government—so the scale of reforms with federal scope is quite large. Most legal academics will think first about the judicial system as the best opportunity for rights-based reform. The law professor's paradigm case of a federal level judicial decision generating substantial systemic change on a national scale is *In Re Gault* in 1967. No judicial decision at any level of government had anywhere near the impact of *Gault* in the 115-year history of the juvenile court. Indeed, only one other modern juvenile US Supreme Court decision had any substantial practical impact on the penal liability of offenders under 18, and that was *Roper v. Simmons* in 2005, holding that the Eighth Amendment prohibits the death penalty for crimes committed prior to the eighteenth birthday. The other successful attempts to use the

US Constitution to restrict penal excesses on young offender cases like *In re Winship* (1970), *Graham v. Florida* (2010), and *Miller v. Alabama* (2012) did not have much significant operational impact on juvenile or criminal justice. These cases sent important signals out to other branches and levels of government that diminished responsibility was a significant legal principle for younger offenders (and this we will mention in the next section), but the Supreme Court has been more than reluctant to use constitutional doctrine to make structural changes in juvenile justice. *Schall v. Martin* (1984) is the most explicit example of this reluctance, and there have been no strong indications that the current court is less cautious.

The rest of the national government is not deeply concerned with youth crime or juvenile justice. The federal office established in the late 1970s, the Office of Juvenile Justice and Delinquency Prevention (OJJDP), is both underfunded and a low priority in the executive branch. The two federal initiatives that this book has identified as hot topics for reform efforts (sex and immigration) are both governmental activities not centered in juvenile justice that threaten both the youth before the court and the court's mission. Federal immigration enforcement threatens to create an adversarial relationship between the court and undocumented juveniles in any of its traditional jurisdictional categories—abuse and neglect, dependence and delinquency. The extension of registration requirement standards to some juvenile sex offenders was a policy spillover in the Adam Walsh Act's crusade against older sex offenders.

The best strategy for juvenile damage control in these collateral damage categories is to mobilize youth welfare lobbies and organizations to create special exemptions for minors in the administration of immigration detection programs (involving both arrest and juvenile courts in immigration) and federal standards for sex offender registration. For sex offender registration some legislative changes will also be necessary, but the federal juvenile offender standards in the 2006 act are unpopular with state governments and may be vulnerable to the kind of reexamination that would best protect young offenders.

The other major involvement of federal policy is an extensive financial and regulatory relationship to education and school governance. Here juvenile justice interest groups can and should become interested and outspoken in reducing police presence in schools and the deemphasis of security in favor of educational priorities. Shifting power back to teachers and away from law enforcement interests and authority can generate common ground between youth welfare groups and both teachers' organizations and school administrators. And support for both alternative secondary schools and federal support for reentry programs and institutions will serve the core interests of at-risk kids. Another tactic for generating at-risk youth friendly federal education policies would be to create a program in OJJDP that focuses on secondary school policies and coordinates with the federal Department of Education.

State Government

The three branches of government in the 50 states are the legislative home of juvenile justice, and often the administrative headquarters for correctional institutions for young offenders and funding for most youth services. The first juvenile court was produced by state legislation in 1899, and the juvenile or family courts of every state are always still the creatures of state legislative invention. All of the rules governing court organization, jurisdiction, sanctions, transfer to criminal courts, funding purposes, and limits are state legislative products. So the first stop in any effort to change the structure and function of juvenile courts is the front door of the state legislature. State administrative agencies located in the executive branch often control institutions that house young offenders and services to many different classes of at-risk youth.

This makes state government not only the place where the rules of juvenile justice are to be found, but also the central focus for efforts to change the laws. Thus the role of the state legislature in juvenile justice is not only foundational, but also dynamic. Thumb through any of the catalogs of legislative change in the 1990s in criteria and procedure for transfer of charges from juvenile to criminal court and note that their footnotes cite almost nothing but state legislation.

So the state legislature is the center of the *action* on changes in juvenile court law, but that is not quite the same as concluding that the state legislature is the sole center of *power* in drafting and passing juvenile justice legislation. Among the many interest groups that consistently try to influence state juvenile court legislation are the people who work in juvenile courts—judges, probation staff, and prosecutors. These local actors—individually or in statewide lobby organizations—bring political power into the legislative arena and also bring legal expertise. The state legislatures constrained by low budgets for staff and term limits for legislators often will lack the technical expertise to draft the legislation they need to consider. As seen in the wave of transfer legal changes discussed in Chapter 2, the detailed legislation passed at the state level was often drafted by local prosecutors (we know of no term limit provisions governing local prosecutors in the United States).

The local level of government is critical to the determination of policy in juvenile justice for two reasons. The first is that the substantive legal principles that govern policing, prosecuting, judging, and sanctioning juvenile offenders invests local actors with vast discretion. Because discretion is the secular religion of American juvenile justice, decisions concentrated at the operating levels of the system play a defining role in determining outcomes. The second reason why local system actors influence policy is that they are the most important interest groups that write the state legislative standards. Discretion means that local actors make the rules that govern case disposition. The collective power of local officials also means that local actors can change the rules at the state level early and often.

But the power of local actors to influence change at the state or national level is easy to underestimate, because local actors seem so, well, *local*. The assumptions and rhetoric of juvenile justice reformers tends to be trickle-down, using the federal government as a focus, or large states. The smaller scale of local actions seems a less efficient method of producing change, but that assumption has not been tested. If sentiments change at the local level in a wide variety of different places, a trickle-up reform strategy might also achieve widespread progress. The scale of any county-level effort is of course much smaller than national or statewide campaigns, but successful grassroots organization might provoke imitation.

Impediments to Reform

Chapter 1's discussion of the rise and fall of youth violence rates in the late 1980s and 1990s noted an asymmetrical pattern of legal reactions to shifts in rates of youth homicide. The sharp increase in youth violence produced a wave of legislative changes designed to increase the power of prosecutors to transfer juvenile defendants to criminal courts and full-scale criminal punishments. The sharp and sustained reduction in youth violence had, with very few exceptions, no legislative impacts at either the state or federal levels. If increased public fear produced punitive legislation, why didn't decreased public fear reverse the process?

The sharp decline in rates of violent crime did have politically important effects in the late 1990s and beyond. The fear and anger of earlier years died down, and thus the pressure for new waves of punitive changes abated substantially. But there was almost no reversal or reform of the earlier legislative patterns. And legal changes in two youth-related areas discussed in Part II—immigration and juvenile sex offenders—put young offenders more at risk during the low-crime decade after the turn of the century.

There are three important barriers to reform in contemporary juvenile justice that intelligent advocates must overcome—inertia, vested interests, and the spillover of moral panics not closely tied to adolescent conduct that put young persons at risk almost as an afterthought.

The ubiquitous obstacle to changing back from the legislative pattern of the 1990s is political inertia—the tendency for legal relationships that have settled into new patterns to stay at rest. The reduction in public worry removed pressure for legal change in the late 1990s rather than creating a reverse dynamic. Increased worry creates a dynamic for altering legal relationships, as happened in the early 1990s. Reducing worry turns down the heat so that the pace of new punitive changes is reduced. But public comfort is not a prod to action.

Closely related to the absence of public concern as a barrier to legal change is the vested interests that won major concessions in the legislative changes of the 1990s and are reluctant to give back any of their recently acquired power. Chapter 2 profiles prosecutors in juvenile courts as both the major beneficiaries of the 1990s changes, and frequently the authors of the legislation that brought those changes. The prosecutor who can now transfer a juvenile to criminal court through a direct file without preparing for an elaborate adversarial hearing and facing the necessity of judicial approval will be reluctant to give back these new powers. Just as those who lost power in the 1990s—chiefly judges and probation staff—might wish to get it back, the winners in the process are now vested interests that will resist changes to preserve newly achieved power.

The third substantial barrier to reform is what can be called "incidental jeopardy," the spillover of punitive policies that did not involve juveniles as a primary concern but extend inappropriate outcomes to juveniles as an incidental outcome. The Immigration Customs and Enforcement (ICE) program to use local police and courts as immigration enforcement tools were not designed with either youth or juvenile courts in mind. The sex offender registration and public notification systems that exploded in the 1990s were concerned with offenders and risks far removed from adolescent delinquents. But both programs spilled over into juvenile offender policy. When the criminal justice system sneezes, the juvenile justice system often catches cold.

And this collateral damage from criminal justice crusades is particularly dangerous because the interest groups and agencies that are most concerned with juvenile justice usually don't see the collateral dangers coming. Advocates for youth must think outside the conventional boundaries of the juvenile court in the United States. And because destructive inclusion of young persons in such penal crusades is harder to reverse once it has happened than it is to prevent, youth advocates must develop better peripheral vision for potential youth hazards in the branches of government dealings with education, housing, drug crime policy, and health policy.

B. Toward a Rhetoric of Reform

The juvenile court is a very young institution by the usual standards of Anglo-American jurisprudence, only now in its second century. And yet this Johnny-come-lately of American legal invention is the single most popular American legal invention by civil law nations—such as Italy and France, which have juvenile courts based on the US invention. England and Scotland embraced this invention of a former colony. Egypt has a juvenile court, as does Canada, Chile, and the Ivory Coast. Tajikistan has one of the many juvenile court systems currently operating in Central Asia.

This almost universal popularity of juvenile justice as an idea and governmental activity should be an important phenomenon to explore while looking for the sentiments and concepts that might support reformist activity in the American present and future. Why does everybody support juvenile justice everywhere? How can reformers capture this essence for use in the tug-of-war of the policy reform process?

The Central Appeal: Institution or Mission?

There are two contrasting versions of the essential appeal of juvenile courts. One account we shall call an *institutional* or *capacity* argument—one that supports juvenile courts because these institutions are effective and competent agencies to both protect society and help delinquent kids. Juvenile courts are worth support because they perform expert tasks with special competence. In this view, what makes juvenile courts superior to criminal courts is that they are more successful at changing delinquencies.

The *mission* explanation for the universal popularity of juvenile courts emphasizes the popular support for the mission of the court rather than the court's particular skills at performance. Juvenile courts are supported because the public would rather endorse an institution that wants to protect and help kids than to merely punish them. If is it the mission that sets the court apart from criminal courts, the court for juveniles need not succeed all the time to earn continued priority. Those who embrace the mission priority of juvenile courts are willing to award As for effort even when the courts may fail in individual cases.

It is not difficult to see the way in which the choice of rationale influences the choice of rhetoric. An institutional appeal is about the quality of the judges and treatment staff of the juvenile court. The stars of the show are the professionals and the institution. A mission-centered appeal is about the kids and the obvious superiority of helping them grow up instead of locking them up. The stars of this show are the 14- and 15- and 16-year-old young people and the adults we hope they can become.

A fair reading of history and present circumstances provides overwhelming support for a mission-centered notion of the central appeal of juvenile courts. Indeed, the universal popularity of the concept of juvenile justice *must* rest on that foundation. Could Tajikistan have created a juvenile court because its citizens thought the local judges were treatment professionals? Is it confidence in the judiciary that makes a court for children popular in both Argentina and the People's Republic of China? And what is true for China on the issue of central appeal is also true for Chicago.

A Mission-Centered Rhetoric of Reform

We propose four principles for a mission-centered argument in favor of youth protection:

1. Kids are different.
2. Kids change.
3. Growing up is effective crime control.
4. Juvenile courts are well-suited to the special needs of young offenders.

Three of the four principles concern the human subjects of youth policy rather than state institutions. And the characteristics of children and youths in the first three principles are not limited to the legal rules encountered in juvenile courts, but apply in full measure in other legal contexts.

1. KIDS ARE DIFFERENT

The most obvious principle for a rhetoric of youth protection is also the most important. The entire architecture of the legal systems of the developed world is based on the assumption that children and youth are different from adults. The defining element of legal childhood is immaturity, which is not only assumed to be universal but is also normative. We not only expect kids to be immature, we also desire many aspects of this trait in our children. And this expectation of immaturity extends well into adolescence—why else do we prohibit young persons from buying alcohol until age 21 and consider youthful marriage and childbearing problematic? Sexual capacities happen early in adolescence, but the culture and the legal system want to postpone permanent commitment such as marriage and childbearing well beyond even legal majority. Why? The reproductive equivalent of the slogan "If you're old enough to do the crime, you're old enough to do the time" would be a catastrophe in any developed nation on this planet.

The logical and emotional implication of knowing that kids are different is to reject the assumption of generality for most legal policies. Rules designed for adults should not be assumed to be equally applicable for children and youth. That is of course the foundational principle of juvenile courts all over the world. But the fallacious assumption of generality crops up like a jurisprudential weed in a wide variety of different legal settings—from sex offender registers to immigration enforcement practices.

2. KIDS CHANGE

The venerable climatological joke is that if you don't like the weather in Chicago, just wait 20 minutes. And the reputation of adolescents for changes in mood, taste, behavior, ambitions, and associations is every bit as notorious as that of Chicago. Everybody knows this about their children and the children of their friends. But the essential changeability of young persons is often forgotten in debates about punishment for young offenders. How does this happen? The rhetorical device that Chapter 1 reported from the 1990s was a new vocabulary to describe young persons who commit crime, as if they were a separate (and essentially non-adolescent) species. The boy is a "chronic offender" (Wolfgang, Figlio, and Sellin 1972) or "life course persistent" offender (Moffitt 1993); boys are "young muggers, killers, and thieves" (Wilson 1995), and, finally, in the immortal phrase of John DiIulio, "juvenile superpredators" on the streets (DiIulio 1996), but he is not the teenager in your house or down the street growing and changing with each new day.

The strategic importance of imagining that young persons who commit crimes are not changeable is that immutable dangerousness can then justify drastic penal isolation. If the superpredator will not change, there might be no alternative for social defense to incapacitation. The high point of this species of negative magical thinking about adolescent offenders was life imprisonment without possibility of parole for 14-, 15- and 16-year-old offenders, sanctions that were sufficiently outrageous to push the United States Supreme Court to strike down such prison sentences as cruel and unusual punishment—the first time in a generation that a cautious Supreme Court struck down sentences of imprisonment as a violation of the Eighth Amendment. What made these punishments particularly obscene was the assumption that 14-year-olds can never change.

The capacity that all kids have to change values and behaviors and capacity for self-control are a powerful argument for second and third and fourth chances. The changeability of kids has policy implications discussed in earlier chapters. Close empirical study of the later careers of juvenile sex offenders (see Chapter 3) confirm what we already should have known—they do not become adult sex offenders. So pushing them on a Megan's Law registry produces two simultaneous bad outcomes: it stigmatizes the young adults who once offended, and it destroys the capacity of a registry to measure and predict public danger. Kids change.

Because kids can change, it is usually best practice to respond to offending with short-term and minimally disruptive interventions, to avoid permanent labels, and to communicate the system's belief in the young offender's capacity to change.

The competing themes in the rhetoric of juvenile policy are for reformers to argue for the policies that the members of the community would wish to see if young offenders were like their own children and their children's friends. The advocates for unrestrained penality are arguing that juvenile offenders are a separate species, and one critical feature of this separateness is the superpredators' fixed and inalterable propensity for evil. Emphasis on the adolescent capacity to change is thus a critical element in progressive youth policies—at once empirically correct and morally appropriate.

3. KIDS GROW UP

For most of the 35 years after 1972, the prison population in the United States grew explosively while the rate at which juvenile offenders were incarcerated grew much less (Zimring 2005 at Chapter 4).

One reason the US imprisonment rate grew by 400 percent was the widely held belief that incarceration was the only available method of preventing high rate offenders from continuing their criminal careers. One exception to this prison-or-nothing dilemma happened in California in 2000, when voters passed an initiative to divert felony drug offenders from what would have been prison sentences to drug treatment programs instead (Zimring and Harcourt 2007 at Chapter 3). This alternative strategy took pressure off the consistent increase of drug imprisonment in California.

But juvenile courts used much less incarceration without public rejection even as the criminal system sank deeper into mass incarceration. Was this passive use of only short-term confinement and probation a crime control strategy? Yes, it was and is. In one powerful sense, what juvenile courts avoided and facilitated did link with a persuasive crime control story—by letting kids grow up in community settings, the system was waiting until kids matured out of the social patterns and temptations toward offending that lead to high rates of offending during adolescence. The best-known cure for youth crime is growing up. And the strategic logic of diversion and minimal sanctions is waiting for maturation to transition a young man from male groups to intimate pairs and from street corners to houses and workplaces.

The juvenile court's strategic commitment to allow youthful offenders to grow out of criminologenic periods is a persuasive alternative narrative to isolation and incapacitation. It promotes and justifies the community's tolerance of second and third changes. The maturation rationale might also explain why the tolerance and restraint of the juvenile court toward young offenders might be more difficult to reproduce in policy toward older offenders. It isn't just the diminished capacities of the young that justify less harsh interventions; it is also the crime control promise of waiting for maturity. This must be a central theme in reform advocacy.

4. JUVENILE COURTS ARE SUITED TO YOUNG OFFENDER POLICIES

The choice of a mission-centered rhetoric over an institution-oriented approach has two implications for statements about juvenile courts in the arguments for youth law reform. In the first place, the court and its competencies are relegated to a supporting role in the dialogue. The kids are rendered more important than the special court for kids. In the second place, a mission-centered approach to juvenile courts changes the nature of the claims about the court being made. What makes the juvenile court desirable is the good fit between its policies and sanctions and the special characteristics of kids, rather than the claim that its judges and probation staff have the power to rehabilitate all kinds of offenders. And what suits the court to the needs of adolescent offenders is as much what it doesn't do as what it does—the passive virtues of community-based supervision that gives kids the breathing room for normal development.

This mission-centered theory of youth crime policy is kid-specific, but not juvenile court specific. It applies as well to other categories of youth regulation but not necessarily to other branches of crime control. While dispute settlement ideologies like restorative justice extend naturally to other types of offenders, a mission-centered theory of juvenile justice is limited to the populations that share the special circumstances of youth. So some of the specific arguments that make the case for progressive juvenile justice more powerful also make the scope of reform generationally limited. But many of the same kid-specific features that apply to kids below the standard eighteenth birthday of the juvenile court are relevant as well to the youngest age groups in criminal court jurisdiction. So it is the youthfulness of the population, rather than the name of the court exercising jurisdiction, that defines the limits of mission-centered arguments for special policy toward the young.

C. Leading Indicators for Reform

We close this survey of the politics of juvenile justice by mentioning three leading indicators of the prospects for progressive reform in American juvenile justice. The first leading indicator on our list is the level of general public concern about crime and violence—an influence no less important because it is obvious. The second and third leading indicators are trust in government and experts and the evolution of specialized professional roles within the juvenile court, particularly for prosecutors. These are low visibility phenomena that we also regard as critical influences on the future of juvenile justice.

Public Crime Concern

Those looking for clear demonstrations of how variations in public fear of crime influence policy in juvenile courts need not travel too far back in American history—the 1990s can stand as Exhibit A, and Chapters 1 and 2 in this volume tell the story. But there are two aspects of public concern about crime on display in earlier chapters of this book that require careful attention in considering its political influence.

The first feature of crime worry as a political force is that it is the level of fear, not the level of crime, that pushes the political process. In the early 1990s, both the youth homicide rate and the level of public concern rose together. But the moral panic around sex crime and sex killers that provoked federal juvenile sex offender registration requirements came after a sharp and steady decline in sex offenses for at least a decade. And fear is no less politically powerful because it has no factual foundation.

The second fact about public concern as a leading indicator for reform is that fear of crime is usually a one-way street in the politics of criminal justice. When citizens are fearful and angry, punitive legislation is likely to result. When citizens are not terribly worried about crime and violence, the inertial forces discussed earlier in this chapter may simply mean that no policy changes take place. So stable levels of public crime concern are a necessary condition for progressive reforms, but not a sufficient condition. A calm public mood means that progress can happen, not that it will happen.

There are three ways we believe public fear and anger provoke punitive distortion in juvenile justice. Public fear and anger can be mobilized in the democratic process to directly produce legislative change for juvenile justice—the pattern for the waves of transfer legislation that were discussed in Chapter 2. Public fear and anger can also create spillover changes directed at criminal court populations that get applied as well to juveniles as an afterthought; this has been the pattern with sex offender registration and immigration. The values of juvenile justice are subverted as incidental damage from conflicts that were not focused on youth or youth crime.

The final way in which public worry about crime undermines juvenile justice is by crowding out concerns about youth welfare. The public always has mixed feelings about youth crime. They want to protect youngsters but also to suppress crime. What should be done when the kid is a criminal but the criminal is a kid? Crime fear and anger distract citizens from their positive sentiments about children and youth and provoke punitive responses to youth crime as if it were no different from other forms of criminality—and the policies produced by angry emergencies distort most people's true (and conflicted) sentiments about youthful offenders.

And one way to overcome the inertial forces that are barriers to reform even when crime fears abate is to emphasize the lack of balance in the policy legacy of more fearful times. The better angles of our nature would never support life without possibility of parole for 14-year-olds, and the penal extremes that fears produced should become one focus of efforts to rebalance policy in a less angry age.

Trust in Government and in Experts

A second important leading indicator of the prospects for progressive reform in legal policy toward youth is public attitudes toward government and experts. Even at its most mission-centered, the juvenile court movement was an investment in allowing juvenile court judges and educational and psychological experts tremendous discretionary power. In the early days of the juvenile court, a Denver juvenile court judge was the eighth most admired man in the United States in an annual survey (Larsen 1972, 7). The huge discretions of juvenile justice and the welfare-oriented risk taking of avoiding sustained confinement requires that the public trusts that judges and clinicians know what they are doing. For this reason, public distrust of government and public distrust of experts poisons support for the juvenile court system.

There is, of course, substantial overlap between punitive penal sentiments and distrust of government and experts. But the distrust of expertise is also a unique negative influence on progressive youth crime policy. And any increases in public confidence in the professionals who supervise and support young people is a bullish leading indicator for financial and legislative help for the core mission areas of juvenile justice. Increased public confidence in youth services such as education also help support for juvenile courts.

There is not likely to be another juvenile court judge in the pantheon of 10 most admired Americans, but any turn toward trust in government in the proximate future will be good news for progressive law reform. And distrust of experts or government will be a negative predictor.

The Evolving Roles of Juvenile Court Officers

The traditional pre-*Gault* juvenile court was an institution with a very powerful judge, influential probation officers, and prosecutors and defense attorneys with much less power than in criminal courts. The explicit impact of *In Re Gault* was to make an attorney for the accused delinquent a much more important part of the system, but this also almost immediately made public prosecutors much more numerous and much more important in the juvenile court.

The years since *In Re Gault* was decided in 1967 have seen dramatic expansion in the prosecutor's power in delinquency cases, usually at the expense of judges and probation staff. Still, when the contemporary juvenile court is compared to criminal courts, the prosecutor is much less powerful in the juvenile than in the criminal system and the juvenile court judge and probation staff are much more powerful. In big city criminal justice, the prosecutor runs a plea negotiation penal system where the punishment is determined in 90 percent of felony cases before a judge ever considers the case.

The role of the prosecutor in the juvenile court is both conflicted and evolving. If the prosecutor in criminal court seeks to maximize convictions and punishments with limited resources, should the prosecutor in the juvenile court have the same ambitions? Or should the juvenile court prosecutor see herself as part of a team with others in the juvenile court who are trying to protect both the kid and the community? There is a basic conflict between injecting the same strategic priorities from criminal justice into juvenile court practice and defining the prosecutor's professional role as helping to achieve the distinctive missions of juvenile court in a cooperative venture. One powerful leading indicator of what will happen with the court is how the juvenile prosecutor's professional self-concept will evolve.

And there are a number of factors that can tilt the balance toward adversarial or juvenile court cooperative self-definitions and values. One influence will be whether prosecutors are transferred in and out of juvenile courts with frequency. Interchangeable and intermittent juvenile court duty will produce prosecutors who are socialized to adversarial criminal court norms and impose them on their juvenile court assignments. That pattern also produces prosecutors who regard the juvenile court as a low status assignment, because the penal stakes are so much lower than criminal court.

The creation of long-term assignments to juvenile court, particularly if they are voluntary and career-oriented, will assure that the juvenile prosecutor is socialized into her role within the juvenile court. And career juvenile court prosecutors are more likely to form sustained working relations with other juvenile court actors. Also, assigning volunteers to careers in the juvenile court will tend to recruit people who identify with the mission of the juvenile system.

With all those distinctions from garden-variety district attorneys, most prosecutors in a juvenile court will have different priorities and values than probation staff, and certainly than defense lawyers. Still, the contrast between juvenile courts with cooperative versus adversarial prosecutors is very substantial, and also leads to sharply different leadership and legal reform constituencies. When cooperative juvenile prosecutors become juvenile court judges (and they will), they are likely to have the values and the expertise that will strengthen the distinctive character of juvenile courts and most of the distinctive power dynamics. So career and cooperative juvenile prosecutors will turn out to be a good leading indicator of a juvenile court that retains its distinctive professional roles and values. Making the judges who sit in juvenile courts specialists who will hold their assignments for a long time will also preserve the special character of the court.

In this sense, the future of the American system of juvenile justice is being negotiated right now in courtrooms and offices in thousands of counties.

REFERENCES

DiIulio, John. 1996. *How To Stop the Coming Crime Wave* (New York: Manhattan Institute).

Graham v. Florida, 560 U.S. 48 (2010).

In re Gault 387 U.S. 1 (1967).

In re Winship 397 U.S. 358 (1970).

Larsen. Charles. 1972. *The Good Fight: The Life and Times of Ben Lindsay* (Chicago: Quadrangle Books).

Miller v. Alabama 132 S.Ct. 548 (2012).

Moffitt, Terrie E. 1993. "Adolescent-Limited and Life course Persistent Behavior: A Developmental Taxonomy," *Psychological Review,* Vol. 100, No. 4, pp. 674–701.

Roper v. Simmons 543 U.S. 551 (2005).

Schall v. Martin 467 U.S. 253 (1984).

Wilson, James Q. 1995. "Crime and Public Policy," in James Q. Wilson and Joan Petersilia (eds.),____ *Crime* (San Francisco: Institute for Contemporary Studies Press): pp. 537–558.

Wolfgang, Marvin, Robert Figlio, and Thorsten Sellin. 1972. *Delinquency in a Birth Cohort* (Chicago: University of Chicago Press).

Zimring, Franklin E. 2005. *American Juvenile Justice* (New York: Oxford University Press).

Zimring, Franklin E. and Bernard E. Harcourt. 2007. *Criminal Law and the Regulation of Vice* (St. Paul: Thomson/West).

ABOUT THE CONTRIBUTORS

Michael F. Caldwell is a Lecturer in Psychology at the University of Wisconsin–Madison, and a Senior Staff Psychologist at the Mendota Juvenile Treatment Center, and he has a private practice in juvenile forensic psychology. He is a coinvestigator with the MIND Research Network at the University of New Mexico. He has served as a consultant to the MacArthur Foundation Research Network on Juvenile Justice, and the National Academy of Sciences Sackler International Scientific Forum on Neuroscience and the Law, and the Sandra Day O'Connor School of Law at Arizona State University. He is currently the president of the Wisconsin Association for the Treatment of Sexual Abusers. His current area of research focuses on the treatment of aggressive and psychopathic juvenile delinquents, and risk assessment of juvenile sexual offenders.

James Forman Jr. is a Clinical Professor of Law at Yale Law School. He is a graduate of Brown University and Yale Law School, and was a law clerk for Judge William Norris of the US Court of Appeals for the Ninth Circuit and Justice Sandra Day O'Connor of the United States Supreme Court. In 1997, along with David Domenici, he started the renowned Maya Angelou Public Charter School, which combines rigorous education, job training, counseling, mental health services, life skills, and dormitory living for school dropouts and youth who have previously been incarcerated. His work has been published in the *Yale Law Journal*, *UCLA Law Review*, *Michigan Law Review*, and *Georgetown Law Journal*, among others. Professor Forman is currently writing a book about the incarceration explosion in Washington, DC.

James B. Jacobs is the Chief Justice Warren E. Burger Professor of Law and Director, Center for Research in Crime and Justice at NYU School of Law. He teaches criminal law, criminal procedure, and juvenile justice. The Guggenheim Foundation named him a 2012–2013 Fellow to pursue his current book project on the uses and abuses of criminal records.

Aaron Kupchik is Professor of Sociology and Criminal Justice at the University of Delaware. His research focuses on the punishment of youth in schools, courts, and correctional facilities. He has published four books, including *Homeroom Security: School Discipline in an Age of Fear* (NYU Press, 2010) and *Judging Juveniles: Prosecuting Adolescents in Adult and Juvenile Courts* (NYU Press, 2006), winner of the 2007 American Society of Criminology Michael J. Hindelang Book Award.

Terry A. Maroney is Professor of Law, Professor of Medicine, Health and Society, and Director of the Social Justice Program at Vanderbilt University. She specializes in criminal law, juvenile justice, wrongful conviction, and the role of emotion in law, drawing heavily on interdisciplinary scholarship. In addition to her scholarship closely examining the use of adolescent brain science in juvenile cases, Professor Maroney speaks and writes frequently about the role of emotion in judicial behavior and decision making. Her scholarship has appeared in journals including *California Law Review*, *Vanderbilt Law Review*, *Notre Dame Law Review*, *Emotion Review*, *American Criminal Law Review*, *Law and Human Behavior*, and *Court Review*, as well as in a number of books in both the United States and Great Britain.

David S. Tanenhaus is Professor and Chair of the UNLV History Department, James E. Rogers Professor of History and Law at the William S. Boyd School of Law, and Immediate-Past Editor of *Law and History Review*. He studies one of the fundamental and recurring problems in the history of law and society—how to treat the young. His books include *Juvenile Justice in the Making* (2004) and *The Constitutional Rights of Children: In re Gault and Juvenile Justice* (2011). He coedited, with Margaret K. Rosenheim, Franklin E. Zimring, and Bernardine Dohrn, *A Century of*

Juvenile Justice (2002). He also served as the Editor-in-Chief of *The Encyclopedia of the Supreme Court of the United States* (2008).

David B. Thronson is Associate Dean for Academic Affairs, Professor of Law, and cofounder of the Immigration Clinic at Michigan State University College of Law. His research and writing seeks to develop frameworks and critical perspectives for analyzing the intersection of family and immigration law, with a particular focus on children. He earned his J.D. degree from Harvard Law School, where he served as coeditor-in-chief of the *Harvard Human Rights Journal.*

Franklin E. Zimring is the William G. Simon Professor of Law at the University of California, Berkeley Law School. His fields of expertise include youth crime and juvenile justice, criminal violence, the etiology and control of firearms violence, and the behavioral effects of crime control policy. He has served on the National Academy of Science Panels on Violence, Deterrence, and Juvenile Justice and as director of research of the Task Force on Violence of the National Commission on the Causes and Prevention of Violence. He has written on issues of youth crime and sentencing policy, penal confinement and the restraint of crime, and gun and drug control policy. Recent books include *An American Travesty: Legal Responses to Adolescent Sex Offending* (2004), *American Juvenile Justice* (2005), *The Great American Crime Decline* (2006) and *The City That Became Safe: New York's Lessons for Urban Crime and Its Control* (2012).

INDEX